Ace of Freedoms

Ace of Freedoms: Thomas Merton's Christ

GEORGE KILCOURSE

University of Notre Dame Press

Notre Dame   London

Manufactured in the United States of America

Poetry excerpts are from:

Thomas Merton: *The Collected Poems of Thomas Merton.* Copyright 1946, 1947 by New Directions. Copyright 1944, 1949 by Our Lady of Gethsemani Monastery. Copyright © 1964 by The Abbey of Gethsemani. Copyright © 1952, 1954, 1955, 1956, 1957, 1961, 1962, 1963, 1967, 1968 by The Abbey of Gethsemani, Inc. Copyright © 1968 by Thomas Merton. Copyright © 1961, 1963, 1965, 1966, 1967, 1968, 1969, 1970, 1971, 1976, 1977 by The Trustees of the Merton Legacy Trust. Copyright © 1977 by William Davis. Reprinted by permission of New Directions Publishing Corporation.

Thomas Merton: *Eighteen Poems.* Copyright © 1968 by The Abbey of Gethsemane, Inc. Copyright © 1977, 1985 by The Trustees of The Merton Legacy Trust. Reprinted by permission of New Directions Publishing Corporation.

Unpublished Merton materials are used with permission of the Merton Legacy Trust.

Library of Congress Cataloging-in-Publication Data

Kilcourse, George, 1947–
    Ace of freedoms : Thomas Merton's Christ / George Kilcourse.
      p.   cm.
    Includes bibliographical references (p.   ).
    ISBN 0-268-00636-9
    1. Jesus Christ — History of doctrines — 20th century.i.
    2. Spirituality — Catholic Church — History — 20th century.
    3. Merton, Thomas, 1915–1968 — Contributions in Christology.
    4. Catholic Church — Doctrines — History — 20th century.   I. Title.
BT198.K53   1993
232'.092 — dc20   92-53741
                                          CIP

To Michael Downey,
midwife for this book

Other masks would be less trouble. This one is never allowed to be familiar: it is often the most naked. It is not without risk in a season of frost. Nothing that is chosen is unbearable.

Cables to the Ace, #79

Contents

Acknowledgments

I would like to express my heartfelt gratitude to those institutions and persons who have made possible the writing of this book. Bellarmine College granted me a sabbatical leave for the academic year 1990–91. This confidence in my research and creativity offered me a welcome support. During the fall semester of 1990, I sojourned in Toronto where Michael Fahey, S.J., Dean of the Faculty of Theology at the University of St. Michael's College, graciously provided visiting scholar privileges, library and office facilities, and access to the resources of the Toronto School of Theology. Various Toronto colleagues, including Ellen Leonard, C.S.J., Annice Callahan, R.S.C.J., Margaret O'Gara, and Michael Vertin were particularly supportive during my months in Canada. The hospitality of George Cerniglia, S.M., and Louis Pinckert, S.M., and the entire Marianist community afforded me the most congenial and pleasant of homes during these months. During the spring semester of 1991, I lived with the monastic community at the Abbey of Gethsemani in Kentucky where the pages of this book were drafted. I owe more than mere thanks to Timothy Kelly, abbot of Gethsemani, and Luke Armour, monk of Gethsemani, for providing me a scholar's paradise in the quiet of the abbey environs, its library, and its rhythms of liturgical prayer.

Anne Carr, B.V.M., Lawrence Cunningham, Michael Downey, and Jean-Marc Laporte, S.J., proved themselves especially generous colleagues by reading my manuscript and offering careful and enthusiastic critiques at various stages of its progress. Michael Mott helped me with his encouragement and insights during my visit to Bowling Green, Ohio, in December of 1990. And Patrick Hart, monk of Gethsemani, supported my work with a careful reading of the manuscript and by contributing Merton publications to my library throughout the past fifteen years. John D. Boyd, S.J., my mentor at Fordham University, first nurtured my interdisciplinary study of Merton. It is a delight to see the tree he so carefully cultivated bear fruit.

My thanks to Peggy L. Fox of New Directions Publishing Corporation for permission to quote from Merton's poetry in this volume. Anne H. McCormick and the Merton Legacy Trust were most cooperative in granting permission to quote from unpublished Merton sources. I am grateful to Ann Rice of the University of Notre Dame Press for her masterful editing and friendship. What many authors approach as drudgery became a welcome and refreshing series of thoughtful, good-humored conversations with her. Marquita Briet, technical services librarian at Bellarmine College, kindly lent her professional expertise in constructing the "Index of Merton Works," and Steve Adams, graduate student at Louisville's Southern Baptist Theological Seminary, carefully constructed the indices of names and subjects.

Finally, I acknowledge my thanks to Jim Flynn, priest of the Archdiocese of Louisville and director of the Kentucky Interreligious Task Force on Central America. He has taught me more than he knows about the mystery of the prophets to whom Merton alluded when he concluded *The Seven Storey Mountain,* heralding "the Christ of the burnt men." Without his witness and insight I could never have fully perceived Thomas Merton's Christ.

Introduction:
The Epiphany of God
in Weakness and Defencelessness

Tell me how it stands with your Christology and I shall tell you who you are.

Karl Barth[1]

When Thomas Merton appropriated that provocative declaration, he both cued and invited us to the very genius of his spirituality as a model speaking to contemporary Christian life. This book explores the full gamut of this unique American Cistercian's writings as a Christ-centered spirituality. But more importantly, it traces the development within Merton's own explicit and implicit christology, which can best be quarried out of his impressive poetry corpus. There one finds the most compelling personifications of the "true self," or "inner self," whose transformation of consciousness articulates Merton's mature christology.

Christology, or the understanding of who is this Jesus, the Christ, and what he has done for humanity, proved to be intimately connected with two dimensions of Merton's experience: (1) the recurring existential question of self-identity, the spiritual dynamic of the false self versus the "true self," or "inner self"; and (2) the unique character of autobiography as dialogue: voicing the discovery of his deepest identity so as to empower readers to wrestle with their own spiritual identity. For Thomas Merton, these remained inseparable strands of the singular mystery of our existence as human persons. By integrating christology, the inner self's identity, and autobiographical voice, I hope to reorient readers to Merton's prose, journals, letters, and especially his poetry, to discover what recommends his spirituality and how it has garnered a unique staying power for today.

There is always something of the pundit about Merton, the monk who delivered sharp aphorisms like, "I have renounced spirituality to

1

find God."[2] Such a flair for paradox became synonymous with the poet's eye for irony. This penchant for the shocking declaration demands careful contextualization. It is rivaled only by his proclivity to exaggerate. Whatever he was reading or commenting upon was all too easily rendered in superlatives: "the best . . . ," "the most. . . ." Merton scholarship faces an equally large task of researching the primary texts and unraveling from the studies on Merton the embroidery that all too often has clumsily burdened the unadorned, the stark, and the immediate lightness in Merton's best writing with commentators' pet themes. After twenty-five years, it vexes many that both the centrality of the mystery of Christ and Merton's own thousand-page poetry corpus have been eclipsed when assessing his legacy.

An obvious starting point for any systematic interpretation of Merton radiates from his own habit of reverencing questions more than answers. "A man is better known by his questions than by his answers," the monk often reminded us. "To make known one's questions," he claimed, "is to come out into the open oneself."[3] It echoes another spiritual master, Holocaust survivor Elie Wiesel, whose autobiographical first book, *Night,* announced: "Every question possessed a power that did not lie in the answer."[4] The method permeated Merton's writing, engaging readers as interrogative confidants. He was not, he said, "in the market for the readymade and wholesale answers so easily volunteered by the public,"[5] though every essay, each poem, and virtually all his correspondence groped for some tentative, provisional foothold in a tottering world. "[E]ach poem is very much the same question but brand new," he volunteered in a critique of a fellow poet, Louis Zukofsky.[6] In the same breath, he could berate the modern church's toying with "mental snake-handling" and "religious vaudeville," and lament a concept of faith that failed to call into question the intimate spiritual ground of one's existence.[7]

Thomas Merton's questions were focused through the effort of aligning Christ, self-identity, and the autobiographical process within a single lens. Jesus' question, "Who do you say that I am?" (Mk. 8:29) perdures as Thomas Merton's ultimate question. Everything converged in the drama: Christ's struggle interpreted Merton; Merton's struggle, revealing the crucified and risen Christ at the center, interprets us. How Thomas Merton grew in his understanding of the mystery of Christ, and how he autobiographically appropriated and interpreted that mystery for us in the vernacular of his prose and poetry, has not yet been the focus of the often labyrinthine Merton industry. Without this focus, the uninitiated who wander unawares into his sprawling work, or that of the tribes of commentators, risk being plagued by a spiritual vertigo.

THE CONTEXT FOR
CONTEMPORARY CHRISTOLOGY'S RENEWAL

To suggest that Thomas Merton developed a full-blown christology would be to exaggerate his contribution. He remained an essayist, allergic to all efforts at systematizing or methodological expositions. What intrigues a theologian, however, is the development of a sustained christological affirmation in his spiritual writing, much of which has quickly achieved the status of a "classic."[8] That Merton succeeded in this enterprise during the very decades when a renewal of christology was erupting is phenomenal. Ironically he read virtually nothing about these formal theological developments. In Roman Catholic circles, much of this literature, subsequent to the close of the Second Vatican Council in 1965, began to circulate in publications only after Merton's 1968 death. Elizabeth Johnson has recently described the "waves" of this renewal, beginning in 1951 with the fifteen hundredth anniversary of the Council of Chalcedon's dogma defining Christ as truly human and truly divine, one person with two natures. The first wave of renewal consisted in remembering the genuine humanity of Jesus Christ. This has been followed by biblical, liberation, feminist, and world religions waves that have made us reconsider a perennial question: What is the contemporary meaning of Jesus as the Christ?[9] To some extent, Thomas Merton trafficked in several of these waves, some much more than others. The impact of Merton's writing, however, proves the resilience of spirituality as a matrix, a source for theology, and for christology in particular. The pages of this book offer a systematic reading of Merton's inchoate christology, an understanding of Christ which proved to be the compass that gave direction to his life and writing.

Acquaintance with Merton's canon leaves one with the impression that his christological understanding derived largely, if not exclusively, from the Greek Fathers' concept of divinization. This fact harbors a potential for distortion, to which Merton himself, at times, succumbed. The classical christology of the church is described as a straightforward "descending christology": God in the Logos becomes human; Jesus is

God. Karl Rahner launched the first wave of new christology when he critiqued the drift in Christian spirituality and piety away from a truly adequate understanding of the fifth-century definition of the Council of Chalcedon.[10] Rahner's nervousness centered on our so mythologizing this mystery that Christians ended up with something quite heretical. We risked a distortion of the dynamic given with the fact of Jesus' true divinity *and* true humanity. The residue of such heresy relentlessly truncates the authentic Christian understanding of human existence: What does Jesus' experience reveal to us about our own humanity? Rahner called this our "practical Monophysitism," the tendency of Christian culture and imagination to deny and swallow the humanity of Jesus in his divinity.

The best Greek patristic thought and writing attempted to balance and maintain this tension. For example, Athanasius taught that the divine became human in order that the human might become divine. But secular currents in Greek culture cultivated a mentality which opposed spirit's becoming matter. These patterns were already deeply encoded in the milieu of the Greek ethos.[11] The dualism of Plato dominated and, eventually, distorted Christian faith. One is reminded of the influence of Augustine's Platonism in Merton's conversion and autobiography, *The Seven Storey Mountain*. The result was a denial of the fuller reality of Incarnation, a trail of Docetism, the heresy that denied the true humanity of Jesus.

MERTON'S TURN TO THE KENOTIC CHRIST

The excesses in theological claims and counterclaims about either the divinity or humanity of Christ determined the course of early Christian theology and the church's creeds and doctrines. When Merton assimilated this tradition, the dry dogmas and formulas of the 1940s lured him, like others, into the very practical Monophysitism that Rahner was diagnosing. But Merton's story is dominated by another tonality. The authentic understanding of the Greek Fathers' theory of divinization includes the shift to an "ascending christology," the capacity of the human for self-transcendence and union with God. The dialectic between descending and ascending christologies is seeded in their writings. Merton ultimately became comfortable enough to take liberties with this Christian tradition. For example, the mature Merton concluded in a 1967 essay that our age of reputed doubt and unfaith offers "authentic assurances of hope and understanding providing we are willing to tolerate theological discomfort."[12] This book will trace the organic development of that christological shift and creative theology within Merton's writing. When Merton reclaimed his experiential bases and was willing to take risks his writing led to something fresh, a radical clarification of Christ's *kenosis,* or "emptying" himself of divinity, in order to immerse himself in the ambiguity of our humanity. In exploring that dynamic of Christ's testing, self-discovery, and radical freedom, Merton almost independently found himself on the whitecaps of the very waves of christological renewal that the contemporary theologians were navigating.

The achievement of Thomas Merton was his discovery in the humanity of Christ of a paradigm for our religious self-understanding. The ground between his early, somewhat saccharine spirituality and the later stark, but poignant writings on the epiphany of God in human "weakness and defencelessness"[13] parallels the expansive geography of contemporary christology.[14]

In fact, the early Thomas Merton went to great lengths to parrot the prevailing, sclerotic christological tradition of the 1940s and 1950s. His prose guardedly claimed a strict Catholic orthodoxy, which in his days as a young novice, scholastic, and fledgling monk translated into the near-Docetist denial of the humanity of Jesus. For the moment, it liberates a Merton reader to jump back to his early works, *Seeds of Contemplation* (1949) and *The Ascent to Truth* (1951), to impress on our memory how far Merton went out of his way to mute and disclaim any adventuresome or creative theologizing on his part. In *Seeds of Contemplation* (1949) Merton introduced the work as rooted in the twelfth-century Cistercians, especially Bernard of Clairvaux and John of the Cross. "This book makes no claim to be revolutionary or even especially original," he protested. "We sincerely hope it does not contain a line that is new to Catholic tradition or a single word that would perplex an orthodox theologian"![15] A similar note, two years later, introduced *The Ascent to Truth* (1951) as "chiefly concerned with the *doctrine* of the Carmelite theologian, Saint John of the Cross."[16] The irony is that Merton later looked back and lamented what he categorized as the "less good" quality of this work.[17] This forthright recognition of his own mediocrity refreshes in an age when self-congratulation has become epidemic.[18]

At the risk of aggravating some uncritical Merton aficionados, it needs to be asserted from the outset that Merton wrote some turgid prose. And often even worse poetry. Most of his early works are theologically banal and inert, even derivative, giving evidence of posturing and imitation. How else explain this embarrassing rendering from the indentured hagiographer of St. Lutgarde: "'[My wounds] tell thee,' Christ replied, 'to labor and to weep, for thy labors and tears will quench the enkindled anger of My Father, and will persuade Him not to hurl sinners down to their death . . .'"?[19] Or the clericalism rampant in the understanding of his ordination: "Once I get those oils on my hands I'll be ready for anything."[20]

The intention for rummaging in such spoiled Merton passages is not to ridicule him. He could be, as biographer Michael Mott has described him, his own worst critic.[21] Even in the final period of his life Merton wryly proclaimed a good-humored judgment: "Every once in a while we have to do a little iconoclasm in our own back yard."[22] Like David Cooper,[23] among others, I propose to place in sharp relief the contrast between the early and the late Merton, without overlooking certain continuities. But the emphasis here will be on the contrast between the christological insights of the mature Merton and the earlier disguised voices and contorted postures which he sometimes permitted himself to adopt as a young monk. For the drama of the "true self" vs. "false self" played out for Merton in christological understandings as well as on an existential level.

Biographer Mott's balanced, comprehensive portrait of Merton affords one particularly fruitful insight for exploring Merton's christology. At first glance, it seems unrelated. But it correlates in an uncanny way when we comb through the monk's christological texts. "The older Merton and the younger Merton," Mott submitted, "showed a gaiety and high spirits, which were largely suppressed during the early years at the monastery."[24] The young Cistercian Merton evidenced that he was well-endowed with blind spots when he succumbed to the christological eccentricities which Rahner and others have diagnosed of that era. For all his unfairness to his younger self, Merton rightly faulted the lingering effects of the earliest monastic period: "I was dealing in a crude theology that I had learned as a novice: a cleancut division between the natural and supernatural, God and the world, sacred and secular, with boundary lines that were supposed to be quite evident."[25] The world, he confessed, was not as simple as it had once appeared in *The Seven Storey Mountain*'s black-and-white categories. The deeper he delved into his monastic roots, particularly the spirituality of Bernard of Clairvaux, the more he discovered the equilibrium of a balanced christology, with both descending ("from above") and ascending ("from below") emphases, encompassing both the true divinity and true humanity of Jesus.

An equally disarming self-appraisal was entered in Merton's 1965 working notebooks, in the context of his reading Dietrich Bonhoeffer's *Ethics*. It coincided with his permanent move to the hermitage, his secluded cinderblock house nestled in cedars above a lovely meadow, a short walk from the monastery's main complex of buildings. Under the heading "My place in the world," he offered: "Obviously in my early writings I said things about 'the world' that had a gnostic or manichean flavor about them." He went on to say he no longer accepted such statements, even though there is a sense in the tradition that gives a basis for the "negative view" of "the world." He specified his antiworldliness as that of "genuine medieval monasticism," and not the reactionary posture of Pope Pius IX's Syllabus of Errors. He concluded, however: "There may be some truth in my pessimism, but the pessimism itself has an evil root, and instead of getting the root out I have been cultivating it in the name of 'spirituality' or what you will. This is no longer honest."[26] Such a conviction dramatically affected the voice of the Abbey of Gethsemani's most celebrated monk. And the final years of Merton's life evidenced endless new vectors toward that recovered optimism, for a world hungering for a spiritual vision.

MERTON'S HIDDEN CHRIST:
CONVERSATIONS AT THE MARGINS

The following chapters examine the autobiography of Merton's inner self converging in the encounter with the inner self of others, all congruent with the hidden Christ of kenosis. It comes as no surprise that Merton gravitated to the margins of the church and society to converse with kindred spirits.[27] For at those margins he met the authentic persons whose searching experience and articulate wrestling with God converged with his own. To name but a few: Albert Camus, Simone Weil, Franz Jaegerstetter, Mohandas Gandhi, Flannery O'Connor, D. T. Suzuki, Edwin Muir, Dietrich Bonhoeffer, Rainer Maria Rilke, Doro-

thy Day, Boris Pasternak, Thich Nhat Hanh, Karl Barth, William Faulkner, a host of desert fathers, mystics, and monastic and contemplative
ancestors of Eastern and Western Christianity, and finally even of Asia.

He spoke directly about his recovered existential style and method
in his preface to *The Wisdom of the Desert* (1960) and the introduction to a revised work, *New Seeds of Contemplation* (1961). Then, in
his prose essays collected as *Raids on the Unspeakable* (1965), the autobiographical rendering of his unexaggerated "testing" and *agonia*
reached lyric proportions. Merton had continuously savored the mystery of Incarnation, which, Piet Schoonenberg reminds, keeps christology from the absolutizing of pure divinization,[28] but now he ranged
out into the precincts of Ionesco's *The Rhinoceros* and Luke's sublime
infancy narrative with its "no room" theme, to deliver a christology
from below, from out of the horrors of dehumanization and alienating
oppression in human history. The epigraph of *Raids on the Unspeakable* from Gabriel Marcel announced the age's greatest need: to guard
the image of God against further dehumanization and to take Christ
in history now with seriousness.

This turn to kenotic christology reoriented Merton to create the
mature prose essays and poetry that make him a paradigmatic figure
for contemporary spirituality. Yet threads of this figure of the hidden,
humiliated Christ also weave in and out of early Merton texts. In this
sense we will trace a certain continuity. Some claim to find in Merton
an almost embryonic, or genetically coded, continuity in his writing.[29]
I dissent from that reading, because Merton negotiated some very public and dramatic shifts. One can detect his writer's persona when it
intruded to eclipse the autobiographical voice that characterized his
successful writing. He had the honesty and courage to admit where
he had misspoken, taken a wrong turn, and humbly needed to strike
out again with mid-course corrections, or even in an entirely new direction. This itself, I would suggest, reflects in an autobiographical key
the same kenotic patterning.

A MAP THROUGH MERTON'S
CHRISTOLOGICAL DEVELOPMENT

While Merton could enjoy the luxury of describing the contemplative experience as "travel[ing] without maps" because the monastic

discipline had so sharpened his own sense of direction,[30] this book will offer definite coordinates to track his path and to route readers through the maze of Mertoniana. Chapter 1 examines Merton's conversion as an *experience* of salvation. Christology and soteriology, the understanding of Jesus as Savior, remained well-integrated in Merton's autobiographical writings: the journals and poetry. Two concerns anchor this appreciation. First, his early monastic formation, dominated by the reigning christology of the 1940s, exacerbated some problematic elements in the young monk's attitude toward the world. Second, the genres of journal, autobiography, and poetry—all grounded in the priority of experience—eluded the constrictions of a narrow christology. Within his own Cistercian tradition, Merton found Bernard of Clairvaux's, Duns Scotus's, and Gregory the Great's optimism about the human condition. Their reverence for the humanity of Christ provided the source for his recovery of a more complete christology and a *sapiential* theology of experience. These subtly reconstituted his Augustinian emphasis on human fulfillment through the will and love of the inner person. In chapter 2 the attention shifts to Merton's poetry. The poet's "paradise ear" recreates and narrates the human person's capacity to recover a lost "likeness" to God. The categories of "poetry of the choir" and "poetry of the desert," suggested by George Woodcock, will be complemented with an examination of the overarching paradisal vision in Merton's poetry corpus. This will be an aid for recognizing in his poems both the personifications of the true, inner self, and ironic symbols and images of the false, masked, counterfeit, illusory ego that obscures and shadows the person's capacity for a fully human self-transcendence in love. A new category, "poetry of the forest," will complete an understanding of Merton's mature poetic voice.

Chapter 3 investigates Merton's dialogue with the theological currents of the 1960s, especially the ecumenical and conciliar theology that re-engaged his social commitment to the world and human history through the civil rights and peace movements. But his geography expanded as well, to Pasternak's Russia, Eichmann's Germany, and the Latin America of poets whose works he avidly translated. In all these currents Merton found at the wounded, suffering margins of the world a new insight into human dignity and the "dangerous memory" of Jesus.[31] His appropriation of the mystery of Christ's Incarnation in terms of a mature kenotic christology, finding Christ in "weakness and defencelessness," dominated the final decade of the monk's life, particularly the concluding three years at the hermitage. Then, in chapter 4, attention shifts to Merton's critiquing the works of a wide spectrum of literary artists. Here his *sapiential* method is illustrated most clearly, and the process yields a constellation of kenotic patterns that Merton finds when he concentrates his critical powers on the fiction of artists like Pasternak, Camus, Faulkner.

Chapter 5 examines Merton's late poetry, the antipoetry of *Cables to the Ace* and *The Geography of Lograire,* and other mature poems, and how they render his understanding of the human condition vis-á-vis christology. His essays on the apocalyptic "cargo cults" of Melanesia, native American spirituality, and contemporary American culture are written against the horizon of the kenotic Christ.

Finally, in chapter 6, I assess how Merton's efforts at Western monastic renewal and the dialogue with Asian spiritual traditions converge during his final years, clarifying his christological understandings and further validating the kenotic patterns of the mature Merton.

In these chapters we retrace Merton's pilgrimage to the sublime compassion of God, Christ's kenosis. It is from this mystery, where "out of strength which abides, he chooses to be weak," that contemporary theologians have reappropriated vital traditions for the renewal of christology.[32] The title of this book, *Ace of Freedoms,* borrows an image from the concluding page of Merton's antipoem, *Cables to the Ace: Familiar Liturgies of Misunderstanding.* As the analysis in chapter 5 develops the understanding of this metaphor, Christ is the source of all human freedoms in Merton's spirituality. But for Thomas Merton, Christ, the "ace" of our freedoms is manifest in intriguing and sublimely kenotic epiphanies. It is no coincidence that this celebrity-hermit ultimately explored the currents of today's more familiar christologies "from below." Only seven months before his December 10, 1968, death, Merton published a terse essay entitled "The Historical Consciousness." There he pointed to the new political movement in Latin America which would subsequently be named "liberation theology" and spoke of the "agonizing mystery in the present crisis." The place where this study, indeed the place where Thomas Merton, ultimately, will arrive is the climax of a christology that reflects upon our primordial experiences of salvation in today's history, politics, and culture. Autobiography, self-identity, and the mystery of Christ, all were to be discovered in this wider context. A characteristic questioning in that essay orients us toward Merton's horizon:

Should contemplatives know about these problems? Obviously they cannot try to follow them in detail. Even experts are baffled by the situation. But contemplatives should have a genuine and deep historical consciousness, since Christ is in fact manifesting Himself in the critical conflicts of our time.

In these conflicts, whether we like it or not, we are all somehow involved. . . . We are not called to feed the hungry, but certainly we cannot ignore them. For the hungry and the oppressed of the earth are the very same Christ who will one day say: "I was hungry and you did not even recognize me, you took the side of those who deprived me." We have to know who is suffering, to have some idea why they are suffering, to be with them and with those who try to alleviate their suffering, and to be conscious of the ways necessary to do this.[33]

This study has a single ambition: to make clear to readers of Merton that his questions and searching christology empower us "to explore a desert area of man's heart in which explanations no longer suffice, and in which one learns that only experience counts."[34] For then, like Christ, like Thomas Merton, we discover that, "Only those who continue to struggle are at peace."[35]

1. Abundance of the Heart:
Merton's Experience of Salvation

In a flashback to the spring of 1932, Thomas Merton commented on what became his posthumously published novel, *My Argument with the Gestapo.* He recollected how he "instinctively jumped into a ditch" when a carful of Nazis sped down the Rhine Valley road where, as a seventeen-year-old student, he was hiking on election day. The Hitler youth, "future officers in the SS," said Merton, had intimidated him by "screaming and shaking their fists." After they quickly vanished, "The road was once again perfectly silent and peaceful," he described. "But it was not the same road as before. It was now a road on which seven men had expressed their readiness to destroy me." While this is the closest Merton came to overt Nazi violence, his novel, he intimated, had explored something different. He described it as a "sardonic meditation" on the world in which he found himself, "an attempt to define its predicament and my own place in it." The self-described "lightly" written novel preceded the actual atrocities of the World War and Holocaust. But for Merton it questioned the "crisis of civilization in general," and in particular "the Germany that *accepted* Nazism." Two particularly revealing comments conclude his January 1968 preface to the novel. First, Merton claimed that in the novel he had gained access to "my own myth." And second, he spoke of "what remains actual" about this "document of a past era" is its awareness that "though one may or may not escape from the Nazis, there is no evading the universal human crisis of which they were but one partial symptom."[1]

This earliest saga of Merton's spiritual odyssey echoes a Paul-like Damascus Road experience. Conversion beckons and pulls the thoroughly secular Merton into an awareness of the vortex of evil and the need for salvation, both personal and global. Here are the syllables of a sober neo-orthodox theology, the theology that emerged between two world wars to remedy the myopia of nineteenth-century liberal optimism. Now sin, tragedy, terror, and death on a scale unimaginable before the modern world's technology, all were shaping the reformulation of Christian thought. Even at this early stage, Merton was already familiar with the stern voice of neo-orthodoxy's master, Karl Barth, whom he mentions in his 1941 Gestapo novel.[2]

On November 16, 1938, Thomas Merton was conditionally baptized as an adult in the Roman Catholic rite, having been baptized an Anglican as an infant. But six years earlier the "universal human crisis" encountered on the quiet country road near Koblenz had awakened Merton to questions which his experience would no longer let him evade. Five months before he composed this preface to *My Argument with the Gestapo*, Merton employed the same metaphor of the road and the escape to a ditch in "A Letter on Contemplative Life." It evidences both extraordinary continuity and development in Merton. Pope Paul VI had requested a message from contemplatives to troubled people in the modern world. The hastily written epistle bristles with the mature Merton's wit and energy. After remarking that "there are few real contemplatives in our monasteries," and "We know nothing whatever of spiritual aviation" or "the language of modern man," Merton confessed that the person in the world "more often comes to me with his wounds which turn out to be also my own." He apologized for the arrogance of addressing people who had not asked for his advice from behind the problematic walls of his monastic enclosure. Luke's parable of the Good Samaritan evoked from the hermit a fresh perspective. "The Holy Father, he can be a good Samaritan, but myself and my brother in the world, we are just two men who have fallen among thieves and we do our best to get each other out of the ditch."[3]

MERTON'S AFFECTIVE CONVERSION

Walter Conn has examined Merton as a paradigm of Christian conversion. His case study of the monk's autobiographical writing traces Merton's development and interprets an ongoing conversion in light of the theories of Lawrence Kolberg, James Fowler, and Bernard Lonergan. Conn's engaging analysis complements Anne E. Carr's study of the "true self" or "inner self" theme in Merton's writings, a theme

Conn pursues in terms of categories of "autonomy and surrender."[4] What most recommends Conn's interpretation, however, is his attention to Merton's mature religious conversion, grounded in what Lonergan scholars term an "affective conversion." Merton's intellectual prowess led him to wrestle with and eliminate misleading and stubborn myths (beginning in the *Gestapo* novel) about himself and the world. His initial attraction to Christianity came through this intellectual conversion experience. His moral conversion reformed his proclivities for selfishly sensual, worldly pleasures. And his religious conversion offered a new horizon that grasped him with ultimate concern. It remained for Merton to ground his religious conversion in affective experiences that would even more dramatically change all his horizons. In other words, Merton had to discover, and to integrate into these other conversions, the language of the heart.

Merton's autobiography, *The Seven Storey Mountain* (1948), records the emotional traumas visited upon him by his mother's distant, cold letter announcing to the six-year-old boy her imminent death in a hospital bed. The boy's heroic adoration of his vagabond artist-father, dead before Tom's own sixteenth birthday, has been convincingly exposed as masking a young man starved for affection. Owen Merton indulged in amorous trysts that left young Thomas feeling rejected, the vulnerable child in a dysfunctional family.[5] Conn orients us to the impact of an affective conversion: "Affective conversion is not first of all loving someone or something new (content), but letting love become the central reality, the dynamic principle of one's life." In christological language, the affective conversion means "to discover the loving God in the depths of one's own being, as Jesus did."[6] Conn argues persuasively that *The Seven Storey Mountain* betrays a "fundamentally uncritical stance," but he recommends it because there, for "the first time we hear the monk's own prose voice speaking about his own experience, rather than the dubbed voice of the earlier pious works of Cistercian spirituality." In autobiography, Conn asserts, Merton's voice "found its sure starting-point, personal experience," though it awaited maturity, when the voice would "discover its proper critical pitch."[7]

One of Merton's former novices and now abbot of Genesee Abbey in New York, John Eudes Bamberger, has best recollected how Merton's affective conversion contributed to his religious conversion. It was something Merton only rarely intimated in conversation, the remembered experience also reviving a woundedness. Bamberger claimed that Merton's later passion for spiritual beauty was earlier rivaled by his passion for all sorts of experiences, which he had indulged too much. "But he never totally identified with that: he always believed in innocence." More importantly, Bamberger says that, "Somehow he was able, because of the experience of God, to believe that God had recreated his innocence."[8]

Merton was never more direct about this experience than when he declared in *The Sign of Jonas* that one simple motive drew him to the monastery: to experience the mercy of God.[9] It echoed those foundational words of Bernard of Clairvaux, arriving with thirty postulants in the year 1112 at a discouraged Stephen Harding's door, just when the future of the Cistercian reforms at Citeaux seemed precarious. In response to Stephen's surprised question, "What do you want?" Bernard simply replied for the group, "The mercy of God, and yours."[10]

In his 1947 poetry collection, alarmingly entitled *Figures for an Apocalypse,* Merton included an autobiographical lyric entitled "On the Anniversary of My Baptism." Its metaphors unmistakably confess Merton's ongoing conversion process. The poem opens with a series of arresting similes, effectively comparing various waters: "Certain waters are as blue as metal / Or as salt as sorrow. / Others wince like brass in the hammering sun, / Or stammer all over with tremors of shadow. . . ." The poet follows with reminiscences of his many Atlantic crossings, and muses on his escape from fatal sea accidents in those years before baptism.

> And this is the ninth November since my world's end and my
>   Genesis,
> When, with the sting of salt in my dry mouth,
> Cross-crowned with water by the priest,
> Stunned at the execution of my old companion, death,
> And with the murder of my savage history,
> You drowned me in the shallow font.
>
> My eyes, swimming in unexpected infancy,
> Were far too frail for such a favor:
> They still close-kept the stone shell of their empty sepulchre:
> But, though they saw none, guessed the new-come Trinity
> That charged my sinews with His secret life.[11]

The baptismal imagery is wrought in metaphors that connote Merton's awareness of ongoing conversion, the infant's unfocussed eyes and Easter's womblike sepulchre that will give yet unimagined life. Merton's affirmation of the Trinity as the animator of his sinewy human life grounds his Christian conversion. This is not just faith in God but faith in the dynamism of the Trinity through creation and history.

Another poem, "Biography," from the 1946 volume, *A Man In the Divided Sea,* rewrites the Passion story in Merton's autobiographical voice: "my life is written on Christ's Body like a map." Its opening stanza recollects Merton's riotous year at Cambridge University in a haunting image that reminds us of the mock crucifixion Merton endured as a student in a drunken party episode.[12] The poem labors under the individualized Passion piety of its era, but the conclusion echoes the appropriation of the paschal mystery which Merton had earlier rendered in the sublime "For My Brother, Reported Missing in Action, 1943" in *Thirty Poems* (1944).

> If on Your Cross Your life and death and mine are one,
> Love teaches me to read, in You, the rest of a new history.
> I trace my days back to another childhood,
> Exchanging, as I go,
> New York and Cuba for Your Galilee,
> And Cambridge for Your Nazareth,
> Until I come again to my beginning,
> And find a manger, star and straw,
> A pair of animals, some simple men,
> And thus learn that I was born,
> Not now in France, but Bethlehem.[13]

A third poem, "St. Paul," also from *A Man in the Divided Sea,* develops the Pauline imagery of blindness and healing more directly; it incorporates the sepulchre imagery in a new dimension. Merton's identification with the Damascus traveler is three times directly claimed: "When I was Saul . . . / My eyes were stones"; "When I was Saul, and sat among the rocks, / I locked my eyes, and made my brain my tomb, / Sealed with what boulders rolled across my reason!"; and "When I was Saul . . . / My road was quiet as a trap." The conclusion is addressed to Christ:

> Oh Christ! Give back my life, go, cross Damascus,
> Find out my Ananias in that other room:
> Command him, as you do, in this my dream;
> He knows my locks, and owns my ransom,
> Waits for Your word to take his keys and come.[14]

The Seven Storey Mountain would deliver the narrative of this same conversion, but often without the directness or economy of Merton's poetry. The titles to individual sections of the autobiography leaned effectively on similar metaphors; for example, the opening section is called "Prisoner's Base"; and the denouement describing Merton's entry into the monastery becomes "The Sweet Savor of Liberty." Midway in the autobiography Merton concludes the description of his adult baptism and communion with the metaphor of gravity's force and God as the Zenlike moving center:

> For now I had entered into the everlasting movement of that gravitation which is the very life and spirit of God: God's own gravitation towards the depths of His own infinite nature, His goodness without end. And God, that center who is everywhere and whose circumference is nowhere, finding me, through incorporation with Christ, incorporated into this immense and tremendous gravitational movement which is love, which is the Holy Spirit, loved me.
>
> And He called out to me from His own immense depths.[15]

In *The Seven Storey Mountain* readers find four particularly significant excerpts which narrate his discovery of Christ. This cluster of experiences in his pre-conversion years is, however, censored through the voice of a Merton *persona:* the young monk. In fact, I suggest that the autobiographer came to transpose these very experiences into the language of doctrine and orthodoxy and thereby robbed them of an immediacy. A residue, nonetheless, has eluded his (or the censors?) retrospective filtering. The first excerpt reverts back to his Italian summer in 1933 (at the age of eighteen), just before entering Cambridge University. Merton says he formed his first conception of who "this 'Christ'" was while sitting in the midst of the magnificent mosaics decorating the historic cathedrals and churches of Rome. "And now," he wrote, "for the first time in my life I began to find out something of Who this Person was that men called Christ. It was obscure, but it was a true knowledge of Him, in some sense, truer than I knew and truer than I would admit. . . ."

> These mosaics told me more than I had ever known of the doctrine of a God of infinite power, wisdom and love. Who had yet become Man, and revealed in his Manhood the infinity of power, wisdom and love that was His Godhead. . . . I grasped them implicitly—I had to, in so far as the

mind of the artist reached my own mind, and spoke to it his conception and his thought.[16]

Later, in his journal *The Sign of Jonas,* Merton alluded to this same experience in Rome and recollected more carefully that the first picture of Christ to appear painted on a wall to be seen by all the people was at the Basilica of St. John Lateran. "It reminded me of the function of art in the life of faith," he noted in a November 10, 1947, entry, adding, "Rome taught me something of that wisdom, fifteen years ago."[17] Despite all his emphasis on doctrine, Merton's deeper appreciation of the intuitive, nondiscursive power of art and symbols stood undisguised in this experience of mosaics of Christ. His declaration, "Soon I was no longer visiting them merely for the art," betrays an art vs. spirituality dichotomy which later plagued and embarrassed him.

When he first visited Corpus Christi Church near Columbia University one summer Sunday during his 1938 pre-catechumen days ("made up my mind to go to Mass for the first time in my life"), Merton recounted the "vital tradition" of Catholic doctrine "tinged with scholastic terminology" in the young priest's sermon:

> How clear and solid the doctrine was: for behind those words you felt the full force not only of Scripture but of centuries of a unified and continuous and consistent tradition. . . .
>
> What was he saying? That Christ was the Son of God. That, in Him, the Second Person of the Holy Trinity, God, had assumed a Human Nature, a Human Body and Soul, and had taken Flesh and dwelt amongst us, full of grace and truth: and that this Man, Whom men called the Christ, was God. He was both Man and God: two Natures hypostatically united in one Person. . . .
>
> Jesus Christ was not simply a man, a good man, a great man, the greatest prophet, a wonderful healer, a saint: He was something that made all such trivial words pale into irrelevance. He was God. But nevertheless He was not merely a spirit without a true body, God hiding under a visionary body: He was also truly a Man, born of the Flesh of the Most Pure Virgin, formed of her Flesh by the Holy Spirit. And what He did, in that Flesh, on earth, He did not only as Man but also as God. He loved us as God, He suffered and died for us, God.[18]

The event is layered over with the language of textbook doctrine. But the experience underlying this mystery unmistakably transformed

Merton. He registers it with a description of how he "looked about . . . at a new world" where all was transfigured in his vision, even the ugly facades of Broadway and Columbia's environs, "streets designed for violence and noise" becoming the "Elysian Fields" as he watched from "the gloomy little Childs restaurant at 111th Street."[19]

A third personal insight came from Merton's encounter with the Hindu monk adopted by his Columbia circle, Bramachari. He directed Merton to the richness of his own Western tradition. Like a bolt, the Indian's advice struck Merton: read Augustine's *Confessions,* and *The Imitation of Christ*! Merton admitted the irony of his blind spot in failing to realize the riches of Christian mysticism. In the context of Bramachari's reorientation, he confessed in a cerebral voice: "I came away from Huxley's *Ends and Means* with the prejudice that Christianity was a less pure religion, because it was more 'immersed in matter' — that is, because it did not scorn to use a Sacramental liturgy that relied on the appeal of created things to the senses in order to raise the souls of men to higher things."[20]

A final episode relates to Merton's study of Huxley, hinted in the passage just quoted. His notions of mysticism appear naive and superficial at this stage. Even embarrassing, in light of his mature studies of Buddhism and mysticism! What is important, again, is the focus on the sacramentality of the world he gains in the experience of reading Huxley at Columbia. But the voice is aloof, intellectual.

> It seems to me that in discarding his family's tradition of materialism he had followed the old Protestant groove back into the heresies that make the material creation evil of itself, although I do not remember enough about him to accuse him of formally holding such a thing. . . . This also made him suspicious, as the Albigensians had been, and for the same reason, of the Sacraments and the Liturgical life of the Church, and also of doctrines like the Incarnation.[21]

An even earlier experience of the Christ mystery is recorded in Part One of *The Seven Storey Mountain.* Merton there recollected that the only really valuable religious moral training in his childhood came from his father, in spontaneous, ordinary conversations—"that has the most effect." He carefully recalled the biblical text: "A good man out of the good treasure of his heart, bringeth forth good fruit; and an evil man out of the evil treasure bringeth forth that which is evil. For out of the abundance of the heart the mouth speaketh." For Merton, the "speech 'out of the abundance of the heart'" not only made an impression, but transformed people. The one such memorable remark he recalled from his father was his telling of St. Peter's betrayal of Christ, "and how, hearing the cock crow, Peter went out and wept bitterly. . . . I have never lost the vivid picture I got, at that moment, of Peter going out and weeping bitterly."[22] This is the ore of a spirituality that tugged with the force of gravity, Merton's *agonia* mirrored throughout the Passion story. It was no coincidence that in his first collection, *Thirty Poems* (1944), nine of the thirty poems center on Passion metaphors and themes. Seven meditate on Incarnation and the Christmas event. The immediacy of the experience of Christ's humanity, the poet appropriating Christ's experience to interpret his own, colors such poems:

> For in the wreckage of your April Christ lies slain,
> And Christ weeps in the ruins of my spring . . .
> The silence of Whose tears shall fall
> Like bells upon your alien tomb.
> Hear them and come: they call you home.
> > ("For My Brother: Reported
> > Missing in Action, 1943")[23]

> Yet it is far from Christmas, when a star
> Sang in the pane as brittle as their innocence!
> For now the light of early Lent
> Glitters upon the icy step —
> "We have wept letters to our patron saints,
> (The children say) yet slept before they ended."
> > ("The Winter's Night")[24]

> To the cold corners of the earth rise up and go:
> Find beggar Faith, and bring him to the holy table.
> He shall sit down among the good apostles,
> And weep with Peter at the washing of the feet.
> > ("The Holy Sacrament of the Altar")[25]

The familiar Passion imagery and symbols are autobiographically transformed in "An Argument: Of the Passion of Christ." It warrants a lengthy quotation:

ii

The worm that watched within the womb
Was standing guard at Jesus' tomb,
And my first angry, infant breath
Stood wakeful, lest He rise from death.
My adolescence, like the wolf,
Fled to the edges of the gulf
And searched the ruins of the night
To hide from Calvary's iron light:
But in the burning jaws of day
I saw the burning Judas Tree;
For, to the caverns of my pride
Judas had come, and there was paid!

iii

Seeds of the three hours' agony
Fell on good earth, and grew from me,
And, cherished by my sleepless cares
Flowered with God's blood, and Mary's tears.
My curious love found its reward
When love was scourged in Pilate's yard:
Here was the work my hands had made:
A thorny crown, to cut His head. . . .

iv

The cry that rent the temple veil
And split the earth as deep as hell
And echoed through the universe
Sounds, in bombardments, down to us.
There is no ear that has not heard
The deathless cry of murdered God. . . .[26]

The selections are still saturated with individualized piety. And the last line quoted strays over the boundary, into vestiges of the Monophysite heresy denying the full humanity of Christ. These poems rely too much on the immature poet's bald similes and are structured on clumsy rhymes and meters. But throughout, they integrate Merton's experience of sin and conversion with the Jesus events in history. His sentiments unfold unashamedly. The poems also claim an immediacy that too easily evades Merton's prose, especially when buried under doctrinal sediment or tailored (by censors' demands?) to conform to the dogmatic stance of the 1940s. Even the poems are not totally immune to clumsy, dogmatic intrusions.

Three passages, early in Merton's autobiography, connect with the affective conversion experience which is most evident in his poetry. He describes one event as coming "in a strange way, suddenly, a way that I will not attempt to explain." Merton places the scene in his room at night, with a light on. It was a year after his father's death. He experienced a vivid and real presence of his father. It startled him, as if he had been touched or addressed.

> The whole thing passed in a flash, but in that flash, instantly I was overwhelmed with a sudden and profound insight into the misery and corruption of my own soul, and I was pierced deeply with a light that made me realize something of the condition I was in, and I was filled with horror at what I saw, and my whole being rose up in revolt against what was within me, and my soul desired escape and liberation and freedom from all this with an intensity and an urgency unlike anything I had ever known before. And now I think for the first time in my whole life I really began to pray—praying not with my lips and with my intellect and my imagination, but praying out of the very roots of my life and my being. . . .[27]

Tears flowed freely, Merton says, in the aftermath of his losing "that first vivid, agonizing sense" of his father's presence. He paints a remarkable portrait of compunction and remorse. His heart had been pricked. He declines to offer any "explanation" of the experience. His only conclusion was that he could be morally certain "that this was really a grace, and a great grace." His only regret in the autobiography was not following it through in the immediate years to follow. The morning after this experience, he climbed to the Dominican church in Rome, Santa Sabina. Now, just walking into the church became "a very definite experience, something that amounted to a capitulation, a surrender, a conversion, not without struggle. . . . " At the altar rail he prayed the Lord's Prayer, but his heart's memory describes the experience as seemingly "at least a half hour of impassioned prayer and tears."[28]

Years earlier, an incident with his younger brother, John Paul, fixed itself upon Merton's memory. It records the most intimate revelation of his childhood's diminished affective life. The context was 1923–25, when Merton and his brother lived on Long Island with his maternal grandparents. The five-year difference in their ages occasioned Merton's recollection of efforts to shake free of John Paul's shadow, while he and peers engaged in the universal enterprise of ten-year-olds: they were building a hut from scavenged lumber and tar paper. He sees in his memory John Paul,

> [S]tanding in a field, about a hundred years away from the clump of su-
> machs where we have built our hut, is this little perplexed five-year-old
> kid in short pants and a kind of a leather jacket, standing quite still, with
> his arms hanging down at his sides, and gazing in our direction, afraid
> to come any nearer on account of the stones, as insulted as he is saddened,
> and his eyes full of indignation and sorrow. And yet he does not go away.
> We shout at him to get out of there, to beat it, and go home, and wing
> a couple of more rocks in that direction, and he does not go away. We
> tell him to play in some other place. He does not move.

John Paul stands, not weeping, but angry, offended, and "tremendously sad" because, Merton describes, the law of his nature ("this law of love") is violated by denying the younger brother the simple desire to be with him. Merton introduced this story with the reminiscence that it filled him "with poignant compunction at the thought of my own pride and hard-heartedness, and [John Paul's] natural humility and love." His reflection leads him to name this experience as a paradigm of sin: "the deliberate and formal will to reject disinterested love for us for the purely arbitrary reason that we simply do not want it . . . in so far as it seems, in our own perverse imagination, to imply some obscure kind of *humiliation*."[29]

When juxtaposed with the later scene of his initial, unexplainable conversion when he experiences his dead father's presence, a remarkable parallel leaps off the pages of his autobiography. Two months after Merton returned from the European tour, he confessed that his religious fervor declined precipitously. Self-consciousness and pride interfered with his prayer. Even approving remarks from the household would test his humility. "It is a kind of quintessence of pride to hate and fear even the kind and legitimate approval of those who love us!" exclaimed Merton. "I mean, to resent it as a *humiliating* patronage."[30] He returned to the Quaker meeting house where his mother had once sat and meditated, a nostalgic longing for affection beneath his purported search for prayer. While his shyness died down, he found the commonplaces uttered in that circle echoed those of ministers in other churches. Beneath Merton's religious conversion, a transforming affective hunger clamored to be fed. The third passage from *The Seven Storey Mountain* recollects the summer of his twelfth year, boarding with the Privat family in Murat, France. His father's solicitude for his physical and moral care was prompted by the boy's discomfort at the Lyceé in Montauban. Merton's reminiscence gravitates to his confessed tendency to resist any kind of "possessive affection" on the part of other persons. His instinct was "to keep clear, to keep free." Perhaps for the first time in his life, he says, he ventured into a reciprocal love with this simple family. Their love did not burn you, he said, nor did it imprison or "trap your feet in the snares of its interest."[31]

There is not only sentiment (sometimes a surplus of it) in Merton's early poems, but also the release/catharsis of his affective appetite. In his three collections of poetry following *Thirty Poems* (1944) religious themes continue to dominate. In *A Man in the Divided Sea* (1946) twenty of the poems examine general religious themes or experiences; five others address the Passion story; and five more celebrate the Incarnation and Christmas. The next year, 1947, sixteen of the twenty-seven selections in the slighter volume, *Figures for an Apocalypse,* take up general religious themes, and only two address the Incarnation and Christmas; a single poem, "The Transformation: For the Sacred Heart," directly employs metaphors of the Passion story itself.

> Why are we all afraid of love?
> Why should we, who are far greater than the grain
> Fear to fall in the ground and die?[32]

Merton frames a poem around his study of six or seven "black and russet" worms who prepare to winter in the crevices of a monastery wall, beside the cemetery. He compares it to St. Teresa's reminder of nature as parable: "For all creation teaches us some way of prayer."

> See with what zeal they wrestle off their ancient, tawny life
> And fight with all their might to end their private histories
> And lock their days in the cocoon.
>
> Walk we and ponder on this miracle
> And on the way Your creatures love Your will,
> While we, with all our minds and light, how slow

> Hard-hearted in our faithlessness, and stubborn as the coldest
>   stone!
> .   .   .   .
> Shall we still fear the fight that wrests our way
> Free from the vesture of our ancient days,
> Killing the prisoner, Adam, in us,
> And laying us away to sleep a space, in the transforming
>   Christ?
>
> O, we, who know from faith and Scripture
> All the scope and end of metamorphosis,
> Run we like these creatures in their glad alacrity
> To our far sweeter figurative death,
>
> When we can learn such ways to God from creeping things
> And sanctity from a black and russet worm!
>   ("Natural History")[33]

Merton sings a hymn to God as Trinity, celebrating the liberty toward which we gravitate:

> Because our natures poise and point towards You
> Our loves revolve about You as the planets swing upon the sun
> And all suns sing together in their gravitational worlds.
>
> And then, as fires like jewels germinate
> Deep in the stone heart of a Kaffir mountain,
> So now our gravity, our new-created deep desire
> Burns in life's mine like an undiscovered diamond.
>   ("Freedom as Experience")[34]

The concluding poem of the collection ends, however, on a sarcastic note. The poet evidences some of the antipathy of his forthcoming (1947) "Poetry and Contemplation" *Commonweal* essay, in which he recommends the ruthless sacrifice of art for the sake of prayer. His envoi to the volume suggests that these poems, "the rhythms that upset my silences," robbed him of contemplative joys in the mornings. He dismisses the collection, "Go, stubborn talker, / Find you a station in the loud world's corners." His negative attitude toward the world reaches its apogee in the declaration that these poems might "ransom some one prisoner" in the environs of what Merton denounces as "the clamor of the Christless avenues."[35]

EXPERIENCE: THE SHIFT TO THE AUTOBIOGRAPHICAL VOICE

In *The Sign of Jonas,* the journals of December 1946 through July 4,
1952, Merton already had reflected crudely upon his habitual autobiographical style. His honesty in this often torturous chronicle of an early
monastic life volunteered more than was first apparent. The prologue
began, remarking how the journal's notes were set down in the "context of ambivalence, of questioning, of supreme spiritual risk" that shared
"the mysterious and secret testing of spirit which was Christ's own Gethsemani."[36] Merton did not let it escape notice that "our monastery was
not named in vain for the Garden of Agony." He disclaimed a sensa-
tional dramatization of his own existence (and then frequently con-
tradicted himself by the tenor of the journal itself!), expressing "a
peculiar horror of one sin: the exaggeration of our trials and of our
crosses." Nonetheless, wrestle he does in these journals, and he points
to each monk's "share in the mysterious and secret testing of spirit
which was Christ's own Gethsemani."[37]

Here Merton was retrieving a devotion to the humanity of Christ
from monastic roots. It paralleled, in some ways, the rediscovery of
the eclipsed humanity of Jesus by contemporary biblical scholars. It
brought Merton to the ascending (or, from below) christology of the
Western church, and the fully incarnational christology found in the
best of the Greek Fathers. Merton gravitated to the humanity and self-
consciousness of the person of Jesus, the mystery of the cross, and creation's "groaning in travail" (Rom. 8:22). By the time he became master
of scholastics in 1951, this deeper dynamic completely claimed him.
He stood, he said, "on the threshold of a new existence," because he
was "doing without asking myself the abstract questions which are the
luxury and the torment of one's monastic adolesence." Now he sought
"the essentials, . . . sinking into the heart of the present as it is."[38] This
turn to personal experience gained momentum in Merton's life and
writing. Yet these were, ironically, the same years when he wrote *The
Ascent to Truth,* a genre and dense style of scholastic theology to which
he would never return. Something of a schizophrenic spirituality
tempted Merton during this transitional period. He was indeed ex-
perimenting with the pitch of his authentic voice. The "true self" vs.
"false self" tug-of-war shifted from being an abstract theory to an existential quandary.

As Merton embraced the dialectical starting point, Jesus truly hu-

man and truly divine, one person with two natures, an equilibrium
and new energy were restored to his writing. He alleged to be traveling
in "the belly of a paradox," Jonas's whale, as he wrestled in *The Sign
of Jonas* with seemingly conflicting identities as monk and writer. But
the metaphor provided for a different set of autobiographical conflicts
expressed in a deeper christological consciousness. The prologue of the
1953 publication read like a manifesto of release:

> I have not attempted to keep what is formally called a "spiritual journal"
> although I have here and there attempted to write, as best I can, about
> spiritual things. In doing so, I have of course tried to put down my ideas
> in my own words, avoiding technical terminology. I have attempted to con-
> vey something of a monk's spiritual life and of his thoughts, not in the
> language of speculation but in terms of personal experience. This is always
> a little hazardous, because it means leaving the sure, plain path of accepted
> terminology and traveling in byways of poetry and intuition. I found in
> writing *The Ascent to Truth* that technical language, though it is universal
> and certain and accepted by theologians, does not reach the average man
> and does not convey what is most personal and most vital in religious ex-
> perience. Since my focus is not upon dogmas as such, but only on their
> repercussions in the life of a soul in which they begin to find a concrete
> realization, I may be pardoned for using my own words to talk about my
> own soul.[39]

Merton's existential, autobiographical method would rarely deviate
from this newly announced trajectory. It took him a decade ("the missing years" David Cooper has dubbed them), during which tentative,
sometimes stiff and formal books came from his pen, to negotiate this
return. The ongoing audition for this voice was unmistakable from the
opening pages of *The New Man,*[40] a book mixing autobiographical soliloquy with pages of dry notes. But the overture of the book honestly
located Merton at the heart of renewing christology:

> Life and death are at war within us. . . .
>   . . . If by chance we become fully conscious of it, not only in our flesh
> and in our emotions but above all in our spirit, we find ourselves involved
> in a terrible wrestling, an *agonia* not of questions and answers, but of be-
> ing and nothingness, spirit and void. In this most terrible of all wars, fought
> on the brink of infinite despair, we come gradually to realize that life is
> more than the reward for him who correctly guesses a secret and spiritual
> "answer" to which he smilingly remains committed. . . .

Indeed, for the man who enters into the black depths of the *agonia,* religious problems become an unthinkable luxury. He has no time for such indulgences. He is fighting for his life. His being itself is a foundering ship, ready with each breath to plunge into nothingness and yet inexplicably remaining afloat on the void.[41]

Merton went on to mock religions that become degenerate, by "simply supply[ing] answers to questions." The "dark terror of the *agonia*" becomes a struggle with the fact that "we cannot be sure of our own choice." He then ends this first meditation with a Pauline summons "to descend into nothingness."

The Christian hope that is "not seen" is a communion in the agony of Christ. It is the identification of our own *agonia* with the *agonia* of the God Who has emptied Himself and become obedient unto death. It is the acceptance of life in the midst of death, not because we have courage, or light, or wisdom to accept, but because by some miracle the God of Life Himself accepts to live, in us, at the very moment we descend into death.[42]

This kenotic pattern unfolds: abundance, scarcity, abundance. Through kenosis, Christ does not exchange his strength for weakness, but precisely out of his strength which abides, he chooses to be weak.[43] Here is born new kinds of strength. Merton's evident preference for this kenotic pattern by the end of the 1950s found him relaxed with such a paschal conviction. The dogmatic formulas having been given their due, Merton risked imaginatively voicing his experience of Christian faith. By the late 1950s, for example, he would write enthusiastically about Boris Pasternak's fiction and poetry in christological terms. For there he discovered one he named the "hidden Christ," and perceived an unorthodox Christian imagination that "gropes after truth in its own clumsy way."[44] It would be among the first of many similar discoveries Merton ventured, observations that mirrored his new integration of autobiographical consciousness, self-identity, and christology.

EARLY SOURCES NURTURING MERTON'S TURN
TO EXPERIENCE

To funnel the myriad sources that influenced Thomas Merton's spirituality would be equivalent to rewriting his biography. This chapter must now focus attention upon three significant theologians who influenced and nurtured the young monk's confidence in human experience and in his own optimistic autobiographical voice: Duns Scotus, Bernard of Clairvaux, and through Bernard, Gregory the Great. An evident tension would nonetheless manifest itself with a counterforce of contempt for the world (*contemptus mundi*), a panicked flight from the world (*fuga mundi*). As the young novice vacillated from one pole to the other, it became apparent that something would "give." Merton moved toward that resolution without dissolving a deeper paradox, rooted in the New Testament's ambivalence toward the world.

DUNS SCOTUS

As early as his Columbia University studies in New York City, Merton had discovered the "bent" of his mind as Augustinian. His lifelong mentor, Daniel Clark Walsh, adjunct professor of philosophy at Columbia, had sized up Merton. He belonged to the spiritual heritage of Augustine, along with Anselm, Bernard, Bonaventure, Hugh and Richard of St. Victor, and Duns Scotus. In Merton's own words, "that meant that my bent was not so much towards the intellectual, dialectical, speculative character of Thomism, as towards the spiritual, mystical, voluntaristic and practical way of St. Augustine and his followers."[45] The convert's autobiographical voice had found its paradigm. Just as Augustine had struggled to reinterpret Christian culture amid the collapse of the Roman Empire, Thomas Merton, arriving at the Abbey of Gethsemani three days after Pearl Harbor and in the midst World War II's chaos, would retreat from the City of Man and reinterpret faith for a world staggering under modernity's crises.

Walsh's perceptive insight revealed as much about himself as his soon-to-be-famous student. Walsh had studied under the most authoritative living Scotus scholar, Etienne Gilson. Only four years before the 1938 class in which Merton was enrolled, Walsh had completed his doctoral dissertation on Scotus, under Gilson's direction. Merton recorded the profound, surprising effect of reading Gilson's *The Spirit of Medieval Philosophy* during his second year of studies at Columbia, with Walsh's tutoring. It launched his unmitigated joy in medieval culture. But more importantly, it opened for him the Catholic tradition's understanding of God's very Being, distinct from the mechanical caricature of God offered by Descartes.

This early, neglected link in Merton's Columbia studies, Duns Scotus, the Franciscan theologian, bears careful scrutiny. For, as we will analyze momentarily, what distinguishes Scotus's theology is his christology. The genius of Gilson and Toronto's Medieval Institute faculty developed a neo-Thomism to reconcile the traditionally opposing Thomist and Augustinian schools. Merton described Walsh's teaching as juxtaposing and placing the two schools of theology in dialogue in order to see them complementing and reinforcing one another, to see the same truth from multiple viewpoints. The effect was to avoid narrowing or restricting Catholic theology and philosophy to a single mindset, an exclusive school or dominant system. This habit of dialogue and reconciling diverse understandings would work into the marrow of Merton's own Catholicity.

Walsh insisted that Scotus deserved to be appreciated in light of his epistemology: Scotus was not a person *with* knowledge but rather a person *seeking* knowledge and, ultimately, the truth. His title, "subtle doctor," captures this dynamic and Scotus's humility in a way that avoids giving the impression of a definitive or final claim on truth. Walsh joined Gilson in lamenting the fact that Franciscan scholars, especially in this century, always attempted to reconcile Scotus with St. Thomas Aquinas, who personified system, order. That was to mute Scotus and to rob him of his own importance and attractive theology. Another primary concern of Walsh was to accentuate Scotus's emphasis on the "person," signifying a relation to divinity in the order of pure love. This contrasted with "rational nature" as Thomas emphasized it. The distinction is an important one: Scotus looked upon St. Thomas's definition of the human person in the perfection of the twin powers of our rational nature (intellect and will) as inadequate for the Christian mystery. Rather, he interpreted the human person's creation in the "image and likeness" of God's self as a basic likeness, not in our rational nature as did St. Thomas, but in our very *personhood.* The model to which God looked in creation was not primarily the divine "idea" of the human person, but the Word, Jesus Christ—Scotus's Christocentric model, distinct from Thomas's theocentric model.

For Thomas Aquinas and much subsequent Catholic philosophy and theology, christology had developed as a reflection on the Christ event as the remedy for the sin of Adam's fall. In fact, christology was often reduced to something of an afterthought in fundamental theology. Scotus sought to remedy this by reclaiming some of the early biblical and Greek patristic traditions of Christ's pre-existence, the "first-born of creation," the *Logos* present at the creation. Put somewhat baldly, for Thomas and the dominant theology, the Incarnation of the Son of God was *necessary* because of sin; for Scotus and the Franciscan school of theology, the Incarnation of the Son of God was *inevitable* because of God's love![46] Scotus's cosmic Christ was not an afterthought of God, but God's first thought, the paradigm of creation, revealing the innate capacity of the human person to be fulfilled in love. Such a theology and christology placed a decidedly distinct emphasis on the will rather than the intellect.

In Scotus's system, the Incarnation holds a prominence that Merton found congenial. The fall of Adam brought a new *state*, not a new human person, not a new nature. Nature for Scotus (unlike Augustine) had been damaged, not depraved. This fallen nature confronted a world of disorder and rebellion. Scientific, discursive reason left to its own resources failed in attempts to reestablish order in the universe. Fallen human persons continued to work to know the order intended by God's creation, but reason was weakened, damaged by original sin. The turning point of history came with the Incarnation. Now there was a new state for human persons through the same nature: a redeemed state, that of the "new man" in Christ; we were indeed fallen but redeemed, and awaiting sanctification. Grace, for Scotus, is restored to nature; nature is not restored, for nature never fell. The effects are cosmic. Not just history or humanity, but the heart of all creation is fulfilled by the Christ event (Rom. 8:21–22). Here germinated seeds of Merton's own optimism about human experience and the innate capacity for love of God and neighbor. Our perfection as human persons depended upon how we exercised our freedom, now that nature had been reoriented by Christ. This tradition, reinforced by Merton's study of patristic and Pauline sources, would lead him back to incarnational christology, yet "incarnational" in a fuller sense, one that seeks a truly temporal and historical meaning for Christ's life, death, and resurrection. Thomas Merton's overarching theme rooted in this soil. The very opening page of his autobiography claimed it:

> I came into the world. Free by nature, in the image of God, I was nevertheless the prisoner of my own violence and my own selfishness, in the image of the world into which I was born. That world was the picture of Hell, full of men like myself, loving God and yet hating Him; born to love Him, living instead in fear and hopeless self-contradictory hungers.[47]

But he quickly relieved this paradox with the optimism he inherited from his father, an artist, whose "way of looking at things" resembles that of Scotus. For Merton, the artist's integrity "lifts a man above the level of the world without delivering him from it." And his father's religious vision respected "the power of God's creation to bear witness for itself."[48]

In 1939 Merton chose Gerard Manley Hopkins, S.J., as the topic of his intended doctoral dissertation at Columbia. The influence of Scotus became more evident. A year earlier he had remarked his increasing consciousness of "the fact that the only way to live was in a world that was charged with the presence and reality of God."[49] But the dissertation never materialized beyond some now lost index cards he mentioned, noting Hopkins sprung rhythms and metrics as he was "trying to figure out manuals on prosody."[50] We find the echo and mirror of Hopkins in Merton's early poetry.[51]

Merton offers a Hopkins-like celebration of creation and the sacramental universe in his poem "The Sowing of Meanings" from *Figures for an Apocalypse* (1947), a song celebrating spring. Birdsong "wound[s] the listener with such bright arrows." They "play in wheeling silences" that define the bounds of solitude. The movement within the poem, as well as the imagery, is reminiscent of "The Windhover" of Hopkins.

> More than a season will be born here, nature,
> In your world of gravid mirrors!
> The quiet air awaits one note,
> One light, one ray and it will be the angels' spring:
> One flash, one glance upon the shiny pond, and then
> *Asperges me*! sweet wilderness, and lo! we are redeemed!
>
> For, like a grain of fire
> Smouldering in the heart of every living essence
> God plants His undivided power —
> Buries His thought too vast for worlds
> In seed and root and blade and flower,
>
> Until, in the amazing shadowlights
> Of windy, cloudy April,
> Surcharging the religious silence of the spring
> Creation finds the pressure of its everlasting secret
> Too terrible to bear.

Then every way we look, lo! rocks and trees
Pastures and hills and streams and birds and firmament
And our own souls within us flash, and shower us with light,
While the wild countryside, unknown, unvisited of men,
Bears sheaves of clean, transforming fire.

And then, oh then the written image, schooled in sacrifice,
The deep united threeness printed in our deepest being,
Shot by the brilliant syllable of an intuition, turns within,
And plants that light far down into the heart of darkness and
    oblivion
And plunges after to discover flame.

("The Sowing of Meanings")[52]

The decade concluded with his 1949 collection of poems, *The Tears of the Blind Lions,* dedicated to Jacques Maritain. The slight volume of seventeen poems includes thirteen on religious themes (solitude, monastic life, saints) and only a single poem meditating on the Passion or Incarnation. The latter is rendered with a Scotist touch:

For we cannot forget the legend of the world's childhood
Or the track to the dogwood valley
And Adam our Father's old grass farm
Wherein they gave the animals names
And knew Christ was promised first without scars.

("Dry Places")[53]

BERNARD OF CLAIRVAUX

This christological legacy of Scotus surfaces in Merton's own writing on Bernard of Clairvaux, the twelfth-century Cistercian theologian, whose vision, like Scotus's, reinforced Merton's optimism about human experience. Two quotations from Hopkins worked their way into a 1954 book-length commentary on the eighth-centenary encyclical *Doctor Mellifluus,* which commemorated Bernard's death. They are pure christology. Merton was attempting to give modern readers access to Bernard's understanding in his sermons on the Canticle of Canticles. Hopkins had attempted to distinguish the Catholic from the non-Catholic meaning of the mystery of Christ, the difference between "a Person" and "a puzzle," as Merton put it. Or, in Hopkins's letter to Robert Bridges:

To you [says Hopkins to Bridges] it comes to: Christ is in some sense God and in some sense he is not God—and your interest is in the uncertainty; to the Catholic it is: Christ is in every sense God and in every sense man, and the interest is in the locked and inseparable combination, or rather it is in the *Person* in whom the combination has its place.[54]

A second quotation from Hopkins focused more clearly on Bernard's idea that by "conforming" to Christ the person claims a real identity. The goal of our creation, this real identity, means "becoming perfectly free, by loving God without limit." Merton borrows a second quotation from Hopkins to illustrate: "This [conformity to Christ] brings out the nature of man himself as the lettering on a sail or the device upon a flag are best seen when it fills." Bernard's Advent and Christmas sermons, as well as his sermons on Mary, the Virgin Mother, complement this doctrine, says Merton. He concludes that Christmas, the liturgical feast of Incarnation, rather than the perspective of the Passion attracted Bernard and the early Cistercians.[55] The importance of the Incarnation was not as a matter of past history. It is a present reality, "the most important reality of all" for Bernard. "Without it," concludes Merton, "nothing in history has any ultimate meaning."[56]

Almost a decade earlier, Merton had written a series of essays on Bernard, which fathom the depth of his discovery of an eclipsed Christ-consciousness within the Cistercian tradition in which he was immersing himself in the 1940s. A 1948 study, "The Spirit of Simplicity," gravitates to Bernard's christology. It contributes a theological anthropology, an understanding of the human person's orientation toward God. When Bernard seeks to understand Adam's fall and our loss in sin, Merton alertly points to an optimism. He identifies Bernard as "augustinian" in the sense of his emphasis on the will and psychology.[57] But he segregates Bernard from Augustine:

One of the ways in which Bernard, departing from traditional augustinian treatment . . . , describes the divine image in the soul is to say that it consists in three things: man's natural *simplicity,* his natural immortality, and his inborn freedom of will. . . . Now the true greatness of man consists not only in his own essential simplicity, but in his ability to rise to a participation in the infinitely perfect simplicity of the Word.[58]

Optimism breathes through Merton's discovery of Bernard's christology. He sees Christ as the contemplator of *"Abba,"* the Father. This grounds Bernard's teaching on humility. Merton describes it as Bernard's insistence on self-knowledge being "not merely that we may be convinced of our 'vileness.'" That half-truth hides "our greatness: our likeness to, our capacity for union with, God." Bernard's christology revolves around an understanding of our lost "likeness" to the Creator; we have retained the "image" of God, even after the fall. The whole of Cistercian life, presented in Bernard's mystical theology, is the "recovery of our lost likeness to God."[59]

The tragedy of our human predicament, for Bernard, was the way in which the human will could conceal this likeness. The fall did not harm our human nature; but for Bernard, something far worse happened. "Our simplicity," says Merton, "was concealed under the disfigurement of a duplicity, a hypocrisy, a living lie that would not and could not be natural to us or part of our nature, and yet which would inevitably cling to us as a kind of hideous second-nature, but for the grace of God, who in his infinite mercy sent his beloved Son to deliver us again by his death on the Cross."[60] These seeds of Bernard's christology will germinate in Merton's drama of the "true self" or "inner self" vs. the "false self." His development of this theme of deformity/disfigurement especially governed his poetic imagination, where the images of the duplicity and hypocrisy multiply: the mask, disguise, illusion, empirical ego, persona, counterfeit, camouflage, cloaking, armoring —all speak the ironic absence of the self in Christ.[61] Merton was "on" to the riches of monastic spirituality, the simplicity and clarity of life and identity that had intuitively attracted him to the Cistercians. "A Letter to My Friends on entering the Monastery of Our Lady of Gethsemani, 1941)" presaged the mystery in Bernard's idiom:

> More than we fear, we love the holy desert,
> Where desperate strangers, hid in their disguises,
> Have come to meet, by night, the quiet Christ.[62]

In a pair of 1949–50 essays entitled "Transforming Union in St. Bernard and St. John of the Cross," he mined from rich veins of Bernard's spirituality an emphasis on the priority of experience. Bernard spoke of the soul being "re-formed" to its lost likeness to God. And only wisdom could so transform a soul. This wisdom is an intensity and purity of love so great that it finds delight in all things. Merton lingered over the Latin term, *sapientia:* "*Sapit*—literally, knows, as it were, by tasting. Hence, *Sapientia,* wisdom, is the knowledge of God by the experience of (tasting) his infinite goodness."[63] What the natural per-

son would find bitter, the person tranformed by wisdom tastes as goodness and finds sweet.

The experience of compunction provided a key for Bernard's understanding of the recovery of our lost likeness to God.[64] We come full
circle here with *The Seven Storey Mountain*'s record of the impact of
his father's story about Peter's weeping, and the footprints of that experience in his own poetry. Merton had experienced this affective conversion, Christ as the love of God, a human person seeking God in
tears of compunction. In Bernard's spirituality, this is the beginning
of the Christlikeness reappearing, an image concealed by sin. No wonder that this imagery of compunction and awakening vision would converge beautifully in Merton's 1949 collection of poetry, aptly titled with
these images: *The Tears of the Blind Lions*. The ultimate question in
Bernard's spirituality was the question of identity, the interrogative voice
underlying every autobiography, asking, "Who am I?"

Merton credited Bernard of Clairvaux with building the simple edi-
fice of Cistercian spirituality upon the foundations of human experience: under divine grace, we find an experience of truth in ourselves;
in the school of charity, we find an experience of truth in the life of
monastic community; and in the silence of contemplative prayer or
mystical experience, we find an experience of truth as it is in itself:
God as the ground of Being. Thus we are initiated, by experience, into
the way to God in "three degrees of truth." Merton introduced this
monastic legacy to an American audience in his popular 1949 history
of the Cistercians, *The Waters of Siloe*. Small wonder that Merton described these waters as intoxicating. The experience could be communicated only in metaphors of ecstasy. Only then did we become our
true self, the self in Christ.

Merton's ability to trust human experience, distinct from more dogmatic formulas, hibernated quietly. Meanwhile, his poetry could tentatively celebrate this optimistic, sacramental vision of the universe,
where Christ is not alien.

GREGORY THE GREAT

There is buried in Merton's 1953–54 essay on Bernard an acknowl-
edgment that the twelfth-century Cistercian echoes not only Augustine but also Gregory the Great in his doctrine on contemplation.[65]
Bernard's dependence on the sixth-century monk-pope and reformer's

spirituality has become more apparent in modern critical research.[66] The footprints of Gregory the Great are curiously faint in Merton's writing. But the clarity and abiding impress of his spirituality on the Kentucky contemplative deserves to be credited as a sustained influence worthy of particular notice. It surfaced in a christological context when Merton published an essay on "The Humanity of Christ in Monastic Prayer." He argued there against the abstract and arbitrary separation of the humanity and divinity of Christ. This had appeared as a pseudo-problem in sixteenth- and seventeenth-century spirituality controversies involving Teresa of Avila and the quietists and illuminists. Merton quotes Teresa's self-reproach for her "high treason" in bypassing the Person of the Man-God because it seemed an obstacle to an experience of the divine essence.

Merton's effort throughout a sometimes meandering chain of patristic and monastic sources is to insist that the appropriate distinction to make in Christian prayer is between the Person of Christ, the God-Man, before the Resurrection, and the glorified life he lives now and forever after the Resurrection. Merton speaks of "'Christ according to the flesh' or the Incarnate Word who no longer lives in that *forma servi* which marked His kenotic and hidden state before the Resurrection"; and the "Christ of glory," who now reigns in heaven and acts through the Holy Spirit until he is manifest and takes to himself all the pure of heart. This latter Christ lives the glory of the risen God-Man, the glorified humanity of Christ. In prayer, the perspective is always that of faith. Merton's emphasis falls repeatedly on this truth and the classical doctrine of the *unity* of two natures in one person.

"The Humanity of Christ in Monastic Prayer" is a study of purity of heart as the ascetic path to contemplation. The recurring source of the monk's pure prayer is the experience of the Apostles, who witnessed the Transfiguration of Christ on Mt. Tabor. By ascending with Christ to the solitude of the mountain, says Merton, "the mature contemplative 'gazes upon the divinity' of Christ."[67] The essay revolves around an understanding of the paschal mystery. "While the Fathers do not draw a sharp contrast between the two abstract natures of Christ," observes Merton, "still less between the Person of Christ and the divine essence," they are very aware of a contrast between the state of the God-Man before his Passion and Resurrection, and after his triumph over death. Christ first lived kenotically, in weakness. He quotes Gregory: "After the Passion, the chains of death having been broken . . . , weakness passed over into power, death into eternity, and humiliation into glory." Gregory describes this *transitus,* or "passing over," as moving from the Word of God descending into our world, "veiling his light in our frail human nature" so that his fidelity to God through death and resurrection might raise us to heaven.

The crucial texts of Gregory center around his image of the Person of Christ, the Word, as *lumen incircumscriptum,* or unlimited light.[68] What we contemplate is not the pure and simple divine essence, but the glory of the Man-God. It is the same as the *lumen Christi,* the light of the risen Christ sung in Easter's "Exultet!" We are called out of darkness to participate in this light. Such is the conversion process, the ascetic climb to the mountain of pure prayer of the Transfiguration, which the monk, and every Christian, lives. Merton returns to the central concern:

> It is the light of the divine, transcendent and life-giving power which belongs to Christ not only as God but also as man, and to exclude the humanity of Christ from that light is to turn away in blindness from the true Mystery of the one Christ. To know Christ *only* as a 'divine essence' is little better than knowing Him only as a frail and mortal man.[69]

Merton here claims two theological insights. First, only abstract theological reflection can separate Christ's divinity and humanity.[70] This mystery, he says, is no longer completely hidden after the Resurrection.[71] We can now experience this *lumen incircumscriptum.* And second, the humanity of Christ does not constitute the real mystery of the Incarnation; rather, it is the fact that human nature now enjoys an inseparable unity with Christ's divine nature.[72] The monk's vocation is to renounce, in Gregory's terminology, whatever opposes the "ineffable light" of God in Christ. When the monk accepts his own total hopelessness and deficiency, his darkness, and seeks in his heart to be transformed by contemplation, he begins to accept the light on its own terms. With an insight that will grow in his own mature spirituality and poetry, Merton remarks: "The ineffable and indefinable light of Christ is a light of extreme simplicity and purity, but it is also a tender and merciful light which does not reject any darkness that is aware of itself and laments its alienation." Love, in Gregory's spirituality, then gives us "eyes with which to apprehend the invisible reality of the *lumen incircumscriptum.*"[73]

Merton concluded this unique study with a paradox: the experience of compunction is first sorrowful and then bursts into tears of gladness at the recognition of God's mercy; the darkness of our sins clears away and we see with our minds in a flash the indefinable light, but we are unable to grasp the *lumen incircumscriptum* and end up baffled, blinded by what Gregory named the "dazzling presence of [Christ's] immensity all about us."[74] Out of these metaphors of blindness and vision, illusion and the "true self" in Christ, was born the mythos of Merton's poetry, which now invites a new scrutiny.

2. Shy Wild Deer:

Personifications of the Inner Self in Merton's Poetry

When Thomas Merton began to read Boris Pasternak's novel, *Doctor Zhivago,* the opening scene could not but rivet his attention. Pasternak's passage describes the funeral of the mother of a ten-year-old boy. The reminder of Merton's inconsolable grief at the death of his own mother, Ruth Jenkins Merton, when he was only six years old, somersaulted onto the text. The Russian family gathers at the grave. The ancient Eastern Orthodox prayers are intoned. Pasternak concentrates the emotional hurricane on the boy, Yura, who climbs onto the hurriedly filled grave's mound. He glances. His face grows contorted and he stretches his neck. "If a wolf cub had done this," the narrator reports, "everyone would have thought that it was about to howl. The boy covered his face with his hands and burst into sobs." An uncle tears the boy away from his torment. The uncle, Nikolai, is a defrocked priest. That night, while caring for his sister's son, he comforts the boy by talking "of Christ." The following summer, 1903, Nikolai, who is working for the liberal newspaper publisher, brings the proofs of a new book on Russia's agrarian and economic crises to the author. Their conversation turns to faith and Christ. In his own critical interpretation Merton enthusiastically quoted Nikolai's affirmation from this early page of the novel:

> It was not until after the coming of Christ that time and man could breathe freely. It was not until after Him that men began to live toward the future. Man does not die in a ditch like a dog—but at home in history, while the work toward the conquest of death is in full swing; he dies sharing in this work.[1]

41

Pasternak spends the bulk of the novel earning the truth of that affirmation. At the end of *Doctor Zhivago,* the author appended a collection of Yurii Zhivago's poems. They are more than a *coda.* Merton's allusion to one entitled "Holy Week" in his *Disputed Questions* essay of 1960 orients us to a keen appreciation of this poetry.[2] These poems, in fact, elucidate more fully the prose of the man awarded the 1958 Nobel Prize for Literature and with whom Merton ventured a correspondence involving considerable political jeopardy for the Soviet Georgian poet. A paradigm for reading Thomas Merton's own work emerges. Poetry stands beside Merton's prose just as panels of a diptych stand, each in dialogue with the other.

This chapter insists upon an integrated reading of Merton's prose meditations on the spirituality of the "true self" or "inner self" and his poetry, where we find its unalloyed personifications. When the poet's contemplative experience tapped the deepest religious center, the self in Christ, then christology, autobiography, and identity converged in the poem. This integrated reading connects directly with the previous chapter because the monk-poet subscribed to a precise theory of poetry as a unique kind of knowledge, concerned with aspects of experience which can never be described but only imitated in action (*mimesis*). The poem recreates an experience and invites the reader to partake of the poet's interpretation of its meaning. In Merton's successful poems he invariably engages his ontological concern in terms of a "paradise consciousness," which I will interpret later in this chapter as Merton's description of the new creation in Christ and not a return to Adam's Eden. The poet seeks to recreate his readers by exposing the illusory false self and summoning the true or inner self, grounded, for Merton, in the experience of Christ, who has restored our lost likeness to God and transfigured human nature. Explications of a variety of Merton's poems reveal this dynamic and orient us to his emergent christology. Their personifications of the inner self manifest the transformation which is rooted in Christ's kenosis, which fathoms new possibilities for the freedom of human persons created in Christ's image. Ideally, a reader would juxtapose the monk's prose meditations on Christ with poems on the inner self written during the same period in order to discern points of convergence or divergence in Merton's christology. The next chapter will independently analyze these christological developments in his prose. In linking these two chapters I hope to make evident the unique christology to be quarried from the strata of poems where personifications of the inner self become Merton's metaphors for the person of Christ.

Thomas Merton's spiritual meditations and poetry are hinged together by his confidence in experience, *sapientia* as we have described it in the first chapter. We can come closer to an understanding of the monk's inner self in his successful poetry than in his prose. This claim is rooted in Merton's temperament as a poet. His mind worked intuitively. He preferred the symbolic to discursive modes of thought. In a 1938 review of John Crowe Ransom's *The World's Body*, a bible of the New Criticism, Merton put the issue sharply: "[Poetry] is a kind of knowledge, and a knowledge that cannot be gained by any other means, for the poet is concerned with the aspects of experience that can never be well described, but only reproduced or imitated."[3] The New Critics of the 1930s and 1940s may have exaggerated the autonomy of the work of art, integral in itself, as a verbal icon. But they restored a necessary balance that emphasized the artist's goal of *mimesis,* the work of art as a structured, meaningful reality, the poem as the miming of an action through which we encounter, in a unique way, the inner self of the artist—and our own inner self. Merton once published a rare letter from his artist-father, Owen Merton, voicing the belief that order and sincerity are closely allied in the artist's vocation. In that context, the elder Merton turned to Van Gogh's remark that Christ "was the greatest artist we ever had, for he dealt with men, not with colours or brushes, he almost created men. If our pictures do not in some measure create the men who look at them or perhaps better re-create them, those pictures are not much good."[4]

George Woodcock's study, *Thomas Merton: Monk and Poet,*[5] deserves credit for coaxing readers to consider the achievement of Merton as poet. For over a decade we have navigated with Woodcock's compass leading us to either Merton's "poetry of the choir" or his "poetry of the desert." This is useful to a point, but like all dichotomies it can force misleading or labored readings. The romanticized Gethsemani poems of the earlier Merton persona, the "poetry of the choir," often betray a world-denying mentality which Merton later disowned; they also include memorable lyrics which celebrate and affirm experiences within the monastic walls. Woodcock does not define the poetry of the choir but describes it as Merton's 1940s verse, influenced by psalmody and its typological and cosmological symbolism, sustained by tones of joy and songs of praise, and structured around an invocatory man-

ner, grammatical repetitions, and "loudness." Likewise, the prophet
or hermit persona's lean and purgative "poetry of the desert" carried
an apocalyptic note. Woodcock describes the poetry of the desert as
a relatively small group of quite distinctive poems characteristic of "Merton's eremetic urge" and characterized by "spareness, control, quite short
lines, [and] a laconic manner that bows toward silence."[6]

But Woodcock's analyses have too tightly segregated, even polarized
these two categories. I would propose two additional categories: (1) the
poetry of paradise consciousness and (2) the poetry of the forest. An
entire constellation of poems, arching across Merton's poetry corpus,
develops a complex of images, symbols, and metaphors of the paradise
consciousness, through which he recreates the experience of the inner
self. They suggest a deeper coherence and continuity among his works.
These poems are reminiscent of both the joy and psalmlike invocations
of the best "poetry of the choir" and the austere, ironic emptiness of
the best "poetry of the desert." My category of poetry of paradise consciousness differs from either of Woodcock's categories because it fathoms Merton's mythos of the spirituality of the true self in poems
which always imply and sometimes explicitly refer to the self in Christ.
The expression "poetry of the forest" fully emerges only late in the
monk-poet's life. As a category it recreates the experience of the true
self as sublimely free and resilient, capable of finding authentic new
life in the wake of personal and social disruptions. Yet it presents an
architectonic by which to reconsider his total poetry corpus, and especially to discern the christological impulse that animates the poet's voice.
It serves, finally, as an arresting metaphor to orient us to his mature
poetry of the hermitage years, the antipoetry of *Cables to the Ace* and
The Geography of Lograire, which chapter 5 explores.

It is arguable whether Merton, the poet, deserves the status of more
than a minor figure in literary circles. His literary beginnings were perhaps auspicious. In 1939 he won Columbia University's Marian Gris-
wald van Rensselaer Poetry Prize for "Fable for a War," the best entry
in the use of the lyric. His early religious poetry was greeted with mixed
reviews, the most enduring suspicion being Robert Lowell's insightful
appraisal, "the poet would appear to be more phenomenal than the
poetry."[7] T.S. Eliot in 1949 judged Thomas Merton's early poetry as
"hit or miss," intimating that the monk wrote too much and revised
too little.[8] A phalanx of Catholic reviewers enthusiastically and often
uncritically celebrated Merton's arrival on the 1940s literary scene as

a sectarian laureate. Other reviewers measured his shortcomings; some critics planted suspicions about the very genre of religious poetry.

What is not arguable is the need to integrate a reading of Merton's poetry with his prose meditations on the spirituality of the inner self, the true self in Christ. One merely pretends to understand Merton by reverently browsing through his thousand-plus pages of poetry, pausing for the obligatory genuflection, if one abdicates any responsibility to wrestle with the poems, indeed to permit oneself to be interpreted and even to be recreated by them. Merton's poetry and prose meditations on the inner self need to be yoked together for an adequate appreciation of his whole contribution.

Many Merton commentators shy away from investigating the epiphany of the "true self" or "inner self" in his poems. Yet, as this chapter will unfold, his poetry manifests the inner self through a dynamic, dramatic process. The inner self is poised to contrast with the "false self." In his 1949 classic, *Seeds of Contemplation,* Merton had diagnosed the spiritual menace: "hell is perpetual alienation from the true self."[9] His poetry manifests a christology by reclaiming the inner self's "homecoming" when various personae in the poems discover a transforming new authenticity and freedom from their marginal vantage points of innocence, weakness, hiddenness, exploitation, or rejection. When the poet discovered that his contemplative experience offered him a newly conceived creativity, the poetry sprang forth as a symbolic matrix in which to portray this ongoing conversion drama. This chapter explores this dynamic, which Merton identified as the poet's "paradise ear." It will encompass: (1) a reflection on the poet's task and how this coincides with every monk's vocation as keeping alive the monk's own experience of God and not just the memory of God. (2) It will also present a schema for distinguishing four types of Merton's poetry, with emphasis on two different constellations of poems which I describe as the "poetry of paradise consciousness" and the "poetry of the forest." My method throughout is to explicate particular poems as personifications of the true self or the inner self in Christ.

THE POET'S TASK: MERTON'S THEORY

Any assessment of Merton the poet not only must address the craft of his collected poetry but also his reflections on the task encompassed by the enterprise of the poet. The poetry ultimately must be judged on its intrinsic literary merits. Nonetheless, Merton's development as poet remains tethered to his own critical appreciation of what literary art intends and achieves.

Under the influence of Mark Van Doren at Columbia University, Merton found new confidence and a rigorous intellectual foundation for his literary interests: T.S. Eliot, William Blake, John Donne and the metaphysical poets, and Shakespeare, among others. It was no coincidence that his literary gifts matured and were polished through the vital contact he sustained with Van Doren. When his first published book review of 1938 hailed John Crowe Ransom's definition of poetry as a unique way of knowing, he was reclaiming a classical tradition along with the charter of a generation of literary insurgents, the New Critics. Their reaction to Romantic theories of poetry and their exposure of fallacies, affective and otherwise, reoriented Merton: "the poet is concerned with the aspects of experience that can never be well described but only reproduced and imitated."[10] *The Secular Journal* (1959) and *The Sign of Jonas* (1953) reveal Merton's early repugnance toward the Romantic poets, with their sprawling emotions and sentimentality.[11]

In Van Doren's Shakespeare class, the young graduate student applauded his teacher's refusal to treat literature as history, or sociology, or economics, or psychoanalysis, or anything other than literature. Merton learned to respect the autonomy of the work of literature. Van Doren avoided reading into poems "a lot of subjective messages" and contemporary issues such as Marxism and political propaganda.[12] For one who considered himself an intellectual gangster during the Columbia years, the experience of Van Doren's class proved sobering in more ways than one.

He would turn to a contemporary of the Romantics, nonetheless, William Blake, as the subject of his master's thesis at Columbia. It was, he said in retrospect, providential. Blake's mystical and supernatural ideal was a reaction against the literalism, naturalism, and narrow, classical realism in art. Merton's study of Blake provided the antidote to his own naturalism and materialism.[13] The discovery of Jacques Maritain's aesthetic theory in *Art and Scholasticism* clued his research to the possibility of interpreting Blake in orthodox Christian categories. What dominates this early study[14] is his understanding of Blake as a "religious artist" and mystic. Merton sees Blake as the antithesis of the Romantic poets, with their Deistic idolatry of nature; for Blake, nature is not intelligible until it is transfigured in Christ. The Incarnation-consciousness of Maritain's aesthetics gave Merton the bridge to understand Beauty as the object of intelligibility.

> If form is the principle of intelligibility, then CLARITAS in a beautiful object is "the glory of form shining through matter. . . ."
> Form is a revelation of essences; to see a thing as it is essentially and how it is filled with God's glory with which all things are alike charged, that is what Blake means by "particularizing." "Distinctness is particular, not general," and so beauty does not conform with certain ideal and unchanging types (That's Plato!). Seeing the world in a grain of sand is the perception of CLARITAS. . . . Look through matter into eternity.[15]

In the poet Blake, Merton had found the seer, the visionary, the mystic. The natural eye proved unimportant for Blake's art. "[O]nce nature had been assimilated and transferred by his imagination," concluded Merton, "it blazed before him in a vision fired with the glory of God."[16]

But even earlier, Merton had gravitated to such a theory of art. Buried beneath the doctrinal accretions that were masking his autobiographical voice in *The Seven Storey Mountain* is his account of an innate trust in the cognitive dimension of art. It is at the center of his reflections in Rome in 1933, some five years before he entered the Roman Catholic Church. He had visited the ancient churches and encountered the great mosaics of Christ. Doctrines of a God of infinite power, wisdom and love "were implicit in every line of the pictures I contemplated with such admiration and love," Merton intuited. He described how the artist's thought reached his own mind and how he implicitly grasped these doctrines. But more importantly, he caught "something of the ancient craftsman's love of Christ."[17] The same aesthetic sensibility provides a threshold for Merton's christology in his poetry.

A POETRY CHRONOLOGY: THE "MISSING DECADE"[18]

In his early monastic journal, *The Sign of Jonas,* Thomas Merton quips, "Perhaps I shall continue writing on my deathbed, and even take some asbestos paper with me in order to go on writing in purgatory."[19] The need to write seemed congenital with Merton. John Howard Griffin caricatured it by remarking on Merton-the-journalist's documentary habit—he could not even "scratch his nose" without writing it down![20] In that same early monastic journal, Merton recollects beginning to read the Book of Job, and he laments: "I know that all of

my own poems about the world's suffering have been inadequate: . . .
[T]hey have only camouflaged the problem."[21] He proceeds then to
vacillate between extremes: first, that of discontinuing all writing and,
then, writing into eternity. Michael Mott has alertly noted the frontispiece photograph of Merton, back turned toward the viewer, which
graces *The Sign of Jonas*. Its haunting pose symbolizes Merton's ordeal, "travelling toward my destination in the belly of a paradox."[22]
He had entered the monastery as a writer and poet of some accomplishment, vowing silence as a Cistercian monk. Yet after the surprising
publishing sensation of *The Seven Storey Mountain* (1948), fame as
a writer pursued him. He would be an enormously successful popular
writer, one who afforded a very public eavesdropping on his search for
the inner self.

The first decade of Merton's life at Gethsemani seemed torturous
to his readers who were following the veiled saga in his books. Would
this self-proclaimed "duck in a chicken coop" really give anything in
the world to be a chicken instead of a duck?[23] What really had gone
lame in the early poems about the world's suffering? How could the
writer coexist with the contemplative? Despite protests that he wanted
to divest himself of the writer's weeds and don only the monk's scapu-
lar, the outcome remained uncertain. For the readers there was, in fact,
little drama, though much tease. One senses through all the self-
consciousness about his literary success that Merton's great fault in the
1940s was cultivating a literary persona.

A chronology of his poetry proves revealing:

1944 *Thirty Poems*
1946 *A Man in the Divided Sea*
1947 *Figures for an Apocalypse*
1949 *The Tears of the Blind Lion*
1957 *The Strange Islands*
1959 *Selected Poems*
1962 *Original Child Bomb*
1963 *Emblems of a Season of Fury*
1966 *Sensation Time at the Home*
1968 *Cables to the Ace*
1968 *The Geography of Lograire*
1977 *The Collected Poems*
1986 *Eighteen Poems*

Even a cursory glance at this record reveals the virtual absence of Merton's poetry in the 1950s, or a nearly ten-year gap in writing poetry between the poetry volumes of 1949 and 1957.[24] In effect, the apparent sacrifice of his poetry announced in the 1947 *Commonweal* essay would appease the conscience and free Merton for more spiritual prose projects, e.g., studies like *The Ascent to Truth* (1951), *Bread in the Wilderness* (1953), *The Living Bread* (1956), *The New Man* (1961, nearly a decade in the making). Responsibilities within the monastery as master of scholastics, and then, of novices, consumed more and more of Merton's attention and energy. He was distracted from, if not ironically robbed of, the leisure and contemplative space in which he could write poetry. Merton boasted that the one compensation of "being a writer" would be that "it brought me solitude."[25]

The stress of Merton's wrestling under the dual pressures of life as a contemplative-poet emerged full-blown in the pair of curious essays in *Commonweal*: "Poetry and the Contemplative Life" (1947), and "Poetry and Contemplation: A Reappraisal" (1958). The former exhibits a discomforting ambivalence. At points Merton speaks patronizingly of the poet, noting that no worthy Christian poetry has been written by anyone "not in some degree a contemplative." But, finally, poetry becomes only a propaedeutic to the "higher" mystical experience of true contemplation; in fact, it can become a "fatal handicap," a distraction: by sharing the contemplative experience one is left with nothing—the "experience of the artist" as Merton grimly paints it.

By 1958 Merton had reversed himself, complaining that he could not merely bury his artistic talent and settle for the career of "professional saint." A distinctively sacramental consciousness is apparent in the second essay, where he emphasizes the "goodness of creation." He has clearly outgrown the two-tiered nature/supernature model. Parallels with the growing optimism in his spirituality and meditations on Christ, identified in chapter 1 and yet to be traced in chapter 3, abound here. Merton concludes by overruling the ruthless and complete "sacrifice" of his poetry. "Indeed, experience teaches us," he writes, "that the most perfect choice is the choice of what God has willed for us, even though it may be, in itself, less perfect, and indeed less 'spiritual.'"[26]

Merton had redesigned and hammered out his poet's tools on the anvil of experience. In the 1940s, the first decade of his monastic life, Merton produced lyric poetry celebrating the claustrophobic comfort of the cloister; in the second decade, the 1950s, he virtually muted his poet's voice; but in the 1960s, the final decade, he reclaimed in a new idiom the unique way of knowing which the poetic experience could recreate. Merton's gregarious personality embraced the contemporary crises of history as the new matrix for the metaphors of his mature poetry, where the epiphany of the hidden Christ coaxed the post-Christian world to awaken to the inner experience.

THE POET'S "PARADISE EAR"

In 1938, the Columbia graduate student Thomas Merton picked up Etienne Gilson's *The Spirit of Medieval Philosophy* and never recovered from the intellectual conversion it sparked. He speaks of it as revolutionizing his whole life when he discovered that the Catholic concept of God's Being, *aseitas,* was not a superstitious, "hangover" belief from some prescientific age. Nor was it Descartes's alternative God. The implications of the discovery that God's very nature was simply "to exist" would lead Merton to a new horizon from which to appreciate God's love for creation, and especially human nature's capacity to participate in a free, loving response to God.[27] From this point on, Merton would be an incurable ontologist, hungering to share the life of this God whose nature it is to exist, to create, and to summon humanity to love. A year before his baptism, ontology was already in the marrow of Merton's Catholic bones.

Paul Tillich has constructed a useful schema of two distinct types of faith, the *moral* and the *ontological.*[28] He divides moral types of faith into *law,* which is concerned with juridical approaches or formal norms leading to holiness; and *prophecy,* which seeks to reform the world's deteriorated structures that defend justice, human dignity, and mercy. When it comes to the ontological types of faith, Tillich again names two distinct types. *Mystical* types of ontological faith are immediate experiences of God as the ground of Being. That is to say, nothing mediates the experience of this divine presence; it is the pure gift of an inner experience. On the other hand, there is the *symbolic,* or sacramental, type of ontological faith, which is a mediated experience of the presence of God as the ground of Being. Concrete, material, historical realities mediate this experience: notes of music; the biblical word; the person of Jesus in his life, ministry, teaching, and preaching; elements of bread and wine in the Eucharist, or water, oil, spoken vows in other sacraments; the poet's metaphors. In mystical and symbolic faith, one participates in, or is symbolically saturated with, the very Being of God.

Merton's struggle with his identity as contemplative and poet mirrors Tillich's distinction between the mystic and symbolic types of faith: both are ontological, yet distinctive, without being exclusive. They are meant to be complementary, not at odds with one another. Tillich's schema suggests that the mature believer integrates dimensions of all four possibilities, rather than isolating in only one of the four. The rhythms of a person's faith life pass from one possibility to another. Various persons may be identified as predominantly attracted to one of these possible expressions, but usually with nuances of the others.

To consider the poet as an ontologist who creates symbols that mediate faith opens up new possibilities for understanding Merton's spirituality of the inner self. It would be a mistake to say that he developed a systematic literary theory, but he indicates certain vectors for the poet, beside which we can plot and test the directions of his own poetry. During his voluntary abstinence from the writing of poetry in the 1950s, Merton ventured to survey the Psalms in the handsome 1953 volume, *Bread in the Wilderness.* A dozen years of immersion in the monastic choir, chanting the metaphoric verses of the psalms in the rhythmic cycle of the Liturgy of the Hours, were subtly transforming Merton. He compared the poet and the original person in paradise, Adam, in a chapter entitled "Poetry, Symbolism, and Typology." Created nature, he said, has been given to humanity as a clean "window." The fall of Adam symbolically rendered nature opaque, so that we no longer look through the transparent window and see all created things in the light of God. We suffer an inability to penetrate the meaning of the world we live in. Our myths and symbols degenerate. Merton called this the "corruption of cosmic symbolism." What makes his description so vivid is the analogy he makes to the poet.

The poet looks through a clear window and reports on reality. Creation owes its being to God. As daylight prevails, the poet sees easily through the windowpane to view the outside reality. The problem begins when lights go on inside his room and night descends. "Then we see ourselves and our own room reflected in the pane." Merton warned that an immense part of reality is lost or abandoned in the process. The poet loses the rich, symbolic character of nature, the world outside the window, and is no longer able to image the "world beyond." The poet becomes self-conscious, absorbed in the self's reflections in the window. We are in danger of a purely subjective, egocentric soliloquy. We are like Adam and Eve in paradise, Merton announced: "They began to worship what they themselves were doing" and this neglect of God was "too often an abomination." Nature was no longer symbol but illusion. In this short sketch, Merton maps coordinates for his poetry of the false self versus the inner self: the paradise consciousness that offers a window on the objective reality of nature, the predicament of the illusory false self, and the poet's ontological ability to see and to experience reality as it has come forth from God and is transfigured in Christ. Adam in paradise, naming the animals and walking with God in the garden, personifies the paradigm of the poet.

In this same chapter of *Bread in the Wilderness,* Merton reiterates his conviction that poetry is a unique way of knowing. Words in poetry are charged with affective and spiritual associations, he insists. The poet puts together words in such a way that they react and release in the reader an enriching experience that touches personal depths. "A good poem induces an experience that could not be produced by any other combination of words. It is therefore an entity that stands by itself, graced with an individuality that marks it off from every other work of art."[29]

The psalms became christological and pneumatological for Merton. Christ's kenotic pattern of transformation again centers Merton's reflection.

> We too, when we chant these verses as the old saints must have chanted them, experience the truth which the Father reveals to us in their writings. We find out that when we bring our own sorrows and desires and hopes and fears to God and plunge them all into the sorrows and hopes of the mysterious One who sings this Psalm, a kind of transubstantiation is effected. We have put all we have — or rather all our poverty, all that we have not — into the hands of Christ. . . . Consecrated by contact with the poverty He assumed to deliver us, we find that in His poverty our poverty becomes infinite riches; in His sufferings our defeats are transubstantiated into victory, and His death becomes our everlasting life.
>
> What has happened? We have been transformed. The process is more than a tragic *catharisis.* . . .
>
> This transformation is operated in us by the power of the Holy Spirit

Who lives and acts in the word He has inspired. He, if you like, is the poet. But He also is the poetry. Or rather Christ, Whose Spirit He is, is the poetry of the Psalms. But the Holy Spirit, besides being the artist, is also the spectator. He is at the same time the poet, the poetry, and the reader of the poetry; the music and the musician, the singer and the hearer.[30]

An even sharper sense of the poet's paradise consciousness is found in the opening pages of Merton's manuscript titled, "The Inner Experience." He explicates the Genesis 3 story of the fall from paradise and the resulting alienation experienced by human persons. Redemption becomes for Merton a recovery of a lost unity—a return, in some sense, to the paradise consciousness. The soul awakens, he says, and now conscious of her alienation, she begins the illuminative way. What becomes crucial is Merton's appreciation of sin as an ontological lapse, not merely a moral lapse. Sin violates the person's very *being*. The distinction approximates contemporary ethicians' understanding of sin as "fundamental option," engaging the deepest levels of human freedom and personal identity. Sin says something about our refusal to be "who" we are created to be.

> The sense of sin is something deeper and more existential. It is not merely a sense of guilt referred to the authority of God. . . . The sense of sin is then something ontological and immediate which does not spring from reflection on my actions and comparison with a moral code. It springs directly from the evil that is present in me: it tells me not merely that I have done wrong, but that I *am* wrong, through and through. That I am a false being. That I have destroyed myself. For sin is spiritual self-destruction.[31]

It is not adequate to define sin simply in terms of categorical actions, which Merton found leading only to the "anxiety of guilt." The contemplative enjoys solitude in which to claim and live the true or inner self. So Merton identified the contemplative's mission for today: "to keep alive a sense of sin" as ontological lapse and not merely the violation of an external code.[32] For Merton, the poet shares an analogous task, coaxing readers to recognize their illusory false self and creating the possibility of an alternative identity. For the monk this ultimately led to the self in Christ. The poet recreates in images, symbols, and metaphors such personifications of the inner self to awaken us.

The German poet Rainer Maria Rilke grew more and more important in Merton's understanding of poetry. He described him as the poet of *Innerlichkeit,* inwardness or interiority. Tape recordings of lectures to the novices at the Abbey of Gethsemani survive to document the influence. The form of Rilke's poems, in particular, provided Merton with what T. S. Eliot called "objective correlatives," or images and symbols that specify the emotions of the poet. To recreate the poet's perception of reality, the reader has no other medium than the poem itself. Rilke presented the poetic phenomenology of the "innocent 'out-gazing' proper to the child, against which the child is systematically educated." In his zoo poems (e.g., "The Panther," a particular Merton favorite) Rilke mesmerized Merton with his report that "the animal simply 'gazes out' without any consciousness of a center which gazes." In the *Duino Elegies* of Rilke, Merton finds the child being taught "to 'be opposite,' to stand against objects, and never to be anything else but a subject confronting object." The full thrust of the ontological task of the poet is described by Merton in a unique published comment on Rilke in *Mystics and Zen Masters.* He contrasts Rilke's poetic sensibility with that of Western mystical tradition and Zen.

> The pure consciousness (as also the apophatic mystical intuition) does not look *at* things, and does not ignore them, annihilate them, negate them. It accepts them fully, in complete oneness with them. It looks "out of them" as though fulfilling the role of consciousness not for itself only but *for them also.* This is certainly a deep spiritual insight on the part of Rilke. The "outgazing" of this *Duino Elegy* throws important light on the characteristic Rilkean "inseeing" (*Einsehen*). Inseeing implies identification, in which, according to Rilke's normal poetic consciousness, the subject is aware of itself as having penetrated by poetic empathy into the heart of the object and being united with it.[33]

In 1967 Merton wrote a review of Edwin Muir's *Collected Poems.* He connected Rilke's "inseeing" power with Muir's "profound metaphysical concern" with the "roots of being": "the poet 'lets himself into the very center' of the particular existent that he sees." "In Rilke's words, he becomes able to see the thing from the very point where it springs from the creative power of God and is 'approved' by God."[34] Merton convinces with his enthusiasm for Muir's poetry. He describes the poet Muir, "compelled . . . to divine in the sense of the water-diviner finding hidden springs; to persuade, not by demonstration but by sharing the water with others."

Finally, only a year earlier Merton had returned to the paradise consciousness in an enthusiastic review of Louis Zukofsky's *Collected Short Poems, 1956–64.* He remarked on the "chaste and sparing" use of language in Zukofsky. The sound of the music actually leads him to structure "the ideas musically instead of logically"—which communicates more meaning than mere words; "so much so," insisted Merton, "that it can not be broken down easily into concepts and the poem has to be respected, left alone, only to be read over and over." The fully mature, sophisticated, and difficult poetry of Zukofsky is, ironically, made up of the "language of children," he observed; "the language of everyday becomes charged with expectations—the language of paradise."

It is this complete acceptance of the *"whole thing"* that one must hear with "the paradise ear," Merton advises. Zukofsky's childlike attitude becomes "the unlimited curious senses of confused anticipation which is the stuff of ordinary life." And this anticipation is "aware of itself as a question that does not provoke an answer to dispose of it." In effect, "each new poem is very much the same question but brand new." Zukofsky had "understood uniquely the reality of the question," Merton surmises, "because here is a poet who has the patience and the good sense to listen." Merton imaginatively celebrated the poet's "ear," cocked to listen for the music of paradise. He does not return to Adam's Eden, but to the "new creation" of the second Adam, Christ.

> All really valid poetry (poetry that is fully alive, and asserts its reality by its power to generate imaginative life) is a kind of recovery of paradise. Not that the poet comes up with a report that he, an unusual man, has found his way back into Eden; but the living line and the generative association, the new sound, the music, the structure, are somehow grounded in a renewal of vision and hearing so that he who reads and understands recognizes that here is a new start, a new creation.[35]

Both vision and hearing are tools of the poet. In the form of poetry, they recreate experience through verbal icons that interrogate the reader. But they also liberate the inner self. Merton's own best poetry invites such a new creation event. Small wonder that he would conclude the author's preface, "First and Last Thoughts," to the 1962 *A Thomas Merton Reader* with the invitation, "I hope we will be together in Paradise."[36]

MERTON'S POETIC VOICES: CHOIR, DESERT, PARADISE, FOREST

POETRY OF THE CHOIR

We have already staked off boundaries to contrast the early and later poetry of Merton by remarking the scarcity of poems in the 1950s. One can effortlessly trace discontinuities of style between the Merton of the 1940s and the 1960s. His dependence in the early poems on similes and an elegant, florid diction is most evident. The writing often labors as self-consciously poetic, even imitative, or worse derivative of Donne, Hopkins, Eliot, and others whose metaphysical conceits Merton envied. Here is an example, from an early verse entitled "Poem":[37]

> Light plays like a radio in the iron tree;
> Green farms fear the night behind me
> Where lightnings race across the western world.
>
> Life, like a woman in the moving wheat,
> Runs from the staring sky
> That bends upon the earth like a reflector.

Or another selection, from "The Greek Women":[38]

> The ladies in red capes and gold bracelets
> Walk like reeds and talk like rivers,
> And sigh, like Vichy water, in the doorways;
> . . . .
> And, opening their eyes wide as horizons,
> Seem to await the navy home from Troy.

Rather than personify, Merton's images and symbols collapse into abstractions in many of these early poems. He frequents the theme of the world's wickedness, even its depravity; pyrotechnic images contrast starkly with the halcyon monastic refuge. Urbanscapes grate the eye and force violent images of decay and moral torpor. "In the Ruins of New York"[39] portrays such a simplistic contrast in this passage:

Oh how quiet it is after the black night
When flames out of the clouds burned down your carried teeth,
And when those lightenings
Lancing the black boils of Harlem and the Bronx,
Spilled the remaining prisoners,
(The tens and twenties of the living)
Into the trees of Jersey,
To the green farms, to find their liberty.

Antitheses remain taut in the imagery: black-white, darkness-light, prisoner-freedom, urban-rural, earth-sky. The monk's condescending tone reaches its zenith in "Senescente Mundo":[40]

> *Senescente mundo,* when the hot globe
> Shrivels and cracks
> And uninhibited atoms resolve
> Earth and water, fruit and flower, body and animal soul,
> All the blue stars come tumbling down.
> Beauty and ugliness and love and hate
> Wisdom and politics are all alike undone.
>
> Toward that fiery day we run like crabs
> With our bad-tempered armor on.

The conclusion of the poem further polarizes the world and the sacred sphere, with Merton's appeal to "Great Christ" in the Eucharist, which the poet trivializes in saccharine imagery: ". . . my fingers touch Thy wheat / And hold Thee hidden in the compass of Thy paper sun."

> And though the world, at last, has swallowed her own
>   solemn laughter
> And has condemned herself to hell:
> Suppose a whole new universe, a great clean Kingdom
> Were to rise up like Atlantis in the East,
> Surprise this earth, this cinder, with new holiness!

There is no decided breakthrough or seasoning of the young poet—although his obvious gift with metaphor, imagery, and diction rehearses, as Eliot well dubbed it, "hit or miss." At his worst, the early poet Merton writes sentimental, romantic poems, stylistically clumsy and burdened with a monastic worldview that spurns the world and hurls invectives in his wake.

Even some pre-monastic poems speak in stark dichotomies. "The Philosophers," for example, proves no less condemning of the world than the novice's verse. Such parody is difficult to suppose as the work of a promising poet. Merton portrays two mandrakes, arguing "in their frozen graves":

> "Body is truth, truth body. Fat is all
> We grow on earth, or all we breed to grow."
> Said one mandrake to the other.
> Then I heard his brother:
> "Beauty is troops, troops beauty. Dead is all
> We grow on earth, or all we breed to grow."[41]

The habitat of the monastery incubates better poems when Merton relaxes his rhetoric against the world, and lets the metaphors unlock the poet's vision and ear to recreate and interpret simple, sublime experiences. For example, "The Reader"[42] halts us with arresting images in a vignette of the monastic refectory.

> Lord, when the clock strikes
> Telling the time with cold tin
> And I sit hooded in this lectern
>
> Waiting for the monks to come,
> I see the red cheeses, and bowls
> All smile with milk in ranks upon their tables.

In this poem the rhythm and meter reinforce the imagery. Merton succeeds with onomatopoeia in the second and third lines' repetitive hard consonants, and again in the round vowel sounds describing the monks' arrival:

> And the monks come down the cloister
> With robes as voluble as water.
> I do not see them but I hear the waves.

Another poem which celebrates monastic simplicity is "Trappists, Working." Its cadence moves as methodically as the laconic monks' labor.

Now all our saws sing holy sonnets in this world of timber
Where oaks go off like guns, and fall like cataracts,
Pouring their roar into the wood's green well.

Walk to us, Jesus, through the wall of trees,
And find us still adorers in these airy churches,
Singing our other Office with our saws and axes.
Still teach Your children in the busy forest,
And let some little sunlight reach us, in our mental shades, and
    leafy studies.[43]

"St. Malachy"[44] is less successful as a poem, but nonetheless captures
the ethos of the monastery in the young monk's imagination:

So the bells rang and we opened the antiphoners
And the wrens and larks flew up out of the pages.
Our thoughts became lambs. Our hearts swam like seas.
One monk believed that we should sing to him
Some stone-age hymn
Or something in the giant language.
So we played to him in the plainsong of the giant Gregory:
Oceans of Scripture sang upon bony Eire.

Then the last salvage of flowers
(Fostered under glass after the gardens foundered)
Held up their little lamps on Malachy's altar
To peer into his wooden eyes before the Mass began.

"St. Alberic"[45] celebrates the monk's love of the forest, interpreting the human predicament of Adam in light of Christ's cross and
resurrection.

When your loud axe's echo on the ponds, at early morning,
Scared the shy mallard from the shallows grey as tin,
The glades gave back your hammers' antiphons—
The din of nails that shamed the lazy spring.
Striving, like Adam, with the barren wildwood,
And with the desolation of the brake,
You builded, in a reedy place,
A cloister and a Ladychurch.

. . . .

When in the church your canticles were done,
Even your silences were better than the birds, whose song
Still fell, like fountains, from the forest to your sunny cloister.
And, when, in the high-noon of contemplation, reason died by
    blindness,
Your faith escaped, and found the flowering Cross—
Loving, in Christ, the agony of Adam:
Body and Spirit tilled and gardened with our penances and
    death.

The "poetry of the choir" consequently forks in two directions: a
scolding of everything in the lost world that has not converted and re-
treated to the refuge of the monastery's walls; and, a heightened consciousness of the immediate events in the monastic environs which
summon a deeper, true self to new life in imitation of Christ's humility. The latter often stray toward romanticized versions of a separate,
holy existence. Themes of alienation, exile, solitude, freedom, and the
identity/illusion quandary alternate in the poetry of the choir. But beneath them are images of transformation and seeds of an optimism
about all human nature. A more incarnational and sacramental vision
of the world auditions in Merton's being ambushed by God's mercy.
But he could not yet expand the orbit of grace beyond the monastic
enclosure.

POETRY OF THE DESERT

Woodcock's category of "poetry of the desert" divides Merton's mature poetry from his early poetry, beginning (with one exception) with
the 1957 collection, *The Strange Islands*. The momentum which he
identifies in this new phase gains throughout the monk's poetry corpus. On this point I choose to expand Woodcock's inventory. There
are obvious desert poems which not only place the poet and reader
in the environs of solitary, marginal existence, but also poems that voice
the existential dread or emptiness of the heart's inner experience. Here
we encounter the monk seeking purity of heart, the precincts of the
inner self in Christ. These poems uncoil the spirituality of the true
self through lean, sinewy verse, and the more dramatic wrestling with
illusion and reality.[46] Few present it as directly as a pair of poems about
the desert father, Macarius.

"Macarius and the Pony"[47] retrieves an anecdote from monastic history. A young girl's parents bring her to the desert father to reverse her perceived change "by magic arts / Into a pony." The parenthetical "(they thought)" triggers the illusion. Macarius responds that his prayers will change nothing. But in his cell "he spoke to God" and anointed the girl. The parents recognize their misperception in a poignant insight:

> And when they saw with what love
> He placed his hand upon her head
> They realized, at once.
> She was no animal.
> She had never changed.
> She had been a girl from the beginning.

Merton uses the ironic depersonalization of the girl by her own parents to heighten their ontological lapse:

> "Your own eyes
> (Said Macarius)
> Are your enemies.
> Your own crooked thoughts
> (Said the anchorite)
> Change people around you
> Into birds and animals.
>
> Your own ill-will
> (said the clear-eyed one)
> Peoples the world with specters"

Here we find the theme Merton will explore in the prose poems of *Raids on the Unspeakable*, where the "herd mentality" of "mass man" threatens to dehumanize society. He has invested in the persona of Macarius the contemplative's attraction to the "true self." And the "love" that characterizes his touch expresses Macarius's ability as the "clear-eyed one" to summon others back to God's approval of her creaturely "true self." It is no coincidence that Macarius's (and Merton's) transcendental freedom ultimately expresses the true self in a symbolic, revelatory encounter: "love" for the alienated, but innocent child, who symbolizes paradise consciousness.

The companion poem, "Macarius the Younger,"[48] draws another portrait of a profound sense of sin as ontological lapse and grace as ontological conversion. Already something cosmic and contemplative resonates in the imagery:

> No road, no path,
> No landmarks
> Show the way there.
> You must go by the stars.

In part three of the poem, monks cross the river in a boat "full of officers." Their identity as "ragged bums" contrasts with the "rich brass" and horses and retinue of the soldiers. The monks, "having nothing," are paradoxically "Free men" whom the tribune calls "the happy ones." The concluding lines play out the dialectic of true self–false self:

> Then the officer saw himself as he was.
> He gave away all that he had
> And enlisted in the desert army.

Both poems are conscious self-congratulation of the monastic ideal. Even the irony of volunteering for "the desert army" in the last line symbolically exaggerates the demands of conversion. But the monks in the poem are now circulating in the world, rubbing shoulders with soldiers. Their identity as vagrant "ragged bums" shatters the brittle veneer of romantically cowled, shadowy figures inside silent enclosures.

Emblems of a Season of Fury (1965) proved a watershed in Merton's transformation as a poet. The style and form change precipitously. This newer "poetry of the desert" wrestles openly with spiritual crisis. The poems open to a more universal experience. And Merton finally ventures into the social turmoil of the 1960s, with metaphors of compassion wrought out of a new affirmation of the human predicament as transformed in the mystery of Christ's life, death, and resurrection.

The desert terrain was the cradle of fourth- and fifth-century monastic life. That legacy provided Merton with a ready complex of symbols. In *The Tears of the Blind Lions* (1949) he included a poem entitled "Dry Places,"[49] one of his first appropriations of the landscape of disaster: with its "rotten verandahs," a place "where / Judas' shadow dwells." The poet conjures up fright in devil-infested environs:

> There the skinny father of hate rolls in his dust
> And if the wind should shift one leaf
> The dead jump up and bark for their ghosts:
> Their dry bones want our penniless souls.

The echo of Ezechiel's vision of the valley of dry bones breathes hope into Merton's christological hymn. It is a song gravitating to images of transformation that are grounded in Scotus's optimism about the human condition.

> We who are still alive will wring a few green blades
> From the floor of this valley
> Though ploughs abhor your metal and your clay.
> Rather than starve with you in rocks without oasis,
> We will get up and work your loam
> Until some prayer or some lean sentence
> Bleeds like the quickest root they ever cut.
>
> For we cannot forget the legend of the world's childhood
> Or the track to the dogwood valley
> And Adam our Father's old grass farm
> Wherein they gave the animals names
> And knew Christ was promised first without scars
> When all God's larks called out to Him
> In their wild orchard.

The Strange Islands (1957) points to the poetry of the desert in a pair of strikingly spare poems. "Stranger"[50] opens with an arresting description of what Merton will later call the *point vierge,* that moment when the new day is born and we become aware of God's presence.

> When no one listens
> To the quiet trees
> When no one notices
> The sun in the pool
>
> Where no one feels
> The first drop of rain
> Or sees the last star
>
> Or hails the first morning
> Of a giant world
> Where peace begins
> And rages end

Merton describes a bird, sitting still and watching God's work: "One turning leaf, / Two falling blossoms, / Ten circles upon the pond." And in that "desert" solitude the inner self shows herself.

> Closer and clearer
> Than any wordy master,
> Thou inward Stranger
> Whom I have never seen

"Elias: Variations on a Theme"[51] likewise relies upon the impressionistic detail. The inner desert converges with the external forest environs; the contemplative experience again is imaged in the journey that paradoxically begins when the pathway dies; and in the bird's song, a symbol of the poet's voice, the desert prophet summons the inner self:

> Under the blunt pine
> I who am not sent
> Remain. The pathway dies,
> The journey has begun.
> Here the bird abides
> And sings on top of the forgotten
> Storm. The ground is warm.
> He sings no particular message.
> His hymn has one pattern, no more planned,
> No less perfectly planned
> And no more arbitrary
> Than the pattern in the seed, the salt,
> The snow, the cell, the drop of rain.

The particularity of these individual creatures, all sharing in the "one pattern," speaks of Scotus's sense of *haecceitas:* all things manifest Christ and God's goal for creation. As the firstborn of all creation, Christ is that first thought of God, the original love of God which will achieve an epiphany in the coming of Christ, who restores the fullness of our freedom. To be free to love is the mystery of the true self, who is Christ, the inner self in all creation.

> The free man is not alone as busy men are
> But as birds are. The free man sings
> Alone as universes do. Built
> Upon his own inscrutable pattern
> Clear, unmistakable, not invented by himself alone
> Or for himself, but for the universe also.

By the time Merton wrote *Emblems of a Season of Fury* (1963), the expansive optimism of his christological reflections wrought new poems to celebrate all the earth's transformation. "Song for Nobody"[52] personifies the manifestation of such an authentic inner self in the "yellow flower." Merton never wrote poetry with more economy of metaphor or imagery. The yellow flower is described as both "Light and spirit" and "Light and emptiness." It "Sings without a word / By itself."

> Let no one touch this gentle sun
> In whose dark eye
> Someone is awake.

The flower's wakeful presence to the inner self depends on the absence of all other identities, parenthetically hinted by the poet: "(No light, no gold, no name, no color / And no thought: / O, wide awake!)"[53]

"O Sweet Irrational Worship"[54] renders an equally chaste and expansive song of praise. The opening image ambushes us with the contemplative's experience:

> Wind and a bobwhite
> And the afternoon sun.
>
> By ceasing to question the sun
> I have become light,
>
> Bird and wind.
>
> My leaves sing.
>
> I am earth, earth
>
> All these lighted things
> Grow from my heart.

Merton achieves the kind of identity at which Rilke had hinted, becoming the subject of the object, earth, now with a universal dimension. The creation process is affirmed, with Hopkins-like audacity; the very act of being of the quail, the trajectory of its flight, becomes the glory of "irrational worship" given to the creator:

> I am earth, earth
>
> Out of my grass heart
> Rises the bobwhite.
>
> Out of my nameless weeds
> His foolish worship.

"Love Winter When the Plant Says Nothing"⁵⁵ pursues the same lithe form and imagistic rendition of the drama of the inner self. Merton addresses the tree in the forest, "Pray undistracted / Curled tree / Carved in steel—Buried zenith!" The allusion to a hidden identity in the "Daily zero" of a snowscape becomes a newborn existence:

> Fire, turn inward
> To your weak fort,
> To a burly infant spot,
> A house of nothing.

For Merton, this is the irony: in winter when the plant "says nothing" by vegetation or foliage, or the song of its leaves, he can acknowledge a deeper being, "Silence, love this growth." With the "unsetting sun" and "golden zero" a new dimension is discovered. This, for Merton, is the real desert: a "mad place" (line 17) of solitude where one wrestles, surrenders, and discovers the inner self.

POETRY OF PARADISE CONSCIOUSNESS

As compelling as Woodcock's dichotomy, choir and desert, at first seems, the majority of Merton's better poems defy these sharply contrasting categories. By analyzing a wide cross-section of his poetry, it becomes apparent that an overarching paradise consciousness transcends both choir and desert environs in a constellation of Merton poems. The significant complex of images and symbols in these poems grows into a mythos of Merton's spirituality of the true self or inner self, wrestling with the illusory, false self. Even when not explicitly christological, the poems imply that the true self or inner self is the self in Christ. Merton's development of a kenotic christology, as will be analyzed in chapter 3, ineluctably manifests itself in the living organism of his poetry.

Among the pre-monastic poems is one written in Cuba, "Song for Our Lady of Cobre."⁵⁶ It was written during his 1940 post-Easter trip. He called it an inspired, spontaneous poem. The Hispanic passion piety and Latin Catholicism stimulated both mind and heart, he reports. Merton admired the steel-like sharpness of the Spanish language for its accuracy as the mystics used it; but it was also soft, gentle and pliant, the language of devotion without sentiment. In this atmosphere and culture of Catholicism, Merton gazed on the "many altars to white and black saints." The poem was "something new." "It pointed the way to many other poems; it opened the gate, and set me travelling on a certain and direct track that was to last me several years," he comments.[57]

The poem is structured on a series of motions, imaged in the lines where we see, alternatively, white girls and then black girls. It is a kinetic poem. And the rhythms of ascent and descent repeat: "The white girls lift their heads like trees" while "The black girls go / Reflected like flamingoes in the street"; "water" and "clay"; "open their arms like clouds" and "close their eyes like wings"; "bow down like bells" and "look up like toys." The climax of the poem comes with the final stanza's cosmic symbol: "the heavenly stars / Stand in a ring," a familiar Marian iconography. The transformation is announced:

> And all the pieces of the mosaic, earth,
> Get up and fly away like birds.

The poem succeeds as a religious lyric because it relies on the pattern of transformation and not on any superimposed dogmatic content. Earth is affirmed in its "mosaic" quality and in its totality. Memory is drawn back to the powerful experience of Rome's mosaics, where Merton learned the early Christian iconographers' love of this Christ. The crux of the poem is the pivotal "because" that introduces the last stanza. It is the christological mystery manifest in Mary's life, a cosmic mystery imaged in the orderly stars, that animates the gestures of praise and adoration by the white and black girls Merton has seen in Cuba. These are authentic acts of the inner self. They reflect the Catholic understanding of Mary's discipleship, having overcome the illusory false self and being able to respond to God's surprising initiative. Merton's Marian devotion draws him into the mystery of Christ. The earth itself shares in transformation. This flight is not from the world. Rather, all creation, the cosmos, is destined for glory because all things have been restored to order in Christ's coming.[58]

During the Second World War, Merton's brother, John Paul, a Canadian Air Force pilot, crashed in the North Sea. Their last visit together at the monastery, earlier that summer, had eventuated in John Paul's baptism. But the brothers' reunion and enthusiasm over the younger brother's upcoming marriage indeed proved short-lived. Arguably the most well-known and successful of Thomas Merton's poems, "For My Brother: Reported Missing in Action, 1943,"[59] was written in the wake of his devastating grief. On Easter Tuesday he learned of his brother's death some ten days earlier. Merton struggled with the experience and gravitated to the symbols of Passion Week and the Easter mystery. Images of transformation abound: lack of sleep, becoming "my eyes are flowers for your tomb"; failure "to eat my bread," becoming "My fasts shall live like willows where you died"; "thirst," becoming "my thirst shall turn to springs for you." John Paul had been buried at sea, in an unmarked grave, beside the survivors' rubber dinghy. The poet sacrificially offers his labors, sorrows, his life and blood, his breath; and in exchange John Paul is envisioned with "a resting place," "a better bed," "a better rest." The poem resonates with Merton's appropriation of the cross in his brother's death and his own sorrow:

> Your cross and mine shall tell men still
> Christ died on each, for both of us.
>
> For in the wreckage of your April Christ lies slain,
> And Christ weeps in the ruins of my spring:
> The money of Whose tears shall fall
> Into your weak and friendless hand,
> And buy you back to your own land:
> The silence of Whose tears shall fall
> Like bells upon your alien tomb.
> Hear them and come: they call you home.

A pacifist note introduces this paschal action. Merton suggests that Christ's cross will be victorious over all war and nationalism. But deeper lies the identity in Christ of both the victim and the survivor. The capitalization of the word, "Whose," reinforces that it is not Thomas Merton but Christ who weeps, to ransom and to summon John Paul to new life, the "home"-coming. The question of the second stanza — "Has your unhappy spirit lost its road?"—evokes the journey motif, which is relaxed in this conclusion. And the realization of John Paul's recent conversion and baptism gives a unique Easter peace to the poet.

The poem might be faulted christologically for the ransom metaphor of redemption in the final stanza. But both the interpretation of his brother's death in war through the symbols of Christ's death and resurrection, and the affirmation that the compassionate Christ, who in his humanity weeps over such tragedy, orient the reader to the inner selves of the poet and his brother. The opening symbols of transformation find their optimism in no less than this paschal mystery.

Ten years later, Merton delivered another poem nearly spontaneously, "Elegy for the Monastery Barn."[60] It recounted the event of a cow barn's burning on a summer's evening in 1953. Merton wrote to Mark Van Doren that this event and the poem were important because they recollected for him a childhood experience in Maryland, and because his poetry began moving in a new direction. Van Doren remarked, "the bearing is in the humor" of the poem: "the slowness of the [fire] truck, the swiftness of the poem, the childhood memory," all "illuminating . . . the happy power awakened in Merton's mind as it races through the realities of his theme."

The opening lines suggest an incongruity:

> As though an aged person were to wear
> Too gay a dress
> And walk about the neighborhood
> Announcing the hour of her death, . . .
> The long barn suddenly puts on the traitor, beauty,
> And hails us with a dangerous cry. . . .

They hold a seductive note, with the lover, fire, destroying in an apocalyptic flash. But the narrative voice summons us to an alternative identity:

> And yet she has another legacy,
> More delicate, to leave us, and more rare.

He remembers the barn's solitude, her peace, and her silence — a contemplative identity. The image of "fifty invisible cattle, / The past years" (which reminds me of Yeats's nine and fifty swans at Coole) speak their summary, an elegy of the barn's shelter and sanctuary. This truer self has been betrayed by destructive fire. The echoes of Luke 21, an eschatological chapter of the gospel, become direct in the last half of the poem: "Here is their meaning found. Here is their end"; and the "presence" of the Lord "thinking upon this barn His gentle doom" in the final, halting line. Merton wrote to Van Doren, "So burning barns are for me great mysteries that are important. They turn out to be the whole world, and it is the Last Judgement."[61] Van Doren replied that "Merton's flight to another dimension . . . starts on earth and gets in its own natural way to heaven." It echoes pure christology. Here Merton, the water-diviner poet himself, finds hidden springs and shares their waters. The inevitable demise of the barn (and all creatures) — all the more dramatic in the sudden disaster of fire ("[lest] that day come upon

you like a snare": Lk. 21:34)—ontologically tugs Merton to the roots
of being in the personified creature "so loved, and so attended, and
so feared." Biblical scholars carefully point out Luke's use of the destruction of Jerusalem's temple as eschatological hope for history ("your
redemption is drawing near": Lk. 21:28). This contrasts sharply with
Mark's purely apocalyptic interpretation. The poem's barn partakes of
that very eschatological hope. Indeed, Merton's dynamic of true self/
false self playfully undergirds the imaginative truth of the personified
barn's intimate identity.[62]

One of Merton's earliest poems, "Aubade: Lake Erie"[63] develops his
use of the child's innocence to symbolize the awakening to paradise
consciousness. The French form of "aubade" is a morning love song
for parting lovers. He reminisces autobiographically about the vine-
yards on the lake, "an artificial France":

> Awake, in the frames of windows, innocent children
> Loving the blue, sprayed leaves of childish life,
> Applaud the bearded corn, the bleeding grape. . . .

Their vantage from the window brings to mind Merton's description
of the Adam-like poet, looking through the transparent window onto
nature. Eucharistic echoes can be found in the "bearded corn" and
"bleeding grape" images. These children spontaneously celebrate and
give thanks. Their dawn rising, "when their shining voices, clean as
summer, / Play, like churchbells over the field," summons the "hitch-
hiking" hoboes who fail to heed or see the morning sun as "our marvelous cousin." These aliens, homeless vagabonds, "fugitives" from the
inner self, can only blindly "grope, in the green wheat, / Toward the
wood winds of the western freight." The poem again conveys much
motion, a kinesis: the children applauding; the train meandering
through the valley; and the shuffling hoboes' scared flight for the western freight train. Unlike the children's world, that of the adults is
pessimistically mired down in the industrial revolution's drudgery: "A
hundred dusty Luthers rise from the dead, unheeding, / Search the
horizon for the gap-toothed grin of factories."

The identification of the child's imaginative life with the true or
inner self reappears in "Dirge for a Town in France."[64] Its title suggests
an autobiographical origin. The children live a mystery which proves
again more real than the adults' exile. Merton constructs a strong metaphor of childhood, the carousel:[65]

> O, it is not those first, faint stars
> Whose fair light, falling, whispers in the river;
> And it is not the dusty wind,
> Waving the waterskirts of the shy-talking fountain,
>
> That wakes the wooden horses' orchestra,
> The fifing goldfinch, and the phony flutes,
> And the steam robins and electric nightingales
> That blurred the ding of cymbals,
> That other time when childhood turned and turned
> As grave as sculpture in a zodiac.

The image of "wakeful" childhood innocence, a paradise consciousness, personifies the imaginative response of childhood. Theirs is a more
real response than the adult despair, or capitulation, which Merton
successfully presents in a stark contrast. They personify, by contrast,
the "new creation" inaugurated by Christ's coming.

> But the men die, down in the shadowy doors,
> The way their thoughts die in their eyes,
> To see those sad and funny children
> Run down the colonnade of trees
> Where the carnival doesn't exist:
>
> Those children, who are lost too soon,
> With fading laughter, on the road along the river:
> Gone, like the slowing calvacade, the homeward horses.

The imagery of death, shadows, and thoughts that "die in their eyes,"
characterizes the men of the poem as spiritually inert. They have for-
feited the life of the inner self. They view the children as "sad and
funny" for chasing the carnival, the carousel. They have consigned these
innocents to being "lost too soon," "gone." But the imaginative world
of paradise consciousness returns with the concluding image: "home-
ward horses." The children, as personifications of the inner self, have
awakened to this archetype of fantasy and imagination. The sights and
sounds of the carousel add circular motion; and the noisy orchestra-
tion, accompanied by steam robins, electric nightingales, and dinging
cymbals, conjures up an archetype of play in childhood's memory.

The poet has intrigued us by identifying the women (mothers) of
the town, perched on the "one-time finery of iron, suburban balconies,"

with the child's innocent response to reality. And even more convincingly, Merton presents the flowers on the balconies as sacramental:
"The roses and the mimosas in the windows / Adore the night they
breathe, not understanding." Again, the vantage of the window suggests a paradise consciousness. Here is intuition in nature, *sapientia*,
that surpasses lesser forms of "understanding."[66]

Another of Merton's most successful poems was occasioned by a surprise. He received from a child named Grace a drawing of her house.
His spontaneous poem, "Grace's House,"[67] continues to refine the symbol of the innocent child as a true self or inner self, the personification
of paradise consciousness. The poem begins with an archetypal picture:

> On the summit: it stands on a fair summit
> Prepared by winds: and solid smoke
> Rolls from the chimney like a snow cloud.
> Grace's house is secure.
>
> No blade of grass is not counted,
> No blade of grass forgotten on this hill.
> Twelve flowers make a token garden.
> There is no path to the summit —
> No path drawn
> To Grace's house.

The house's security hints at the inviolability of the inhabitant. The
solicitous drawing of blades of grass and a full dozen flowers in the
garden reveals Grace's love for this place where she dwells. The in-
decipherable mailbox lettering makes it universal; her inner self's identity defies naming or labeling. The mailbox is filled with Valentines,
which leads the reader to understand that Grace herself is loved and
has many friends. There is a Zenlike wakefulness in the child's vantage, at the window again:

> All the curtains are arranged
> Not for hiding but for seeing out.
> In one window someone looks and winks.

The animals in the picture share Grace's posture of Rilkean "out-
gazing," the innocent pose of paradise consciousness:

> Two gnarled short
> Fortified trees have knotholes

From which to look out.
From behind another corner of Grace's house
Another creature peeks out.

Merton returns at the end of the poem to the all-important detail, that there is no path to Grace's house. Like in "Macarius the Younger," there is no external path, no ordinary way to this truth.

A spangled arrow there
Points from our Coney Island
To her green sun-hill.

Between our world and hers
Runs a sweet river:
(No, it is not the road,
It is the uncrossed crystal
Water between our ignorance and her truth.)

O paradise, O child's world!
Where all the grass lives
And all the animals are aware!
The huge sun, bigger than the house
Stands and streams with life in the east
While in the west a thunder cloud
Moves away forever.

No blade of grass is not blessed
On this archetypal, cosmic hill,
This womb of mysteries.

I must not omit to mention a rabbit
And two birds, bathing in the stream
Which is no road, because

Alas, there is no road to Grace's house!

There is an echo of baptismal imagery in this passage. The name "Grace" reinforces the initiative of God in her salvation. The poet invites us to cross over, to convert, to her truth. For Grace and her imaginative world are more real than our false, Coney Island selves.

These poems of childhood remind readers of Merton's poetic models: William Blake's *Songs of Innocence* and *Songs of Experience;* and Gerard Manley Hopkins's "Spring and Fall." Taken literally, they could be naively misinterpreted. But interpreted as symbol, they collectively present a pattern of confidence in human nature, an optimism about an innate capacity of persons to love, as the true self or inner self liberated by Christ. They are admittedly introspective, lacking the horizon of social consciousness which Merton's mature poetry will assimilate. But they are nonetheless asymptotes that lead us through his spiritual development.

Another even more autobiographical poem, written in the same period as "Grace's House," creates a striking metaphor of the inner self. At first glance, readers are tempted to categorize "Night-Flowering Cactus"[68] as the epitome of poetry of the desert. But at a deeper level the poem dramatizes the epiphany of the inner self of the monk, a paradise consciousness. Bob Lax, Merton's fellow poet and Columbia University classmate, once dubbed this poem the monk's spiritual autobiography. The desert landscape defines the scene of this poem as in none of the other Merton poetry. Its marginal locale, the poverty, aridity, and isolation are the environs for the solitary's encounter with the dynamic of transformation. Moreover, the scene is night, the hour of the contemplative's death of the senses, adding to the hushed and remote drama, pregnant with epiphany. The poem unfolds in a soliloquy of the personified cactus. The themes of identity and manifestation tease the reader, with time and the sudden bloom poignantly imaged in the abrupt unfolding of the white bell flower. But irony lies in the fact that the cactus flower often blooms unnoticed. It is none the less for escaping notice, just as the monk's contemplative life seeks to be hidden, avoiding notoriety and celebrity.

> I know my time, which is obscure, silent and brief
> For I am present without warning one night only.
>
> When sun rises on the brass valleys I become serpent.
>
> Though I show my true self only in the dark and to no man
> (For I appear by day as serpent)
> I belong neither to night nor day.
> Sun and city never see my deep white bell
> Or know my timeless moment of void:
> There is no reply to my munificence.

The poet transforms this delicate, alluringly scented cactus flower into a "sudden Eucharist" lifted "out of the earth's unfathomable joy" in the next stanza. The christological foundations of the poem become transparent. An incarnational and sacramental consciousness converge in the realization that the cactus obeys "the world's body." From the mosaic of the desert floor, reminiscent of the icon-painting techniques that use only earth's elements—pure, unadulterated elements like the egg and natural pigments—the flower becomes a radiant transfiguration of the cactus. A genius for sacrament plays in Merton's haunting stanza, where the simultaneity of revealing and concealing meets the witness. Who would imagine that this ugly bearded cactus, clutching the dry, barren desert floor, could create such beauty?

> I neither show my truth nor conceal it
> My innocence is descried dimly
> Only by divine gift
> As a white cavern without explanation.

This mystical image of the knowledge of God in love leads Merton to the mute response of those who experience this cactus flower's blooming. No one questions the cactus flower for the silence of its "impeccable bell" bloom; "He who sees my purity / Dares not speak of it." The poem ends with Merton's question, "Have you seen it?" This dialogue reminds the reader that the transformation of the poet, under the metaphor of the cactus and its flower, recreates the reader's possibility to be transformed in the echo of Merton's own "quickly ending" mirth. John Howard Griffin quoted from Merton's private journals a late aphorism: "The desert is a desert as long as you try to escape it. The moment you accept it, it becomes a paradise."[69] In this poem, all the lines of Merton's poetic myth intersect.

A poem from 1966 personifies the inner self, or paradise consciousness, in Merton's mature poetry about experiences in the monastery. "Elegy for a Trappist"[70] was written about the death of Father Stephen at the Abbey of Gethsemani. The dynamic of inner self versus false self animates the poem with new confidence. The poem, again a more spontaneous verse, celebrates an eccentric gardener-monk. One of Merton's taped conferences (October 16, 1966) contains an entertaining retrospect on Father Stephen at the time of his death. It begins quaintly with Merton reading from one of the old monk's "document[s]" which was written (characteristically) on the back of a brown paper bag. Merton launches with a description of Father Stephen as a "camp" artist. But he quickly notes that he uses the word not out of contempt, but to compliment a man "who learned to see that stuff that nobody ever looks at has worth." He describes Stephen's "whole spiritual life" centered on the magnanimous project of cultivating roses to choke out weeds! Here, he says, was a man with a "snowball imagination" which he has to carry all by himself. The beauty of the monastery, he affirms, is that it defies an assembly-line monastic identity and makes room for the utterly unique and eccentric personalities who could be admired without your getting involved in the snowball they imaginatively create.[71]

Some of Merton's most successful imagery and lyrics capture Father Stephen:

> Whom we will always remember
> As a tender-hearted careworn
> Generous unsteady cliff
> Lurching in the cloister
> Like a friendly freight train
> To some uncertain station. . . .

His identity as "boundless love" centers Merton's praise for the "true self" which nonetheless could "vainly" try to smuggle "some enormous bouquet / to a side altar / In the sleeves of your cowl." It was this same solicitude that placed flowers throughout the monastery, surprises for guests or monks on special occasions. The poet proceeds to describe an event on the day of Father Stephen's burial. A truck "moved like a battle cruiser" "past your abandoned and silent garden." Its glaring lights swept over grottos and "presences" Stephen had placed, as it passed through the "red gate." The poet names the intruding truck "Leviathan" and whimsically comments (directly to Father Stephen) that the truck "had passed you by / And never saw you hiding in the flowers." It is as if Father Stephen had become the "subject of the object," to use Rilke's phrase, as if he had completely identified himself in the flowers. Here was his inner self. It is "inseeing" and "outgazing" simultaneously. That he is "hiding" ironically reinforces the poet's discovery of this true self, and encourages the reader to find not only Father Stephen, but the reader's true self.

POETRY OF THE FOREST

Much of the power of Merton's appeal to readers revolves around his autobiographical wrestling with the superficiality of an external persona, a seductive "false self" that paralyzes the authentic power of love and communion. The "true self" is easily chased into hiding or appears wearing a disguise. Merton frequently referred to his own quarrel with the "shadow" of the celebrity-seeking writer who followed him into the monastery. For himself and for every person, however, Merton developed a spirituality of the "true self," an inner person whose freedom was born in solitude and the contemplative experience of God's unconditional love, mercy, and grace at the heart of reality. His poetry celebrates this christological pattern of transformation. Once a person had experienced this transforming moment, the capacity for unity and global dialogue among "true selves" could be actualized.

One revealing example of the unique knowledge experienced through the poet's metaphors occurs in the very opening paragraphs of the unfinished and much-revised important work "The Inner Experience." Merton opens his notes on contemplation with a familiar litany of warnings to recognize the seductions of the illusory and fictitious "I." The alienated or "false self" masks a deeper, hidden, interior "I." Our Promethean false self, he cautioned, can wrongly ("slyly") manipulate the "true self" by making spiritual life into another "project" or "accomplishment." Merton's riveting metaphor wonderfully ambushes this compulsive false self:

> The inner self is precisely that self which cannot be tricked or manipulated by anyone, even by the devil. He is like a very shy wild animal that never appears at all whenever an alien presence is at hand and comes out only when all is perfectly peaceful, in silence, when he is untroubled and alone. He cannot be lured by anyone or anything, because he responds to no lure except that of the divine freedom.[72]

It is this "true self" (or "inner self") and the assaults upon it by contemporary society which Merton develops throughout his spirituality. He prescribes no technique, but speaks in terms of "awakening" and "discovery" of the inner person beneath our superficial pursuits. The poems of paradise consciousness already have manifested this dynamic.

Merton's use of the "shy wild animal" metaphor captures the imagination when juxtaposed with his recently published journals of 1964–65, *A Vow of Conversation*. There he ten times narrates or alludes to the experiences of observing, sighting, and encountering the shy wild deer near and around the hermitage on the rising knoll at the Abbey of Gethsemani. The first entry records an especially dramatic episode:

Yesterday a small deer fell into the reservoir by the new waterworks and thrashed around trying to climb out. But the concrete wall was not negotiable. I was afraid it might drown, but it squeezed through the narrow joists of the footbridge and to the other end, where there was a foothold, and trotted off across the road into the woods, looking beat and confused.[73]

The descriptive details and emotional bearing of the narrated experience ("I was afraid") exemplify Merton's powers as a writer. What fascinates a close reader, however, is the recurring mention of the deer as Merton begins to spend more and more time at the hermitage in late 1964 and during 1965 before he permanently took up residence on August 20. In late December 1964 he recorded a frozen, moonlit morning walk down to the monastery, "with the hard diamonded leaves crackling under my feet, a deer sprang up in the deep bushes of the hollow, perhaps two."[74] The encounters continued on the feast of Epiphany 1965 with the description of "A lovely moment that stretched into ten minutes or more" as monk and deer "stood looking at me and I at them" in the evening light. "They did not run . . . but eventually they walked quietly away into the tall grasses and bushes, and, for all I know, they slept there." At this point he numbered as many as ten deer.[75] By mid-March the deer approached the hermitage porch, allowing him to walk "in the dim dusk and moonlight" only twenty feet away. "They remained peacefully, quietly, until finally I began moving about. Then they lifted up the white flag of their tails and started off in a wonderful, silent bounding flight," only to stop a hundred yards away.[76] A week later he discovered a dozen places where the deer had been sleeping in the thick bushes only thirty or forty yards from his own bed, exclaiming, "They are my nearest dormitory neighbors. . . . How wonderful!"[77] We could celebrate these narratives, recall "The Inner Experience" metaphor of "a shy wild animal," and relax complacently in the monk's compassion and charm.

But the meaning of this symbol of the deer can be further teased out. Buried in Merton's "Uncollected Poems" selections there lies a poetic reworking of the first deer incident, the episode of the deer's struggle in the reservoir and retreat to the woods from *a Vow of Conversation*. "Merlin and the Deer"[78] speaks for itself; but I will situate the experience of this poem within Merton's "false self"/"true self" or "inner self" dialectic. The poem opens:

After thrashing in the water of the reservoir
The deer swims beautifully
And so escapes
Limping across the country road into the little cedars.

Followed by Merlin's eye
Bewitched, a simple spirit
Merlin awakes
He becomes a gentle savage
Dressed in leaves
He hums alone in the glade
Says only a few phrases to himself
Or a psalm to his companion
Light in the wood.

The poet interrupts to consider the intruding reality of hunters, who can kill both doe and deer "in and out of season." He constructs a parallel threat with:

And messengers also
Come to bring him back
To hours and offices of men.

The poet returns to the trauma of the deer:

But he sees again
The curved and graceful deer
Fighting in the water
And then leaving

So he pulls out
Of all that icy water himself
And leaves the people

"Il revient a ses forets
Et cette fois pour toujours."

Now caught in many spells
Willing prisoner of trees and rain
And magic blossoms
The invisible people

Visit his jail
With forest stories
Tales without sound
And without conclusion
Clear fires without smoke
Fumbled prophecies
And Celtic fortunes.

There are obvious baptismal symbols in the poem: the pool of water, the "light in the wood" and "Clear fires without smoke," all suggesting the imagery of the Easter Vigil. The images of threatened chaos and death, and the "awakening" of the persona of Merlin—a fable-name of the magician, remarkably and fancifully resembling Merton's own name!—sustain this baptismal motif. His metamorphosis ("He becomes a gentle savage") suggests a new innocence. He leaves the "icy water" and the people for a forest where he has been before ("And this time forever"). The time of the writing of this poem would coincide with Merton's first overnights and long days at the hermitage, the 1964–65 transition to full-time life there. The irony of his status as "willing prisoner of trees and rain" situates the poet's decision for freedom in the forest, where he is "caught in many spells" of contemplative prayer and "invisible" visitors. There is subtle humor in exchanging a monastic cell for this ironic forest "jail." For all the preoccupation with Merton the autobiographer, it intrigues us to realize the neglect of such important poems which are a barometer of his quest to articulate a new consciousness.[79]

Earlier in 1964 Merton had recorded in his journal some enthusiastic reflections on Rudolf Bultmann's essays. "He has made clear to me," Merton writes, "the full limitations of all my early work, which is too naive, insufficient *except in what concerns my own experience*" (emphasis added). Merton seizes upon Bultmann's quotation: "Man comes into his present situation as in some way under constraint, so that real freedom can only be received as a gift." His sustained spirituality of the "true self" speaks directly to the point: "The dread of being oneself is the great obstacle of freedom," he surmises, "for freedom equals being oneself and acting accordingly." The entry is dated January 6, Epiphany—an apt feast for his starkly contrasting the "safety" of his own and society's past ("the familiar constraint") with the "freedom to respond to the new gift of grace in Christ."[80] Epiphany is the feast of the manifestation of Christ to the Gentiles, the event of the fullness of salvation for all people. The freedom of all human persons to recognize and to respond to this mystery ("equals being oneself and acting accordingly") would become ever more critical in Merton's own more inclusive christological reflections, particularly in the hermitage years and the Asian journey.

Merton undoubtedly experienced the vocation of hermit in solitude as such an exercise of transcendental freedom. The identity of his "true self," indeed his salvation, was engaged in this "serious decision," as he described it: "no longer a question of desire but of decision."

> I am not too sure just where the encounter [with the Word] is except that my heart tells me that in this question of the solitary life there is for me a special truth to be embraced. A truth which is not capable of fully logical explanation. A truth which is not rooted in my own nature or in my own biography, but is something deeper and something that may also cut clean through the whole network of my own recent works, ideas, writing, experience and so forth. . . .[81]

The proviso that recommends this "poetry of the forest" category is a reminder that the forest of "trees and rain" spans Merton's entire Gethsemani career.[82] Nowhere is this more evident than in the airy frontispiece of his 1946–52 journal, *The Sign of Jonas,* where Merton is photographically portrayed walking deeper into the woods, his back turned to the reader. The portrait should not be misinterpreted as flight but as the invitation of Merlin's "simple spirit" ("true self") that "escapes" only in the sense of finding authentic new life in the forest, like the "limping deer." A decade before the hermitage was built Merton had been named the monastery's "fire watcher" at the Vineyard Knob tower. During his years as novice master (1955–65), he frequently took the young monks to the woods for tree plantings in his forester's role. Merton's "poetry of the forest" transcends Woodcock's categories, both the cloister and the desert. Its solitude nurtures the ecology of the "true self," the "shy wild deer," Merlin's voice in the environs and habitat of glade and rain. The "poetry of the forest" will aptly describe the antipoetry of Merton's hermitage years, but it overarches all the expressions of his poetic voice — choir, desert, paradise, and forest — recreating the experience of the inner self which cannot be lured but only divined, like the water-diviner.

Merton hints at the convergence of poetic and contemplative identity when he complains about the "cliche of 'meaningful' experience,"
as distinct from authentic inner experience.

> "Experience" is thought to be made "meaningful" by being referred to
> something else—a system, or perhaps a report of someone else's experi-
> ence—and therefore its quality is diminished. So the ambiguity of "mean-
> ingfulness" is exposed. When experience becomes "meaningful," it also,
> in some sense, becomes unreal or less real. To live always outside of ex-
> perience as if it were the fullness of experience! This is one of the basic
> ambiguities of Western thought.[83]

The real experience of Merton's "poetry of the forest" is the encounter with the "true self," the "inner self"—of the poet, of the creature(s)
he encounters, of one's own person as awakened by the experience
of the poem. It is an immediate and innocent ontological intuition,
recreated by the experience of the poem. In this sense, the poetic experience is more real than a merely sensory experience because it is
interpreted (and thus meaningful) experience. It is again Merton's
confidence in poetry's unique way of knowing.

Merton's own sense of Rilke's experience of "inseeing" or "inwardness" echoes in a journal entry on December 9, 1964, where he realized, "I was happy!" What follows from this inner experience is described
by Merton as a transforming experience. His own self-emptying is a
consequence of Christ's kenosis, a life enacted as self-emptying gratitude.

> I said the strange word, "happiness," and realized that it was there not
> as an "it" or object, it simply was and I was that. . . .
>
> The only response is to go out from one's self with all that one is (which
> is nothing), and pour out that nothingness in gratitude that He [Christ]
> is who He is.
>
> All speech is impertinent. It destroys the simplicity of that nothingness
> before God. . . .[84]

Only this "true self" can be happy. Or celebrated in the christological pattern of "poetry of the forest."

One particularly overlooked source of this "poetry of the forest" is
the 1985 collection *Eighteen Poems* which were occasioned by Merton's love for a nurse, "S." They are not only fine lyric and ironic poems
but extraordinary late poems by which to measure his sense of the "true
self." The selection "Louisville Airport: May 5, 1966"[85] especially de-

serves our attention. The imagery and symbols of the "poetry of the forest" converge with Merton's confidence in his own experience:

> We with the gentle liturgy
> Of shy children have permitted God
> To make again His first world
> Here on the foolish grass
> After the spring rain has dried
> And all the loneliness
>
> Is for a moment lost in this simple
> Liturgy of children permitting God
> To make again that love
> Which is His alone
>
> His alone and terribly obscure and rare
> Love walks gently as a deer
> To where we sit on this green grass
> In the marvel of this day's going down
> Celebrated only
> By all the poets since the world began
>
> (lines 5–20)

Michael Mott's biography, *The Seven Mountains of Thomas Merton,* carefully reviewed the monk's intimate journal accounts of this abandoned love relationship. Nonetheless, the recurrence of the imagery of "spring rain" and the "green grass," along with the imagery of "Love walks gently as a deer," mark this as an important poem in the poetry of the forest genre. In particular, feminist commentators on Merton will find warrant for new affirmations of the true self in this and other selections from *Eighteen Poems.* Merton's overt reference to "shy children" in an Edenic context works effectively with "all the loneliness / Is for a moment lost" in a love "terribly obscure and rare." He has tethered it all to the symbol of the deer, the docile and vulnerable creatures who frequent the pages of his later journal. It is a graceful rendering of the true self's desire.

The prose poem "Rain and the Rhinoceros" (and to a lesser degree, "The Day of a Stranger") affords a unique reflection by the poet from the forest hermitage. Merton reads the sixth-century desert father Philoxenos and quotes: "One who is not alone has not discovered his identity." Such "individuals" experience the illusion of "collective existence," he laments, having "no more identity than an unborn child in the womb. He is not yet conscious. He is alien to his own truth. . . . He has life but not identity." Merton celebrates the freedom of the true self: "The discovery of this inner self," he says, "is an act and affirmation of solitude." Otherwise, to "live in a womb of collective illusion, our freedom remains abortive. Our capacities for joy, peace, and truth are never liberated." In the night rains of the Nelson county forest, Merton celebrates the "uselessness" of rain and its "wonderful, unintelligible, perfectly innocent speech" because, he says, "Here I am not alien."[86] The true self seeks fulfillment in relationship, a communion of persons for Merton. In this sense, the hermit becomes the most social of creatures. So he writes on Shrove Tuesday, 1965: "One thing the hermitage is making me see is that the universe is my home and I am nothing if not part of it. Destruction of the self that seems to stand outside the universe. Get free from the illusion of solipsism."[87]

Rain in the forest ("the murmur of water in the buckets") again found Merton immersed in poetry, lines from Lancelot Andrewes:

> The heart is deceitful above all things.
> The heart is deep and full of windings.
> The old man is covered up in a thousand wrappings.

He described them as "sad words" whose truth was felt because of so much solitude. "I cut wood behind the house and enjoy the faint smell of hickory smoke from the chimney," he narrated, preparatory to focusing on his true self's struggle; "while I taste and see that I am deceitful and that most of my troubles are rooted in my own bitterness." Merton refused to despair. "The heart is deceitful and does not want this [to bear solitude's rigors]," he confessed, "but God is greater than my heart."[88]

These riveting declarations became the matrix of Merton's "poetry of the forest." It is the same voice, a forest's "true self," that speaks in the best of Merton's poetry. In this sense we can experience his poems as icons of a presence, the presence of the true self, or inner self, who reflects for Merton the person of Christ.

The concluding entry of *A Vow of Conversation* returns to the shy wild deer outside the hermitage windows. The poet who had, like the deer, "trotted off / across the road into the woods, looking beat and confused," now expresses himself in a graceful gesture of the true self. Merton describes:

Last evening, when the moon was rising, I saw the warm burning soft red of a doe in the field. It was still light enough, so I got the field glasses and watched her. Presently a stag came out of the woods and then I saw a second doe and then, briefly, a second stag. They were not afraid. They looked at me from time to time. I watched their beautiful running, their grazing. . . .

The thing that struck me most—when you look at them directly and in movement, you see what the primitive cave painters saw. Something you never see in a photograph. It is most awe-inspiring. The muntu or the 'spirit' is shown in the running of the deer. The 'deerness' that sums up everything and is sacred and marvelous.

A contemplative intuition, yet this is perfectly ordinary, everyday seeing—what everybody ought to see all the time. The deer reveals to me something essential, not only in itself, but also in myself. . . . Something profound. The face of which is both in the deer and in myself. The stags are much darker than the does. They are mouse-gray, or rather a warm gray-brown, like flying squirrels. I could sense the softness of their brown coat and longed to touch them.[89]

This pastiche integrates Merton's spirituality of the true self in a fitting climax to the journals of his earliest hermitage days. Four particular elements recapitulate the disclosure of his authentic voice in what I have proposed as the "poetry of the forest":

(1) "*. . . they were not afraid*"—Throughout Merton's spirituality, the ability of persons to encounter one another is preconditioned by the capacity to claim a self-possessed contemplative center. If, for him, fear is the root of alienation, greed, and war, then this absence of fear proffered new possibilities. The symbolic expression of this truth in the "shy wild deer" metaphor opened for Merton wider paths of global spirituality and inculturation. The true self again and again overcomes fear, especially any timidity about our deepest identity, to claim the "freedom [which] equals being onself and acting accordingly."[90] It is the epitome of Christ's own inner self-possession.

(2) "*. . . the 'spirit' is shown in the running of the deer*"—What Merton identified as "deerness" eludes photography (or any superficial copying) and demands immediate experience. The unique ontological essence of a creature could only be revealed through things in their true identity. A long debt to Duns Scotus's *haecceitas,* the "thisness" of individual created realities, had come to Merton through the

poetry of Gerard Manley Hopkins. Merton transformed that existential insight about God's Christ who "plays in ten thousand places"[91] with a fidelity to his own experience and his readers' experience when he ventured the event of each new poem. This element reinforces the first (". . . they were not afraid") in a "sacred" moment, the primitive religious instinct of simultaneous fear-and-attraction in the presence of the holy.

(3) *"The deer reveals to me something essential . . . also about myself"*—The poet's ability to see likenesses where comparisons might seem inappropriate gives rise to metaphors. But the ultimate purpose of such unique poetic knowledge is a self-knowledge by both artist and reader. Merton's spirituality of the true self imitates (*mimesis*) this dynamic by creatively experiencing the deer's "profound" simplicity. For Merton, this meant entering the "subject of the object" (in Rilke's sense), or claiming more deeply his own true identity as a contemplative. Therefore, Merton became more aware of the presence of God by love.

(4) *"I could sense the softness of their brown coat and longed to touch them"*—The mystic's contemplative experience does not end, as Merton himself cautioned, in a solipsistic bubble of individualism. The mysticism of the unifying vision seeks the reconciliation and harmony of persons and creation. In this light, the final line of the journal climaxes Merton's spirituality of the true self in a longing for touch, a symbolic fullness of encounter. The gesture signals mutual acceptance. It incarnates the presence of true selves, one to another. His debt to Scotus's christology becomes apparent in this confidence in God's inevitable intimacy with human persons through Christ's fully human experience.

In the innocent poem of "Merlin and the Deer" we have identified a matrix for an understanding of Thomas Merton's "poetry of the forest" wherein the monk offers the dynamics of a spirituality of the true self, who is the inner self in Christ. T. S. Eliot wrote of "the hint half guessed, the gift half understood."[92] In the Merton canon, such are the poems, the "poetry of the forest," wherein we encounter Merton's true self and our own. To use his own phrase, Merton has left us in the mythos of these poems "another legacy, more delicate, more rare."[93] But how poignantly he touches and summons a response from our own deepest true self through these verbal icons. Merton's own "true self" found a voice in such a poetry of the forest:

He hums alone in the glade
Says only a few phrases to himself
Or a psalm to his companion
Light in the wood.[94]

A hermeneutical key to interpret these poems was emerging simultaneously in the organic development of Merton's prose, in which he explored a kenotic christology, the epiphany of Christ in our "emptiness," as the paradigm of the true or inner self. Merton's readers must integrate the monk's poetry with these emergent christological insights in his prose, dialoguing them like panels on a diptych.

3. Dance of the Lord in Emptiness:
Merton's Kenotic Christ

Thomas Merton's prose poem "Hagia Sophia" was published in 1962 by the Stamperia del Santuccio press of his Lexington artist friend Victor Hammer. The work originated with a February 28, 1958, dream and subsequent March 4 imaginary love letter. In the dream he had been embraced by a young Jewess, Anne, whom he named "Proverb." Weeks later, on March 18, Merton stood at the corner of Fourth and Walnut Streets in Louisville and experienced what he describes as an overwhelming sense of solidarity and love for the people surrounding him in the busy shopping district. The alienation of the young monk, who, three days after the bombing of Pearl Harbor in 1941, "spurned New York, spat on Chicago, and tromped on Louisville, heading for the woods with Thoreau in one pocket, John of the Cross in another, and holding the Bible open at the Apocalypse"[1] had dissolved. He describes the event as "liberating," "like waking from a dream of separateness, of spurious self-isolation in a special world, a world of renunciation and supposed holiness." Six times in the brief passage, edited and embellished seven years later for *Conjectures of a Guilty Bystander,* he uses the word "illusion" to critique flaws in his monastic self-understanding. An aura of self-righteousness clings to the text, however, when he attributes solely to the monk a consciousness of all human persons' common belonging to God. Even while acknowledging humanity's absurdities and mistakes, Merton can breathe an optimism grounded in the event of Christ's Incarnation: "[Y]et with all that, God Himself gloried in becoming a member of the human race. A member of the human race! . . . I have the immense joy of being a *man,* a member of a race in which God Himself became incarnate. . . . Now I realize what we all are."[2]

89

He has transformed the original, spare journal entry with a lyric description of the crowds and "the secret beauty of their hearts," the "depths" of the person known to God. He borrows an image from Louis Massignon to describe the center of our being as *le point vierge:* "a point of nothingness which is untouched by sin and by illusion," the *"absolute poverty"* which is "the pure glory of God in us."[3] The image is rendered in terms of a "spark," "like a pure diamond, blazing with the invisible light of heaven." Spiritual maturity has come to mean not a program but seeing "these billions of points of light coming together in the face and blaze of a sun that would make all the darkness and cruelty of life vanish completely." The imagery echoes Bernard's therapy for the contemplative's reclaiming the true self and Gregory the Great's *lumen incircumscriptum.* "There is no way of telling people they are walking around shining like the sun,"[4] concluded Merton.

The independent poem "Hagia Sophia" celebrates the feminine principle, *Sophia,* personified in the dream as "Proverb," in a dramatic reenactment of the mystery of Christ. At dawn, the liturgical hour of Lauds, Merton describes awakening from a dream which perhaps coincides with the "illusions" of the Louisville vision: "It is like the One Christ awakening in all the separate selves that ever were separate and isolated and alone in all the lands of the earth . . . [and coming back] into unity of love." With the high morning hour of Prime, light imagery dominates the prose poem. The echoes of Gregory the Great's *lumen incircumscriptum* and Gerard Manley Hopkins's "That Nature Is a Heraclitean Fire and the Comfort of the Resurrection" introduce us:

> The Sun burns in the sky like the Face of God, but we do not know his countenance as terrible. His light is diffused in the air and the light of God is diffused by Hagia Sophia.
>
> We do not see the Blinding One in black emptiness. He speaks to us gently in ten thousand things, in which His light is one fulness and one Wisdom.
>
> Thus He shines not on them but from within them. Such is the loving-kindness of Wisdom.

Julian of Norwich's feminine description of "Jesus our Mother" is integrated into the poem. God is both Father and Mother, "and as Mother God is experienced as mercy and love": "As Mother His shining is diffused, embracing all His creatures with merciful tenderness and light." Merton's language, clumsily using the masculine pronoun for God, stalks ahead. Sophia is described as "infinite light unmanifest, not even waiting to be known as Light." Sophia is the center, "obvious and unseen," alias *le point vierge,* manifesting Light as pure gift to those who pursue solitude. Merton offers a striking image of contemplative transformation, of the Wisdom of God, Sophia: "That which is poorest and humblest, that which is most hidden in all things is nevertheless most obvious in them, and quite manifest, for it is their own self that stands before us, naked and without care." He returns to the kenosis of Christ in the final section of the prose poem, at sunset and the liturgical hour of Compline. The Cistercians' Marian devotion climaxes his celebration of femininity, Mary's nothingness as "the perfect expression of Wisdom in mercy." In Christ's Incarnation, "God enters without publicity into the city of rapacious men. She crowns Him not with what is glorious, but with what is greater than glory: the one thing greater than glory is weakness, nothingness, poverty."[5] This paradoxical language is not new to Merton, but it has developed to new proportions by 1960–62 when "Hagia Sophia" came from his pen. In *The Sign of Jonas* he had intimated a similar image. "God's glory and God's shyness," he wrote, "are one." For "God seeks glory by giving glory."[6] What is new is the creative connection between Merton's affective experience, in both the "Proverb" dream and the vision at Fourth and Walnut Streets, and the mystical theology and symbolism, which before now he had compartmentalized in his too often stiff, cold, and formal books on spirituality. These experiences of 1958 act as a catalyst for Merton's discovery of a new, wider matrix for writing about the contemplative inner self's compassion.[7] Even a cursory attention to the imagery he uses in recounting both experiences points to a deeper convergence of christology, autobiography, and the identity of the inner self.

A useful distinction made by Karl Rahner suggests a method for analyzing the development of Merton's christology. Rahner has sketched a contemporary classic presentation in his essay "The Two Basic Types of Christology." He distinguished between metaphysical christology — "incarnation" is the central category and emphasis is placed on the descent of God's Word into the world, the taking flesh of God's own self-expression for the sake of making human life like God's; and salvation-historical christology — the story of Jesus' life is central, with its movement ascending toward the God in whom he trusted absolutely and whose kingdom he proclaimed with absolute fidelity.[8] These "poles" of christology have been variously labeled: descending/ascending, christology from above/christology from below, high christology/low christology, speculative/praxis, ontological/functional, divinization/humanization. Michael L. Cook has distinguished successful contemporary christologies which "seek to integrate the four dimensions of historical Jesus, cross, resurrection, and incarnation by centering upon the concrete, personal existence of Jesus of Nazareth." "They all seek," he says, "to avoid the thought process that first separates and then reunites the divinity and the humanity of Jesus." He finds indispensable Piet Schoonenberg's conviction that "Jesus' divine sonship is his humanness to the utmost."[9] Merton had claimed these very insights in the 1964 essay "The Humanity of Christ in Monastic Prayer."

Merton's turn to human experience, linked with his reclaiming an optimistic confidence in the goodness of creation and nature as already examined in chapter one, mirrors the transition from an exclusively metaphysical christology to the incorporation of a salvation-history christology. He never self-consciously uses Rahner's precise categories. The later, contemporary technical language of ascending/descending, or from above/from below christologies was foreign to him. But the enlarged context of the dynamics of history as the arena for the experience of salvation in Christ comes up repeatedly in Merton's last decade.

The year 1958 proved a watershed for Merton. The experiences of the Louisville vision and Proverb dream unlocked long dormant possibilities in his christology. This chapter will suggest how this reunion of christology and a broader, global sense of soteriology as ongoing salvation history grew in Merton's consciousness and writing. *Conjectures of a Guilty Bystander* proves to be the barometer of such growth, a journal/readings notebook spanning the years 1956 through 1963. Merton's own personal context had changed significantly, and the historical contingencies affecting the church and secular society registered seismic shifts. He had become master of scholastics in 1951 and then master of novices from 1955 until he retired to the hermitage in 1965. He resisted opportunities to transfer to the Carthusians and live a more eremetical lifestyle, and spurned a scheme to retire to the Abbey of Gethsemani's firetower as a Cistercian hermit because it carried a proviso that he abandon writing projects.[10] In the mid–1950s the United States convulsed with the birth of the civil rights movement and aggravations of the cold war with the Soviet bloc. In 1958 an unlikely caretaker, the seemingly geriatric Angelo Roncalli, became Pope John

XXIII and surprised Catholicism and the world in 1959 by announcing the convocation of an ecumenical council to renew and reform the
church, despite its reluctance to being ushered into the modern world.
The call for openness and dialogue precipitated a period of exploration and unexpected discoveries for both Merton and Roman Catholicism. Meanwhile, the early sixties erupted with war in southeast Asia,
the Vietnam conflict that triggered a response of protest and peace
making from the Kentucky knob where Merton perched, now "present everywhere by hiddenness and compassion."[11]

The arthritic manuals of theology in use during Merton's novitiate
had retarded his christology with algebraiclike formulas. In *The Sign
of Jonas* he evaluated a year and a half study of Sabetti's moral theology and Tanqueray's dogmatics as "dull."[12] A visiting French abbot com-
miserated, wishing that Merton had a good theologian to guide him
in his writing.[13] The theological curriculum he sketched as master of
scholastics mixed mysticism, dogma, scripture, and patristic literature.[14]
He had confessed that he found theology "too technical. . . . I need
the living God."[15] He found more theology in the "Exultet" than in
the pages he wrote of *The Ascent to Truth,* pages he tore up because
he could not write "theology."[16] "God is not a theory," he wrote; therefore, God could not be "weighed" out in doctrines.[17] He mocked himself, styling his theology as the "theology of Job's friends"[18] when he
began teaching, on November 16, 1949, the eleventh anniversary of
his baptism. He confessed that he preferred to open the windows of
Augustine and there find theology.[19] But most of all, Merton struggled and gave birth to a theology from the crucible of his own experience, what his self-deprecation dubbed "my little pawnshop of second-
rate emotions and ideas."[20]

In *The New Man,* a book written in 1955 but only published in
1961, he focused his method: "The spiritual anguish of man has no
cure but mysticism."[21] God's "terrible but healing mercy," he wrote,
"allows us to approach him as we are." But it proves a "long and patient struggle."[22] Mystical theology, or contemplation, is the monk's
knowledge of God won through this searing experience. It is helpful
to distinguish this from a more analytic, systematic sense of theology.
Merton's turn to the experience of mysticism is reflected in a similar
distinction between intellect and reason.[23] The highest understanding
of God, contemplation, comes by what the scholastics call "connaturality," contemplating God in creation and God's action of providence

in the world. Contemplation happens as the person surrenders to a gift in the realm of experience, as intuitive knowledge and imaginative, recreative understanding. Merton gravitated toward the scriptures, the desert fathers, and patristic literature in order to retrieve this tradition of contemplation. As chapter four will show, his artistic temperament and literary critical skills fathomed the same sapiential method in modern novelists and poets. There, too, he found the imaginative and intuitive rendering of God's providential presence (or, God's ironic presence by absence) in the density of human experience and creation. But the story gallops ahead. Preambles to the mature voice of the Merton of *Conjectures of a Guilty Bystander* stand like signposts and deserve to be plotted on the map in order to guide readers through his spirituality.

PREAMBLES OF MERTON'S MATURE CHRISTOLOGY

It is an understatement to say that Merton's publications were theologically uneven. This fact can be indexed, in part, by the diverse voices of the early Merton. He ventured into trouble — and that paralyzing "false self" he often describes — when he tried to write abstractly, speculatively. While some of the essays from his mature days as a hermit improve upon this fault in his prose, his forte remained narrative, autobiography, the existential meditation laden with imagery and metaphors, poetic language. Early journals and poems reveal a more playful, personable, and honest Merton; the early books of spiritual meditation tease with the theme of personalism, but keep the reader at arm's length and only permit an occasional honest self-revelation. Nonetheless, they are important signposts in Merton's development. Other books were banal hagiography, uncritical biographies of Cistercian mystics, penned by an indentured young monk. Still others bear the earmarks of their lengthy postponement; a publication date might be five or six years after the actual writing.

Anne E. Carr[24] has brilliantly excavated a cross section of Merton texts and identified the development of his spiritual dynamic of the false self versus the true self, or the inner self. There is no need to rehearse her masterful score. This chapter instead addresses the same line of development as her study, but with a focus on the christological content of his writing. Merton gradually shifts from a formal, exclusively metaphysical christology to a fuller salvation history christology. This shift is congruent with his autobiographical habit, turning to experience, and his eventually revolutionary recognition that "Christ is in fact manifesting Himself in the critical conflicts of our time."[25]

SEEDS OF CONTEMPLATION

Merton set out to revitalize the monastic and patristic sources for a contemporary audience in the style of spiritual meditations. The first such collection was the 1949 classic, *Seeds of Contemplation,* which he described in the author's note as disconnected thoughts and aphorisms. Two chapters in the Cistercian-looking, burlap-bound volume bear the special footprint of Scotus. "Things in Their Identity" celebrates the very individuality of all created things, reminiscent of Scotus's doctrine of *haecceitas.*[26] Hopkins had cultivated this important principle in his sacramental vision of the world, celebrating the uniqueness and particularity of singular creatures. Merton rendered it more prosaically: "A tree gives glory to God first of all by being a tree."[27] Merton's debt to Hopkins for the technique of inscape, which the latter had developed out of the Scotist tradition, appears directly in this context when Merton writes, "Their inscape is their sanctity."[28] In the chapter "Everything that is, is Holy," he borrows the title from William Blake (*America: A Prophecy,* plate 8, 1. 130), the subject of his Columbia University thesis. When he describes creation as "the Art of the Father," reflecting God's reality and presence, the debt to the Franciscan tradition of Bonaventure's *Itinerarium* is apparent.[29] He addresses chapters on solitude, integrity, humility, liberty, detachment, renunciation, and inward destitution to an audience "in the world." The dynamics of the "transforming union" with God summons the perfection of humility, the quest of persons in the monastery and in the world to discover their own true selves in Christ. Life becomes the project of denying the illusory false self, the self-centeredness of original sin. The entirety of *Seeds of Contemplation* becomes a series of concentric circles around the mystery of the true identity of the inner self. "Who am I?" becomes the recurring question. The answer dawns in the inner self's discovery that in our humility, poverty, and abandonment, we begin to live "in Christ." Merton returns to the monastic infatuation with the biblical myth of the fall to pose the christological mystery of recovering the image and likeness of God.

You seem to be the same person and you are the same person that you have always been: in fact you are more yourself than you have ever been before. You have only just begun to exist. You feel as if you were at last fully born. All that went before was a mistake, a fumbling preparation for birth. Now you have come into your element. And yet now you have become nothing. You have sunk to the center of your own poverty, and there you have felt the doors fly open into infinite freedom, into a wealth which is perfect because none of it is yours and yet it all belongs to you.

And now you are free to go in and out of infinity.[30]

This thread of nothingness and poverty as the threshold of the new self in Christ gingerly auditioned within *Seeds of Contemplation*. Merton tentatively played the note of Christ's kenosis in his chapter "Electa ut Sol" by transposing the christological mystery of one person, with both a truly human and a truly divine nature, in a metaphor reminiscent of the eighteenth-century metaphysical poets: humanity, in the person of Mary, was the glass through which God's light, Christ, has shone.[31] But the metaphysical christology of Incarnation still eclipses anything outside a privatized piety at this stage of Merton's development.[32]

As a magnifying glass concentrates the rays of the sun into a little burning knot of heat that can set fire to a dry leaf or a piece of paper, so the mysteries of Christ in the Gospel concentrate the rays of God's light and fire to a point that sets fire to the spirit of man. . . . Through the glass of His Humanity He concentrates the rays of His Holy Spirit upon us so that we feel the burn, and all mysterical experience is infused into the soul through the Man Christ.[33]

Merton declared that "in Christ" the divine and supernatural becomes "connatural," or accessible, to us. There is a cosmic extension of God's love through the humanity of Christ. Paul's cosmic christology echoes faintly in *Seeds of Contemplation*. But it matured only much later in Merton's writing. This book plants seeds of the contemplative's true identity, seeds of contemplation.

The theological anthropology in *Seeds of Contemplation* occasionally veers close to pessimism. Merton writes of the false self that the structures of pleasures and ambitions are destined to be destroyed. "And when they are gone there will be nothing left of me but my own nakedness and hollowness, to tell me that I am a mistake." At times it is difficult to distinguish the false "I" from the true self, or inner self. Merton voices the confidence that the true self will be discovered in the discovery of God. And that means that "the secret of my identity is hidden in the love and mercy of God."[34] Christ comes as God's love, and transforms us, so that we might discover "who I am," and possess a true identity.[35] Merton picks up the Pauline concept of Christ's "emptying" (*kenosis*) in a larval theme that draws a distant horizon on the boundary of *Seeds of Contemplation*'s christological reflections. The mystic's paradox revolves around the fact that you cannot enter to the deepest center of your inner self unless you pass out of yourself and "empty" yourself, giving yourself to others in the purity of selfless love.[36] He images the self-hypnosis that avoids this dynamic as a barricading, behaving like a turtle, relying on narcotics. The mystical relationship with Christ becomes a kenotic understanding of the cross. Christ is the humiliated person of poverty. And with Mary, the Mother of Jesus, Merton finds the exemplar of "absolute emptiness," "the most perfectly poor and the most perfectly hidden," the one whose "nothingness" adores God. Because Mary is full of God, she gives birth to Christ. We share her mission to bring Christ, born out of our nothingness, to others.

The concluding chapter, "Pure Love," however, virtually retracts the kenotic christology of these earlier passages. The "emptiness and unfathomable incomprehensibility of God" can come through the arid desert experience, but Merton finds this painful to nature and human faculties because it is infinitely above them. Contemplation comes to be identified exclusively with the divinity of Christ. The book closes with a retreat into the christological formulas of the 1940s, a near-Monophysite eclipse of the humanity of Christ. A decade later Merton's revised *New Seeds of Contemplation* (1961) gave ample evidence of the salvation history christology, which by then was dramatically refashioning his meditations on the Christ.

THE ASCENT TO TRUTH

The only thoroughly systematic theological study Merton undertook was his next major book, *The Ascent to Truth* (1951). He attempts to define the nature of contemplative experience and its relationship to the ascetic life and mysticism. He elaborates on the apophatic mystical tradition, the mysticism of "dark knowledge," or knowing God by "unknowing," in Gregory of Nyssa and John of the Cross. The crux of the book is his juxtaposition of John of the Cross with the system of Thomas Aquinas. Again the book gravitates to the metaphysics of Incarnation. By this time Merton's study of the Greek Fathers had begun to exercise a decided impact on his work: Christ is God become incarnate in order to effect a mystical transformation of humanity, the person's *divinization*. He credits the Greek Fathers with the refusal to divide the human person by a narrow escape into angelism or the Gnostics' teaching, which did violence by discrediting our humanity and the material creation. The ascetic seeks to elevate humanity and to elevate our faculties and gifts to perfection. By the same token Merton cautions against the Pelagian temptation to perfect our humanity by our own efforts, without God's initiative.

A primary source of Merton's presentation of the transformed vision is Gregory of Nyssa's *Commentary on Ecclesiastes*. He borrows from it to criticize the vanities of the world and the psychology of attachment and illusion, vision and detachment, to explain the Christian mystic's relationship with the world. "Only Christ, only the Incarnation by which God emerged from his eternity to enter into time and consecrate it to Himself, could save time from being an endless cycle of frustrations."[37] The false self, a prisoner of illusion, suffers under concupiscence and seeks idolatrous value in created things. Merton cautions that the mystic speaks only figuratively of the world as "illusion" and "nothingness." He credits Gregory of Nyssa with an affirmation of the ambiguity of "nature" as both vanity and symbol. In Christian Platonism, Merton reminded, "contemplation of nature does not consist in an intellectual tennis game between these two contrary concepts of nature."[38] For the Greek Fathers' *theoria physica* proposed a contemplation of God in nature, or created things, through the ascetic gift of discernment.

In chapter 7, "The Crisis of Dark Knowledge," Merton ponders the seemingly irreconcilable opposition between body and spirit, natural and supernatural, concepts and contemplation. He insists that divinization does not allow human persons to attack our own nature. We are not angels. Nor are we Stoics, with a soldierly endurance of suffering for its own sake. A whole family of dualistic heresies, descended from Gnosticism and Manichaeism, are discredited by Merton because they violate the essential nature of humanity by annihilating the flesh in the victory of the spirit, a radical departure from Gregory of Nyssa's incarnational divinization. Merton identifies the logical terminal point of this attitude: "As soon as the phenomenal world ceases to be an intelligible manifestation of the Absolute, and as soon as our thoughts and our words cease altogether to provide us with an objectively valid means of communicating with God, we fall into agnosticism." And agnosticism, for Merton, results ultimately in moral indifference. He then balances the scales with a rich observation that for the first time presages the wider context of a salvation history christology. While the mythic, symbolic, and magic consciousness of primitives is neither "merely external forms" nor, strictly speaking, "spiritual," "they are at least interior: they spring from the soul, the psyche of man. And they also have a marked effect on his body. . . . They can take possession of a man's whole being."[39]

Part Two of *The Ascent to Truth* attempts to reconcile reason and mysticism in John of the Cross. Merton's reconstruction of John's Thomist education at Salamanca, Spain, includes the Carmelite's familiarity with the 1567–68 lectures of the famous Dominican, Mancio, on the third part of Thomas's *Summa,* which deals with the Incarnation.

> God's revelation of Himself to the world in His Incarnate Word forms the heart and substance of all Christian mystical contemplation. This is just as true of St. John of the Cross as it is of Saint Bernard of Clairvaux, or Saint Bonaventure, or any of the mystics who are esteemed for their special devotion to the Humanity of Christ.[40]

There occurs here a nodding assent, but only abstractly, in the direction of the social responsibility of the mystic. Because contemplative life is a life of charity, love of God and neighbor are integrated. "Charity is always twofold. It has but one object: God. But it reaches Him both directly, in Himself, and through other men."[41]

Merton concludes the third and final section of the book, "Doctrine and Experience," by invoking the popular caricature of the mystic as anti-incarnational. It offers an important christocentric realignment.

> Their supraconceptual experience of God cannot in fact be achieved without Christ. What is more, it cannot even be arrived at without a Christian mysticism. "No man comes to the Father but by Christ." (Jn. 14:6)[42]

This unique systematic effort by Merton, which he later lamented as a style foreign to his temperament, concludes with a dramatic image to describe the mystic's radical transformation of consciousness: "God must move and reveal Himself and shake the world within the soul and rise from His sleep like a giant."[43] Merton had earlier created a metaphor to articulate the mystic's transfiguration: the mystic is transformed in God "like a bar of iron in the heat of a furnace. The iron turns into fire." The soul then becomes "translucent in the flame of divine love."[44] Merton's poetic symbols of awakening and transformation of the real self were grounded in these very analogues of mysticism and contemplation. *The Ascent to Truth* remains a period piece, the effort of a young monk to write theology in the idiom of mid-century Thomism. Merton's unease and disorientation during its writing, as well as his subsequent displeasure with the finished work, gauge the creative block. The dry, doctrinal abstractions were holding him hostage to a sclerotic metaphysical christology.

NO MAN IS AN ISLAND

In 1955 Merton continued the "occasional pattern of reflections on the spiritual life" which *Seeds of Contemplation* had launched, "leaving systems to others." The mystery of Christ radicated his outline of spiritual life: "The meaning of my life . . . is seen, above all, in my integration in the mystery of Christ."[45] The key to our development as persons, he emphasizes, involves a discovery not of ourselves but of Christ, the Logos who becomes incarnate.[46] The metaphysical christology is unmistakable in this language. It became more apparent in Merton's parallel writings, but is already implied here, that his allusions to the humanity of Christ at this point mean the *glorified* humanity of the risen Christ. Merton's earthly Christ enjoys the beatific vision, as the orthodox vernacular of then contemporary metaphysical christology would prescribe. There is disappointment in reading a chapter promisingly entitled "The Word of the Cross." One might hope to find Merton turning to the historical Jesus' passion, given this reflection on the problem of human suffering. Instead, he wrote:

> The death of Jesus on the Cross has an infinite meaning and value not because it is a death but because it is the death of the Son of God. The Cross of Christ says nothing of the power of suffering and death. It speaks only of the power of Him who overcame both suffering and death by rising from the grave.
>
> . . . For Jesus is not merely someone who once loved men enough to die for them. He is a man whose human nature subsists in God, so that

He is a divine person. . . . And it is of the very essence of Christianity to face suffering and death not because they are good, not because they have meaning, but because the Resurrection of Jesus has robbed them of their meaning.[47]

His use of a romanticized image of suffering becomes abstract and banal.

Baptism engrafts us into the mystical vine which is the body of Christ, and makes us live in His life and ripen like grapes on the trellis of his Cross. . . . My suffering is not my own. It is the Passion of Christ, stretching out its tendrils into my life in order to bear rich clusters of grapes, making my soul dizzy with the wine of God's love, and pouring that wine as strong fire upon the whole world.[48]

What does mature in this book is Merton's study of the phenomenology of interpersonal human love. He probes deeply how the human person recovers identity in Christ. Midway through *No Man Is an Island* a glimpse of the relaxed Merton claims the tentative voice of a more sacramental and incarnational spirituality. He suggests the importance of recovering the neglected ability to respond to reality, "to see the value and beauty in ordinary things" of creation that surround us. He is ambiguous about withdrawal from the world's bombardment, mentioning the stimuli of advertising, in particular. The idiom has shifted abruptly: "[W]hat we must do is begin by unlearning our wrong ways of seeing, tasting, feeling, and so forth, and acquire a few of the right ones. . . . [L]earn to see life as if it were something more than a hypnotizing telecast."[49]

THOUGHTS IN SOLITUDE

In the transitional year 1958, whose revolutionary events in Merton's life were noted at the beginning of this chapter, the last book of his spiritual meditations was again dominated by metaphysical christology. *Thoughts in Solitude* returns to the theme of humanity divinized by the Incarnation. The book affirms the axiom that grace builds upon nature; thus, Merton can speak of grace being "engrafted" without uprooting human persons and transplanting them in the realm of angels.[50] Contemplation is demythologized, no longer a special state that removes or separates a person from ordinary things because God penetrates all.[51] When he announces flatly that "Christianity is not

Stoicism," he criticizes false ascetics who deaden their humanity instead of developing its capacities as the Greek Fathers' concept of divinization suggests. The christocentric focus is restated: "Christ, the Incarnate Word, is the Book of Life in Whom we read God."[52] Here only a passing voice is given to Christ's kenosis, but Merton's enlarged spirituality now gives a new place to emotion and human feeling. The attractiveness of his famous, much-quoted prayer, "Lord, I have no idea where I am going . . . [b]ut I believe that the desire to please you does in fact please you . . . ",[53] accepts the human condition within a newly perceived eschatological horizon: "Although [the human person] is a traveller in time, he has opened his eyes, for a moment, in eternity."[54] Merton voices an unselfconscious kenotic christology in a lyric prayer. It will remain for events and later books to probe and reflect on the christological meaning of the human heart's compassion. But now he was walking in the direction of a salvation-history christology. This personal spirituality, appropriating the mystery of Christ, made Merton attractive to his audience, indeed unique in an era of otherwise either pietistic or cerebral Catholic spirituality. A descending christology begins to be balanced by an ascending christology, a christology from below.

> You do not wait for me to become great before You will be with me and hear me and answer me. It is my lowliness and my humanness that have drawn you to make me Your equal by condescending to my level and living in me by Your merciful care.
>
> . . . I know that You have called me to live long with You and to learn that if I were not a mere man, a mere human being capable of all mistakes and all evil, also capable of a frail and errant human affection for you, I would not be capable of being Your Son. You desire the love of a man's heart because your Divine Son also loves You with a man's Heart and He became Man in order that my heart and His heart should love you in one love, which is a human love born and moved by Your Holy Spirit.
>
> If therefore I do not love You with a man's love and with a man's simplicity and with the humility to be myself, I will never taste the full sweetness of Your Fatherly mercy, and Your Son, as far as my life goes, will have died in vain.
>
> It is necessary that I be human and remain human in order that the Cross of Christ be not made void. Jesus died not for the angels but for men.

And *this is the mystery of our vocation:* not that we cease to be men in order to become angels or gods, but *that the love of my man's heart can become God's love for God and men, and my human tears can fall from my eyes as the tears of God because they well up from the motion of His Holy Spirit in the heart of His incarnate Son.* [55]

THE NEW MAN

While *The New Man* was published in 1961, the book had been written in the mid-1950s. The working title of this book, "Existential Communion," hinted strongly at a change in Merton's voice, from speculation back to experience. His prescription, "The spiritual anguish of man has no cure but mysticism," [56] perhaps overstated a truth. But embracing the long, patient struggle now meant that we could approach God as we are, in the fullness of humanity, and find God's "terrible but healing mercy." [57] The familiar struggle of *Seeds of Contemplation,* the conflict between the illusory, false self and the true, inner self returns, now undergirded by Greek patristic sources and Paul's christology. The human person's real power, Merton signals, gravitates to our identity in Christ. That power lies hidden in the agony which makes a person cry out to God; and there we are at the same time helpless and omnipotent. [58] Merton distances the mystic from the philosopher. The contemplative participates "in a concrete action of God in time." The historical consciousness gains a nudging momentum in Merton's spirituality. Having given with one hand, though, he takes back with the other, quickly privatizing the act of the God-Man as "capable of communicating itself spiritually and repeating itself over and over again in *the lives of individual men.*" [59]

The sixth chapter, "The Second Adam," alludes to the speculations about the fall which divided Scotists from Thomists. But in the Greek Fathers he retrieves a view of redemption from the perspective of a cosmic christology. He describes the Promethean frustration, our trying vainly, on our own power, to regain what was lost by sin.

Even before Adam existed Christ was a Cosmic Mediator. . . . and He was, at the same time, already exercising another Mediation which would include all men in Himself in His Incarnation. The very fact that men were made in the image of God meant that they were already potentially united with the Word of God who was to come and take human nature to Himself. [60]

This optimism from his research in the early 1950s, studying the patristic scholarship of writers like Henri DeLubac and Hans Urs Von Balthasar,[61] was grounded in Gregory of Nyssa and Maximus the Confessor. Adam was already created in the image of the Image of God, Merton said, because God "has decided from all eternity to become man in Jesus Christ."[62]

Paul's captivity epistles, especially Colossians 1:15–17, breathe for Merton the life of a neglected cosmic christology. Creation is oriented toward fullness (*pleroma*). He volunteers that the gospel narratives cause us to regard the strangeness of this because, for the most part (e.g., Jn. 1:1–15), in them "the Incarnation suggest[s] that God enters into His own world as a stranger and an alien." The mystery of Christ's kenosis depends on the paradox of his infinite distance from us and his infinite nearness to us.[63] This hidden Christ is manifest as simple and unobtrusive. Merton borrows from the recapitulation (*anakepheliasis*) theory of Irenaeus, who echoes St. Paul's cosmic christology: Christ recapitulates or "sums up" the whole of salvation history, beginning with Adam. Adam's loss of paradise is described as spiritual blindness. The error of our Promethean habits, Merton laments, is that they take no account of anyone but the false self and end in a narcissistic, isolated, and unfulfilling anguish.[64] Only grace as interpersonal relationship, revealed in Christ's love, can reorient us to that friendship with God.[65] Merton's christological reflections were not only growing, but evidencing a new complexity. He poised on the threshold of a new decade, and a new context in which to recognize the hidden, kenotic Christ who is not alien but at home in our weakness and defencelessness.

NEW SEEDS OF CONTEMPLATION

The rewriting of the 1949 classic, *Seeds of Contemplation,* occupied Merton's attention during 1960.[66] He confessed that the original work had been written in the vacuum of his lack of experience in confronting the needs and problems of other persons. But *New Seeds of Contemplation,* "in many ways a completely new book," had been changed by contact with other solitudes. The loneliness of his novices and fellow monks coincided with the loneliness, he intimates, of people even outside the church. The true measure of Merton's reworking the coordinates of his spirituality comes when he acknowledges that he, the monk, is a debtor even to the experience of people without formal religious affiliations. In retrospect, *Seeds of Contemplation* compares as a more brittle, insular vision of spirituality than the supple, expansive new life of the revised book.

New Seeds of Contemplation begins with two additional chapters on what contemplation is and is not. Everything radiates from the christocentric mystery, "It is now no longer I that live but Christ lives in me." Merton emphasizes that contemplation explores this mystery, the *"experience* of what each Christian obscurely believes."[67] He goes on to describe in arresting imagery what contemplation is: it is an experience that "awakens a tragic anguish and opens many questions in the depths of the heart like wounds that cannot stop bleeding." The paradox of Christ's kenosis now becomes the center of gravity for Merton's journey. To be holy now means to be something beyond understanding, a hidden, apparently contradictory mystery: "for God, in Christ, 'emptied Himself,'" and was condemned and crucified because he did not measure up to human conceptions of holiness. The paradigm of the kenotic Christ confounded the world that witnessed his abandonment, "as if the Divine Power and mercy had utterly failed." Merton put it paradoxically:

> In dying on the Cross, Christ manifested the holiness of God in apparent contradiction with itself. But in reality this manifestation was the complete denial and rejection of all human ideas of holiness and perfection. The wisdom of God became folly to men. . . .
>
> If, then, we want to seek some way of being holy, we must first of all renounce our own way and our own wisdom. We must "empty ourselves" as He did. We must "deny ourselves" and in some sense make ourselves "nothing" in order that we may live not so much in ourselves as in Him. We must live by a power and a light that seem not to be there. We must live by the strength of an apparent emptiness that is always truly empty and yet never fails to support us at every moment.[68]

When Merton turned to the existential dilemma of humanity's disunion in his chapter entitled "A Body of Broken Bones," he pointed to the fork in the road leading either to love or to hate. The tragedy of every weak, lost, and isolated person is in giving life to hatred, out of our loneliness, unworthiness, and inadequacy. Ironically, he said, such hatred consumes the self that hates and not the object of its hatred. Again he turns to the mystery of the cross. For when Christ conquered death, "He opened their eyes to the reality of a love which overcomes hatred and destroys death." Everything depends upon the free decision "to love in spite of all unworthiness whether in oneself or in one's neighbor." For Merton, this is ultimately not a matter of will but of faith. Christian love is rooted in *the faith that one is loved.*[69] He portrays the "Moral Theology of the Devil" as a distortion of the mystery of Christ. Today we would term it a form of divine child abuse, to say that God takes pleasure in delivering Jesus to his executioners, or that Jesus became human because of a desire to be punished by God, *Abba*. Merton rejects any concept that God rejoices in suffering or that God wills or plans a universe of misery. Such a theology would have no place for mercy, only revenge. But for Merton the cross is mercy.

Christ is identified by Merton as the power and wisdom of God, Light, echoing the poem, "Hagia Sophia."[70] In Christ God is no longer separate, remote, but accessible.[71] He faults a superficial grasp of dogma for precipitating the artificial "problem" of whether the contemplative should abandon the humanity of Christ in order to pass directly to Christ's divinity. Our love of Christ does not terminate, for Merton, in his human or divine nature, but in his *Person*. "To love Him merely as a *nature* would be like loving a human friend for his money or his conviviality," Merton objects. "We do not love Christ for what He has but for *Who He is*." In the end, this unites us with Christ, "*two subjects in one affective union.*"[72]

A chapter on "Detachment" now finds in Christ's cross the model for the human person's striving for complete emptiness and freedom, opposed to the "exclusive [false] self."[73] The kenotic motif becomes sublime in Merton's description, "God touches us with a touch that is emptiness and empties us."[74] This empty self, concludes Merton, is nothing in our own eyes or in the eyes of the world, but in the eyes of God the kenotic self in Christ is our true reality. He nudges readers to cross "the threshold of the abyss of purity and emptiness that is God."[75] It is a pattern that imitates Christ's poverty and weakness as the precincts of God's epiphany.

The concluding chapter of *New Seeds of Contemplation*, "The General Dance," signals Merton's incorporation of a salvation-history christology rooted in Christ's kenosis. The entire chapter is new material. It opens with a disclaimer of the theology of creation that proposes God as a dominant, judgmental, willful creator who intends to reject creatures. "God creates things by seeing them in His own Logos,"

Merton counters. So the world becomes a garden, and the human person is the gardener in paradise. Adam is co-creator with God, giving names to the animals in paradise. The truth that Adam brings to creation by the light of intellect is distinct from what Merton calls "the dark light," an echo from Gregory the Great. No names are given in this light. God confronts our simplicity in God's simplicity, in love unmediated, in contemplation. This experience forms, he says, "as it were, an emptiness" in which names are not given, but taken away. The inner self wears no such disguise or labels of identity. Identities disappear. Four times in this text Merton alludes to God's hiding and the inner self as hidden. The mystery of God as Trinity reveals God not only loving the creation as *Abba,* but entering creation, "emptying Himself, hiding Himself, as if He were not God but a Creature." The motive is simply God's love. "[God] could not bear," says Merton, "that His creatures should merely adore Him as distant, remote, transcendent and all powerful." Such suggestions of God's glory mislead and become models for our own exploitative claims. Merton repeats the kenotic theme. Taking on "the weakness and ordinariness of man, [God] hid Himself" and became an anonymous and important person in a very unimportant place. And this "hidden, unknown, unremarkable, vulnerable" Christ can be killed.[76]

In interpreting the crucifixion of Jesus, Merton plumbs the experience of dense human suffering. All humanity's suffering became Christ's. "[T]heir weakness and defenselessness became His weakness and defenselesness; their insignificance became His."[77] Evil and death now have no power over the inner self. This, for Merton, is the truth of Christ's resurrection. And Christ's humanity ultimately means God has potentially become every woman and man who ever exists. The crux of the mystery is our decision to become "aware of [Christ's] presence, consecrated by it, and transfigured by its light."[78] Merton distinguishes this from God's presence as creator, which depends on no one but God. Our own hidden, inner self, he adds, is taken up in the mystery of Christ, "so that in secret we live 'in Christ.'"

At this point Merton fathoms new depth in his category of the exterior self, which often wears a mask. He cautions against necessarily reproving the exterior self. "The mask that each man wears may well be a disguise not only for the man's inner self but for God, wandering as a pilgrim and exile in His own creation." The convergence of the inner self and Christ becomes complete for Merton.

This chapter, freighted with kenotic christology, closes with the poet's image: the dance. We are called to surrender our false self-consciousness and join Christ in the cosmic dance in the emptiness of the garden of creation. "For the world and time are the dance of the Lord in emptiness," Merton celebrates. Echoes of its music, which "beats in our very blood," abound in the gift of sublime contemplative moments: in the solitude of a starlit night; a chance autumn sighting of migrating birds, resting and eating in a grove of junipers; seeing children being real children; "when we know love in our own hearts"; or, hearing the old frog "land in the pond with a solitary splash." These are moments of paradise consciousness, the awakenings celebrated in the poet's personifications of the true self. Merton says they invert all our values. They are an emptiness that gives pure vision, providing "a glimpse of the cosmic dance." The self-forgetfulness summoned by the dance becomes ecstasy, "cast[ing] our awful solemnity to the winds," as the inner self dances with Christ.[79] Here Merton had struck gold in his af- firmation of the sacramental and incarnational dynamic in history.

MERTON'S SALVATION-HISTORY CHRISTOLOGY

How Merton followed the thread out of the labyrinth of metaphysical christology and embraced a fuller salvation history christology is the story of the transitional years, 1958 through 1965, when he finally retired to the hermitage. His writing provides a barometer for this christological development. Five major texts best record the process and extent of the change: (1) *Conjectures of a Guilty Bystander,* an edition of his journals for 1956–63; (2) *Seeds of Destruction;* (3) a 1964 essay, "The Humanity of Christ in Monastic Prayer"; (4) *A Vow of Conversation,* an edition of his journal for 1964–65; and (5) *Honorable Reader,* a posthumously published collage of retrospective introductions and prefaces written for foreign editions of early spiritual writings.

CONJECTURES OF A GUILTY BYSTANDER

This freer voice of Merton in the journal *Conjectures of a Guilty Bystander* is dubbed "a personal version of the world in the 1960s." He disclaims any attempt to be systematic. And despite the expansive horizon by venturesome reading of major contemporary Protestant theo-

logians such as Von Rad, Bultmann, Tillich, Marty, and most promi-
nently Karl Barth and Dietrich Bonhoeffer, he advises that it is not
a book of professional ecumenism.[80] Yet these perspectives, particularly those of Barth and Bonhoeffer, catalyze new insights in Merton's
christological reflections.

1. Karl Barth

Part One of *Conjectures* is entitled "Barth's Dream." Merton identifies Barth as a kindred spirit because of the predominant Wisdom,
or sapiential, tradition at the heart of his theology. He begins by recollecting Barth's dream about Mozart, who rejected a Protestantism which
he had accused of being "all in the head." In that dream, Barth was
appointed to examine Mozart's theology. Merton describes the dream
in terms of Barth's own salvation, for the Mozart he played each morning before writing his theology in the shadow of the Swiss Alps would
prove more important, said Merton, than the volumes of dogma he
wrote. Merton characterizes the music of Mozart as "unconsciously seeking to awaken, perhaps, the Sophianic Mozart in himself, the central
wisdom that comes in tune with the divine and cosmic music and is
saved by love, yes, even by *eros.*" This hidden self is distinct from what
he calls the theological self that seems more concerned with love as
agape. Such stern, cerebral love, he cautions, "is not in our own heart
but *only in God* and revealed only to our head." Merton quotes Barth's
own statement that "it is a child, even a 'divine' child, who speaks in
Mozart's music to us," and remarks that Mozart was always a child "in
the higher meaning of that word."

> Fear not, Karl Barth! Trust in the divine mercy. Though you have grown
> up to become a theologian, Christ remains a child in you. Your books (and
> mine) matter less than we might think! There is in us a Mozart who will
> be our salvation.[81]

The coincidence of Merton's and Barth's death, both on December 10,
1968, has magnified the link betweeen these contemporary theologians.
The paradise consciousness of the child, as imaged in Merton's poems,
comes for Barth with Mozart's music.

Merton points to Barth's famous 1932 Christmas sermon for the remarkable insights the Reformed Church theologian auditioned there.
He identifies with Barth's affirmation that the Light born at Bethle-

hem is "certainly *the most unprincipled reality* one can imagine." Barth asks if an unconditional faith in all sorts of principles is not the typically German form of unbelief. Here Merton agrees with Barth on the nature of revelation. It is the primary act of God's gratuity. His own experience of *lectio divina,* the monastic reading of Scripture as the event (*dabar*) of grace was perfectly congruent with Barth on this point. And so the Incarnation, Christ's epiphany, was surprise, gift. "The Incarnation is not something to be fitted into a system," he concludes. Merton's aversion to scholastic theology echoes Scotus's resistance to the proposal of the necessity of the Incarnation because Adam had sinned; with Barth, Merton shared an affinity for the inevitability of the Incarnation because of God's love, God's sheer gratuity.

There is a reminder couched in the monk's enthusiasm for Barth, an almost casual remark in the preface of *Conjectures,* where he describes the book as a Catholic sharing in the Protestant *experience,* not a critical analysis of Protestant thought by a Catholic. So he can signal that "I am not in perfect agreement with everything in Barth and Bonhoeffer."[82] He is more specific later in the journal, where he points to problems in Barth's system with the rights and dignity of nature — Barth early on saw nature as depraved[83] — and philosophical reason and natural law knowledge.[84]

Any interpretation of Merton's fondness for Barth in *Conjectures* deserves to be situated in the context of two articles which develop in greater depth their common attraction to Anselm's twelfth-century classic, *Cur Deus Homo,* the treatise on Christ's Incarnation and the Redemption. As the Cistercian more than once suggests, Anselm is the source for Scotus's theology.[85] He quotes Barth's aphorism, "Tell me how it stands with your Christology and I will tell you who you are," from Barth's 1960 study *Fides Quaerens Intellectum.* The point of Merton's return to Anselm as a source is his affirmation that christology is the foundation for the doctrines of theological anthropology, creation and the world, and the moral life. Anselm's doctrine of the human person's *rectitudo,* or justification, means for Merton that christology is inseparable from the doctrine of "the freedom and dignity of the human person created in the image and likeness of God" and subsequently redeemed by the Incarnation and cross.[86] Merton is quick to analyze how Anselm's salvation theory, or soteriology, as expressed in the notion of *rectitudo,* is not a purely juridical concept. Anselm's is not an apologetics by way of "proofs" to convince unbelievers. It is, contends Merton, theology as contemplation.

It is commonplace to describe Anselm's concept of salvation as a matter of restoring God's "honor," along the lines of the tenth-century Lombardic code. Because of Adam's sin, only a God-Man could satisfy God's honor; hence, the Incarnation. Merton contests this, saying that it distorts Anselm. He finds Anselm's concept of salvation suggesting a profoundly contemplative view of God's plan for humanity and for the cosmos. Rather than sin offending against God's honor in terms of God's nature, Merton suggests an interpretation of sin as offending God's *Person*. Sin has disordered God's plan for harmony, so reparation must restore the violated order which God's wisdom and love have willed. The theology of the cross takes its meaning not in terms of blood vengeance, says Merton, but in the mystery of love united with this sense of justice. God's honor is restored not by violence but by the reconciliation of Christ's liberty, a spontaneous, sacrificial fidelity to *Abba*. Merton's reflection on this kenotic christology and soteriology crystalized and opened new paths for him:

> The *rectitudo* of Christ in the Redemption does not consist for Anselm primarily in the acceptance of a condemnation to death imposed by the Father. . . . Christ was not condemned to death by the divine justice. He came into the world, was made man in order to live perfectly as man, in the freedom and truth of man, to do what was fitting for man, and thus to save other men. . . . He preferred explicitly *to save man by a renunciation of power.* Therefore he willingly and freely underwent death. The Father willed the salvation of man but left Christ entirely free to choose His own means. What is pleasing to the Father is not precisely the suffering and death of Christ, but the fact that the Son uses His freedom to choose that which He thinks best and most perfect in saving man — that which is in fact the purest exercise of freedom without any afterthought of self-interest. Hence, strictly speaking, the Father's will did not arbitrarily impose suffering and death on Christ, but *sent Him into the world to use His freedom to save man.* It was out of love for the Father that Jesus chooses this particular way, the way of humiliation and of the total renunciation of power, in order to save man by love, mercy, and self-sacrifice. . . .
>
> . . . It is the *human* will of Christ that makes this choice of the renunciation of a divine power that He could justly use. God's will was that the

human will of Christ should freely specify by what means man should be saved. Christ as a man chose the way of total poverty, humiliation, self-emptying, since in this way He was most completely identified with man, and also most freely witnessed to the nature of love as supreme freedom —a freedom that is not limited or stayed even by death. . . . Such freedom is not accessible to us outside the love of Christ, which means also love of the *humanity* of Christ, that is to say of man.[87]

Merton insists that God's honor demanded nothing for itself in terms of reparation; it did demand humanity's salvation and restoration. And this demonstrates God's commitment to justice and love, following a "higher necessity" than a juridical concept of justification. The coming of Christ in the Incarnation perfects the good God had begun, even having foreseen Adam's defection.

A 1966 essay, "St. Anselm and His Argument," again addresses the key issue of "honor." Merton places the Christ event against the existential reality: "Creation is dishonored . . . because the place that should have been occupied by one of his chosen creatures is left conspicuously empty."[88] He promotes Anselm's *Cur Deus Homo* as perhaps the greatest of meditations on authority and freedom, reconciling God's justice and mercy in the events of Christ's incarnation and death.[89] In this process he reaps a harvest for an understanding of the human person, a theological anthropology grounded in human freedom and God's universal salvific will.

2. Dietrich Bonhoeffer

Merton's most significant notes on Bonhoeffer's christology date from the exact time of his beginning life as a monastic hermit at the Abbey of Gethsemani, August 1965. Some thirty pages of holographic reading notes on Bonhoeffer's *Ethics* ushered the monk into a new sense of social responsibility applied as "worldliness" in terms of the Incarnation. The epigraph of Part Two of *Conjectures* quotes from Bonhoeffer: "The news that God has become man strikes at the very heart of an age in which the good and the wicked regard either scorn for man or the idolization of man as the highest attainable wisdom."[90] Structures and cultural developments of the world have been profoundly changed by the revelation of Christ in history. Bonhoeffer assessed our unfaithfulness to God's entry into history.[91] Merton borrows Bonhoeffer's critique of an "escalator to unworldliness and devotion" spirituality. And he goes on to lament the misunderstanding of the theoretical distinction of natural and supernatural. The scorching analysis proves as autobiographical as prescriptive:

> We "believe" with our mind, but heart and body never follow. . . . The damnable abstractness of our "spiritual life" in this sense is ruining people. . . . As long as thought and prayer are not fully incarnated in an activity which supports and expresses them validly, the heart will be filled with a smothered rage, frustration, and a sense of dishonesty.[92]

In Bonhoeffer's ethical system, social life becomes the arena where a Christian participates in Christ's redemptive work, liberating human persons. Merton sums up with a christological affirmation: the Christian choice is "simply a complete, trusting, and abandoned consent to the 'yes' of God in Christ."[93]

Early on in *Conjectures,* he remarks that God's revelation in history is the key to the dynamic sense of history which is basic to both the Bible and Marxists. It recalls the passage he quoted, at the opening of Pasternak's *Doctor Zhivago*: "Man does not die in a ditch like a dog — but at home in history, while the work toward the conquest of death is in full swing. . . ." He contrasts this dynamic summons of history with the "static essences and abstract moral values" of modern Christians.[94] Bonhoeffer insinuated that the Hitler *Jugend,* or youth groups, caused the church to be apathetic and acquiescent to Hitler for fear of losing youth and its own future. Merton suggests that such a temporal, worldly sense of church survival implicitly denies the victory of Christ and resurrection faith. He castigates the notion of God looking at history "from outside," and joins Bonhoeffer in emphasizing the Christian's incarnational responsibility in the world.[95] In October 1965 the hermit reevaluated his former attitude toward the world while reading Bonhoeffer's *Ethics.* He found that the German martyr's "Christian worldliness" did not absolve the world of all guilt. It was not the freewheeling and breezy optimism of some of Bonhoeffer's later alleged disciples. Merton quotes Bonhoeffer's optimism, describing it as "entering into the fellowship of guilt for the sake of other men."[96] He embraces Bonhoeffer's locating God's presence in the world in humanity (1 Cor. 3:17).[97] As was his custom, he occasionally recorded a journal reflection on a facing page of his reading notebook. In this instance he headed the page, "My place in the world." He admits that in his early writing he obviously said things that had a Gnostic or Manichaean flavor. He claims a legitimate ambiguity in the New Testament about "the world." Then Merton splits his own writing into two categories. The world as nature, work, literature and culture, Asian philosophy, he notes, along with humanity are all "fully accepted" in our historic reality. What Merton does not accept is the world in its contemporary confusions. And in Bonhoeffer's fashion, Merton concludes his christological confession with a radical commitment.

> There may be some truth in my pessimism, but the pessimism itself has an evil root, and instead of getting the root out I have been cultivating it in the name of "spirituality" or what you will. This is no longer honest. My task is to come to terms *completely* with the world in which I live and of which I am a *part,* because this is the world redeemed by Christ — even the world of Auschwitz. . . . [Auschwitz, Hiroshima, and Southern racism] too must be "redeemed." The great task of redemption is in *America* which imagines itself Christian! That is why I am here, and must stay here.[98]

Merton now joined Bonhoeffer in bearing the presence of Christ to the world. Christology would no longer waft away in metaphysical vapors. Jonah's whale had finally coughed and belched up the prophet on the shores of the secular city.

3. Eastern Orthodoxy

Books like *The New Man* evidenced Merton's attraction to the theology of the Greek Fathers. Eastern Orthodox Christianity, with its liturgical and mystical traditions and its spirituality of icons, afforded the matrix of a common ethos with monastic life. Merton turned to the creative renewal within Orthodoxy and found an encouraging rejection of the frantic, so-called progressive forms represented in the secular theologies. The works of Bulgakov, Evdokimov, Meyendorf, and Schmemann reinforced his own sense of the world as a "cosmic liturgy," a eucharistic view of creation. Alexander Schmemann's *Sacraments and Orthodoxy* garners from Merton one of his most enthusiastic reviews. It coincides with the very period when he is reading Bonhoeffer and retires to the hermitage. His departing conference to the novices, August 20, 1965, previews a written review of Schmemann's attempt to avoid dividing the sacred–secular, spiritual–material, natural–supernatural so as to make them absolutely irreconcilable, both in theory and practice. Merton prefers Orthodoxy's eucharistic view of creation, to celebrate the world as the sacrament of God's presence.[99] He shares the Greek Orthodox theologian's distemper with secularists who are stoically resigned to accept the world as a "cosmic cemetery." Merton agrees with Schmemann that the desacramentalization of the autonomous, natural world results in a dangerous clericalism. Religion gets organized as a transaction with the supernatural, administered by the priest. But that only aggravates the separation. "It is precisely from this state of affairs that secularism arises: 'Clericalism is the father of Secularism.'"[100]

Schmemann voiced Orthodoxy's spiritual vision of transforming or transfiguring nature, as Christ's body was transformed in the resurrection. In this paschal action, the cross is all-important. This christological center of gravity attracts Merton. To avoid or evade death, to use the cross as a magic charm to neutralize death is to turn from the resurrection, Merton warns, and that means compromising with the cult of death. The theology of the cross which he finds in Schmemann's book sharpens the theology of the cross in his christology. It is easy, he says, to overlook the "transforming action of the cross," which is *only* "by virtue of the cross." To deny the cross is to deny half of the picture of Christianity: the restoration of all things in Christ. Merton cautions against the pseudo-spirituality that pretends that our righteous moral lives can reverse the crucifixion. We cannot act, he repeats, as if there had never been a crucifixion. That is the false gospel preached by the secularists. But Orthodoxy's sacramental and eucharistic vision of the world affirms that with the crucifixion the dead world ("the cosmic cemetery") comes to life through Christ's victory. The very sense of *presence* becomes the key to our life in the world. The transformation of the world, the cosmic liturgy, converges with Bonhoeffer's Christian worldliness: "And so the disciples at Emmaus—their vocation is our vocation—came running back to Jerusalem bubbling over with joy and happiness not because they understood the mysteries of another world but because they had seen the Lord," Merton quotes from Schmemann. In these ancient sources of Eastern Orthodoxy, the monk was glimpsing the christological mystery that ineluctably led him back to the world with compassion and confidence in the capacity for human transfiguration.[101]

4. Teilhard de Chardin

The dialogue between Merton and the works of Jesuit paleontologist Pierre Teilhard de Chardin provides a striking insight into the monk's christology and incarnational spirituality. There are only four references to Teilhard in *Conjectures of a Guilty Bystander,* but the enthusiasm and evidence of Merton's reading of his revolutionary theory of the universe converging toward a Christogenesis, or Christ consciousness, warrants special attention. He heralded Teilhard's success because the French writer had enabled Christians to believe they belonged in the world and had convinced them that a posture of contempt for the world was now meaningless. In so doing, Merton says, Teilhard has enabled thousands of Christians to be reconciled with themselves and prepare for the renewal of religion in our day. He agrees wholeheartedly with Teilhard that the great danger of modernity is the human person's refusal of humanity and thus the refusal of our potential for creativity, which leads to destruction.[102]

In several parallel contexts, Merton developed his appreciation for his Jesuit contemporary. Teilhard, he says, offered a new horizon in Christian spirituality as one who "can speak the language of contemporary man without totally compromising his faith in God and in Christ."[103] He was excited by the prospect that Marxists and non-Christians would welcome the scientific expression of Christian experience in Teilhard. But there are reservations. He hesitates about a Teilhardian movement.[104] He views the religious-scientific mystique as a poetic protest against the mechanical, dehumanized worldview. It activates "inner forces for transformation," but Merton cautions against what he named the myopia of Vitalism. Its danger was to make a leap of faith "into the stream of self-perfecting creative evolution in which even God is 'becoming.'"[105]

A critique of Teilhard's *Divine Milieu* finds Merton characterizing the scientist-priest's vision in terms of grace building on nature and congruent with the Greek Fathers' concept of divinization. He identifies the heart of Teilhard's spirituality as "sublimely eucharistic," because for him Jesus Christ, God Incarnate, gave himself to us "in matter sanctified and sacramentalized."[106] The tenor of Merton's apprehension over Teilhard becomes more apparent in a 1967 *Commonweal* essay, "Teilhard's Gamble: Betting on the whole human species."[107] He applauds Teilhard's cosmic and incarnational mystique, and the radical anthropocentrism he has restored to theology. But in the final analysis, Merton criticizes Teilhard for gambling "entirely on the future" and naively polarizing yesterday and tomorrow in the evolutionary optimism of his spirituality. Is this, asks the Cistercian, "purely and simply the theological hope of the Gospels and of the Church"? He quotes from Henri de Lubac's critical study of Teilhard which remarks on the scientist's complacency about his own originality and laments Teilhard's lack of even an elementary knowledge of the history of Christian thought. Bringing the discussion back to the arena of existentialist reflection, Merton charges that Teilhard has overlooked the present in his panoramic angle of future vision.

In a trenchant critique of Albert Camus's *The Plague,* the then-hermit compares the paleontologist and the French-Algerian novelist in their acceptance of nature and material creation. He credits Teilhard with a Christian mystique of matter. But the crux of their difference begins with Camus's suspicion of totalitarians who appeal to the principle of evolution to justify an infallible progress to the new era. The novelist protested against the sacrifice of the human person in the present condition to the lure of an ideology that attracts us to some "future." Merton calls it a superficial eschatological hopefulness based on evolution, the very ideology that precipitated the German extermination camps, napalm, and the H-bomb. He sees Teilhard as choosing the kind of optimism "which tends to look at existential evil and suffering through the small end of the telescope"—unable to scruple and anguish with Camus over the murder of an innocent child, but somehow able to glory in the new atomic-powered bomb without pausing over its human toll. Merton sees a flaw, a collision ahead. He contrast Teilhard with his Jesuit confrere Father Paneloux in Camus's novel *The Plague,* who personifies a pessimism which stands at the opposite pole from Teilhard. But he finds both attaching more importance to an abstract idea or mystique or system than to the fallible, existential human reality here and now. Merton agrees with Camus on resisting this great temptation: "Lured by an ideology or a mystique, one goes over to the side of the executioners, arguing that in so doing one is promoting the cause of life."[108] This flaw compromised, for Merton, Teilhard's kenotic christology, which had initially led both to be passionate about the things of the earth. In the arena of history, the cross becomes apparent in the contemporary crises and anguish of suffering persons and in our collective history. For all Teilhard's virtues, Merton regretted that this

christology was unable to offer adequate mercy for weakness and defencelessness.

SEEDS OF DESTRUCTION

No book better signaled Merton's involvement with the world's traffic
in moral crises than the 1964 volume *Seeds of Destruction*. The book
overlaps with a late midpoint in the journals of *Conjectures*. The author's "Note" which introduces the essays redefines his vocation as monk.
He explains that the contemplative life cannot be mere withdrawal or
negation, a turning of our backs on the world's sufferings, crises, confusions, and errors. To ignore the world, he confesses, makes us accomplices in the implicit political decisions that result in exploitative
economic and social structures. The monastery, he says, is deeply im-
plicated; therefore, he claims a moral obligation as monk to respond
to the contemporary social crises. Yes, the monk had fled to the desert,
but it was as a social act to dissent from the deluded, egotistic, and
sinful world. Now Merton turns to the Incarnation to center his voice
of dissent. Christ's coming centers "on a historical event which has
changed the meaning of history," he reminds. It was a "freedom *in*
time," liberating human persons to cooperate redemptively to shape
the course of history in the direction of the eschatological Kingdom
of God.

Karl Rahner's retrieval of the "diaspora" metaphor for the contemporary church captured Merton's imagination in describing the changed
historical context of Christianity. He develops in *Seeds of Destruction*
a key essay entitled "The Christian in the Diaspora" to mark the passing of Christendom's triumphalism, clericalism, and church privilege.
In the post-Christian world, the culturally disenfranchised church now
sees that the world, secularity, and even the profane do not exclude
or obstruct grace but are fully embraced by the redemptive order. Christian faith, for Rahner like Bonhoeffer, needs to be brought to this
awareness of heroic witness in the world.[109]

What dominates *Seeds of Destruction* is Merton's interpretation of
the black revolution in the United States and the compassionate protest he registers for racial justice. "Letters to a White Liberal" remains
one of the most provocative and candid essays of social criticism in the
Merton corpus. The companion essay, "The Legend of Tucker Caliban,"
analyzes black novelist William Melvin Kelley's *A Different Drummer,*

asserting that the heart of the novel is the black's realization of a historical hour of destiny, the *kairos*. Merton points out the paradox of the novel in the blacks' mission to free whites, which begins by freeing themselves. For Merton, part of this paradox involves the whites' own enslavement. He finds a prophetic and Christlike identity in the black, who knows a spiritual freedom that white society needs for its own sake. Indeed, *"we need him to be free,"* the monk speaks, on behalf of all white society.[110] There is an acid irony in his challenge to the "white liberal."

Seeds of Destruction also marks a controversial watershed in Merton's claiming social responsibility for peacemaking in a bellicose era. He had edited a small book, *Breakthrough to Peace,* two years earlier in which he contributed an introduction and an essay, "Peace: A Religious Responsibility." Pope John XXIII's 1963 encyclical on peacemaking, *Pacem in Terris,* relieved much of the Cistercian censors' pressure that reined Merton's protest for peace and international justice. He integrates problems of violence, hatred, and power politics.[111] The monk reverses the questions: it is not a matter of whether we can avoid total war, but what are our real intentions? He gravitates to the christological mystery to ground his social criticism. Being more than our sisters' and brothers' keepers, he insists that more is demanded than avoiding evil. Because the Word was made flesh, we must regard every human person in light of the principles of human dignity and the common good over against the particular good of our political self-interest.[112] Why not reject the necessity of force as our unquestioned starting point, he asks. He credits Pope John XXIII with opening the Catholic ghetto and insisting that dialogue with other ideologies and cultures communicate the fundamental goodness and cooperative capacities of human persons. He distinguishes the work of peacemaking from a pacifist refusal to participate in war. It requires a greater sacrifice, a greater heroism, he admits. Then he proceeds to expose the flaws in Christianity's just war theory from Origen to Augustine. He criticizes the excessive naiveté in regard to the "good" to be attained by violent means, and the double weakness of stressing the subjective purity of intention (all too easily manipulated) and a tendency to pessimism about human nature and the world. A complementary essay, "The Legacy of Machiavelli," critiques power politics as an obsolete practice from the era of individual monarchs. Merton provides a commentary on *Pacem in Terris,* with its optimism about human persons as cooperative, constructive, responsible peacemakers. He reclaims from Paul's letters and the gospels a confidence concerning the Incarnation as underwriting human nature's ability to overcome the stark challenges of evil that infect the modern world. Merton describes this belief in the human, rooted in the mystery of Christ, as Franciscan optimism, a mission to cultivate in the world.[113]

The voice of the social critic now specified the crises of history. In these craters of the human spirit, racism and war, the suffering Christ of emptiness and poverty manifest a way of transfigured hope for those who would do justice and walk humbly with the hidden God of compassion.

"THE HUMANITY OF CHRIST IN MONASTIC PRAYER"

Within the same time frame of the *Conjectures* journal, 1964, Merton published a dense, scholarly article entitled "The Humanity of Christ in Monastic Prayer." One wonders what provoked this piece, so seemingly different in voice and style from the other writing of the 1960s. The chain of monastic and patristic sources he cites makes it evident that the subject has occupied his attention over an extended period of time. The conclusion to the piece is most likely the best key. Merton alludes to the fact that the patristic tradition distinguishes the humanity and the divinity of Christ in order to unite them in his Person, not to separate them. Thus, the Christ of monastic tradition is the unity of two natures, human and divine, in one Person. At several points in the encyclopedic article Merton takes pains to avoid the Nestorian heresy, which separated the two natures of Christ. The mysteries of Christ's human life on earth, he claims, can be the object of our *meditation,* our devotional admiration and love, but the ultimate resting place of our *contemplation* is in the light received from the risen Christ, which reaches to the depths of our being.

The article begins with Teresa of Avila's reproach of herself for "high treason" in straining for an experience of the divine essence and bypassing the Person of the God-Man as if it were an obstacle to prayer. Merton attempts to resolve the problem by asserting that we cannot contemplate the divine essence except in and through the Person of Christ, the Man-God. But he credits Teresa with rightly distinguishing the humanity of Christ before his resurrection and the glorified humanity of Christ after the resurrection and forever.[114] Several times he speaks of the kenotic and hidden state of Christ, in the form of a servant, before the resurrection.[115] The echo of Logos christology can be detected in Merton's emphasis on Jesus' risen humanity. Without becoming a low christology, Merton's emphasis opens toward a christology from below and refuses to bypass the merely human. That had been the suggestion of the Quietists and mystical illuminists, as well as Teresa's temptation.

It is hard to credit Merton with clarity or system in such pages. Perhaps some of the difficulty lies in his sources, sources which he himself critiques. For example, he cautions that Gregory the Great's explanation that meditation on the mysteries of Christ's life and death is seen as a *transitus* or *pascha,* a passage from the human to the divine, suggests a separation of natures. He quotes Gregory's comment that Paul could not communicate his own contemplative experience of the divine vision, so he preached Christ crucified. Merton suggests that we not exaggerate the statement but see it as a rhetorical trope and not a theological principle. The paschal mystery sees the death of Jesus from the perspective of his risen glory. Gregory's *lumen incircumscriptum* is none other than the *lumen Christi,* the light of the risen Christ, for Merton.

> [The uncircumscribed light] is the light of the divine, transcendent and life-giving power which belongs to Christ not only as God but also as man, and to exclude the humanity of Christ from that light is to turn away in blindness from the true Mystery of the one Christ. To know Christ *only* as a 'divine essence' is little better than knowing Him only as a frail and mortal man. The Christian and monastic contemplation of Christ is that of a man who is God, who is totally transfigured in the light of God and who calls us, His brothers, out of darkness to a participation in that "admirable light" (I Pt. 2:9).[116]

There are two passages which immediately follow and situate the kenotic motif, by now writ large in Merton's christology. The first occurs with his description of the monk's coming to this ineffable light of contemplation. He describes the light of this risen Christ as tender and merciful. It does "not reject any *darkness that is aware of itself and laments its alienation* from His truth."[117] This lamentation resides in complete honesty, it removes all obstacles between its inner self and Christ. Here Merton presages his discovery of the christological mystery in voices of poverty, helplessness, weakness, and even the silence of defencelessness.

A second kenotic motif suggesting such a christology from below occurs in Merton's borrowing from Gregory the Great's homily on the woman seeking the lost groat being like God seeking the divine image in humanity. When this light of glory is lit in the "'lamp' of the risen Christ," it strikes directly at our conscience and shakes our very foundations: "the lost drachma, or man's likeness to God, is found when the *lumen incircumscriptum* enters the conscience, turning everything upside down and *purifying the heart with tribulation.*"[118] This compunction, which evokes tears of both sorrow and joy, cleanses and welcomes us to the "homeland" of conversion. It is the parable of the prodigal son revisited. And the reclaiming of every human experience of anguish, all "tribulation," sets the stage for the crises of history to become Christ's never-ending Garden of Gethsemani.

A VOW OF CONVERSATION

The sequel to *Conjectures* is the less self-conscious, honest, simple, and searingly deep journal of 1964–65, *A Vow of Conversation.* The very fact that it was written from the environs of the hermitage, where Merton began spending lengthier visits during the days until he moved there on August 20, 1965, suggests a catalyst for the relaxed intimacy of these mature pages. The monk examines himself and discovers a new level of decision making, a fundamental option, in his quest for authentic freedom. The tempo of the sun and the days invites a new harmony with everything around him. At the same time, in these pages he can scold monastic structures that frustrate the monastic charism, or ponder the heart's deceit, or complain about the attempts to embargo *Seeds of Destruction* with its peacemaking talk.

But these are porous pages of journal writing, and Merton lends insight into his developing christology in seemingly enigmatic entries. An April 17, 1964, passage wanders from remarks about work on his Gandhi book, *Gandhi on Nonviolence,* a French translation of his black revolution essays (from *Seeds of Destruction*), and the abbot's renovated suite, to a halting declaration and a question: "[T]he great religious issues today turn out also to be political. Can one look attentively at Christ and not also see Auschwitz?"[119] He remarks on October 19, 1964, about reading Hans Urs Von Balthasar's *Word and Revelation,* which he judged to be excellent. He connects it with Julian of Norwich's saying "all manner of things shall be well" because after Christ judges and separates the good from the bad, "the rejected will turn out to have been those chosen with a greater and more mysterious mercy." He asks, in Anselm's terms, "Can there be a limit to the mercy of Christ who has fully satisfied forever all God's justice and now has the world in his hand to do with according to his merciful love?"[120] He intimates in a December 1, 1964, entry that Christ "pulls all things in me together" to save him from misdirection or lassitude, the "mask for despair" which he so easily experiences.[121]

On Ash Wednesday, March 3, 1965, Merton comments on his discomfort with Simone Weil's description of her experience of Christ. While he admits some authenticity to her mysticism, he cannot accept "her dogmatic ambiguities." He is impressed by "her intuition of suffering and love," the way she insists on identifying with "the unfortunate and the unbeliever," which he relates to the core of the mystery of Christ: "the realization that God's love must break the human heart." He quotes from her beatitude: "Blessed are they who suffer, in the flesh, the suffering of the world itself in their epoch. They have the possibility and function of knowing its truth, contemplating its reality, its suffering of the world. But unfortunate are they who, having this function, do not fulfill it."[122] The sublime christology from below radiates from Merton's concern with the suffering of the weak and defenceless.

A final entry, May 15, 1965 muses over the difficulty in making an act of faith that all of history is in God's hands. The context is what he describes as the disastrous decisions of President Johnson and the Pentagon in conducting the war in Southeast Asia, which he compares to the police tactics used in Alabama during the civil rights movement: "beating people over the head because we believe we have a right and a duty to do so since they are inferior." Merton's christology from below, seen from the vantage of the woundedness of human persons in history, now radicates in the Passion of Christ:

> We have to see history as a book that is sealed and opened only by the Passion of Christ. But we prefer to read it from the viewpoint of the Beast. We look at history in terms of hubris and power—in terms of the Beast and his values. Christ continues to suffer his passion in the poor, the defenseless, and his Passion destroys the Beast. Those who love power are destroyed together with what they love. Meanwhile, Christ is in agony until the end of time.[123]

PREFACES AND INTRODUCTIONS TO FOREIGN TRANSLATIONS

Augustine set a fine precedent when, toward the end of his life, he penned his *Retractiones.* A scholar's delight is to find an author's own backward glance, a bit more nuanced or subtle restatement of earlier stances. We have something of that genre in over fifteen prefaces or introductions which Merton wrote for foreign translations of his early and middle works.[124] Merton did more than merely introduce these books, he reflected on them and even augmented the emphasis in each carefully crafted essay. Some are apologetic, even confessing serious limitations ("and a consequent danger of misunderstanding"), like the 1953 preface to the French *Exile Ends in Glory.* In a 1960 introduction to a South American translation of his *Complete Works,* Merton offered an important reorientation for his definition of contemplative life, which he argued "does not exist only within the walls of the cloister. . . . I can satisfy my vocation with nothing that is partial or provincial."[125] The diverse spectrum of audiences reveals the global Merton: these pages were written for Catalan, Argentine, Brazilian, Japanese, Spanish, Korean, Vietnamese, and French readers. "My Catholicism is all the world and all ages,"[126] declared an ecumenical Merton. A 1958 preface to the French edition of *Monastic Peace* situated monastic life for him squarely within the struggle for justice: "The monk, man of poverty, must live with the unfortunate of his time, sharing their problems and their thirst for justice."[127] The same solidarity broadcast from his 1963 French preface to *The Black Revolution* (a reworking of some material in *Seeds of Destruction*), an important preface translated for the first time in English in the collection *"Honorable Reader."*

But it is in the four new Japanese prefaces that Merton hands us a hermeneutical key to his own development that is anchored in the kenotic Christ. In the much quoted 1963 preface to the Japanese *The Seven Storey Mountain* Merton asked, what has changed for the author? Answer: his attitude and the assumptions behind the "irrevocable" decision to become a monk. No longer can he be negative toward the world. Compassion permeates. The monastery, he confesses, can no longer be justified as an "escape from the world." Merton will participate in "the struggles and sufferings of the world" by "mak[ing] monastic silence a protest."[128] The preface to the Japanese edition of *Seeds of Contemplation* finds him offering a summary outline of the meaning of Christian contemplation, "this journey without maps." Throughout these later prefaces Merton questions Western Christianity's fear of solitude. The 1965 Korean preface to *Life and Holiness* disclaims the priority of dogma and doctrine in Christianity, preferring the hidden God, love. For Merton, Christianity is a "way of life, rather than a way of thought."[129] By the 1966 preface to *The New Man*, Merton condemned Western Christianity's Promethean passion for will, power, action, and domination. Such pragmatism sadly eventuated in the "worship of visible results." The contemplative way of the true self meant "love replace[s] the will to get visible results." Thus Merton could hauntingly conclude: "We [in the West] have perhaps misrepresented Christ, and given a strange, distorted idea of Him to the other peoples of the earth."[130]

This chapter has surveyed Thomas Merton's prose — including the familiar books of spirituality and later journals — to trace the development of his christology from what Karl Rahner describes as a "metaphysical christology" to a salvation history christology. The famous 1958 vision of solidarity and universal love which Merton experienced at Louisville's Fourth and Walnut Streets reoriented him to a new compassion and protest on behalf of abandoned others. The social dynamic of history, in all its contingency, expanded to become for him the new precincts of Christ's epiphany.

We have contrasted Merton's preoccupation with an individualized contemplative and apophatic mystical experience in early works (*Seeds of Contemplation, The Ascent to Truth, No Man Is an Island, Thoughts in Solitude*) with a mature spirituality that accepts the changed diaspora context of contemporary Christian life in his later works (*Conjectures of a Guilty Bystander, Seeds of Destruction,* "The Humanity of Christ in Monastic Prayer," *A Vow of Conversation,* and his foreign prefaces and introductions). While both expressions of spirituality are christocentric, Merton refined early allusions to Christ's kenosis, or emptying himself of power in order to be weak, into a new expression of christology in dialogue with Protestant theologians Karl Barth and Dietrich Bonhoeffer, Eastern Orthodoxy, and Pierre Teilhard de Chardin. The resulting appreciation of Christ's use of human freedom to renounce power and accomplish God's universal salvific will liberated

Merton to discover Christ's presence in "weakness and defencelessness." Grounded in such a radically kenotic christology, he emerged with a profound compassion for the human experience "from below." As we now explore, it would be through the voice and imagination of contemporary literary artists that he discerned the living Christ in human poverty, nothingness, rejection, and seeming despair.

4. Son of the Widowed God:
Merton's Sapiential Reading of Fiction

With the characteristic bluntness that colored his mature writings, Thomas Merton addressed the prospect of lay contemplatives near the conclusion of "The Inner Experience." He sarcastically remarked that if you were waiting to be spoon-fed the contemplative life, it would be a long wait, especially in America. "You had better renounce your inertia, pray for a little imagination, ask the Lord to awaken your creative freedom," he advised.[1] Nowhere would Merton find greater natural nourishment for authentic contemplation than in the creative freedom and imagination of contemporary literary artists. He contrasted the theology which is most interested in correct dogmatic formulas, which do not call into question the intimate spiritual ground of one's existence, and the existential theology encountered in the literary artist's work, which vividly unmasks the flight from the true self. Empty gestures of religious conformity contrasted starkly, for Merton, with the authentic commitment summoned by novelists' imaginative awareness of the spiritual crises we are in.[2]

It was a long journey from the complaint lodged in *The Sign of Jonas* that it was no fun to live the spiritual life with the equipment of an artist[3] to Merton's later reverence for isolated and lonely artists, many of whom were not church-goers or conventional believers but who experienced, he confessed, the depth and existential dimensions of religious problems. A slight book written in his last year, *Opening the Bible,* describes these imaginative writers as profoundly biblical in the sense that "the Bible goes beyond religion . . . [when] it preaches the kenosis or self-emptying of God and his identification of himself with man as person and as community."[4]

Spirituality and the literary imagination gradually became more inti-

mately connected in Merton's vision for contemplative life. The evidence
of his personal reading habits suggests that he nurtured his mature
contemplative life by reading a diverse spectrum of novelists: Boris Pasternak, James Joyce, James Baldwin, Flannery O'Connor, William Melvin Kelley, J. F. Powers, Albert Camus, William Styron, Julien Greene,
William Faulkner, and Walker Percy, among a host of others. This
chapter analyzes what Merton came to define as a "sapiential method"
for the theological criticism of contemporary fiction. The task includes:
(1) an appreciation of what Merton describes as our predicament—
"the cramp of the imagination"—and how the novelist overcomes this
superficial ego, or false self, in the existential drama of the person and
grace; (2) a definition of the "sapiential" method; and (3) an interpretation of Merton's development of sapiential criticism in his essays
which apply this method to Pasternak, Camus, and Faulkner.

RELAXING THE "CRAMP OF THE IMAGINATION": PERSON AND GRACE

In his posthumously published essays on monastic renewal, *Contemplation in a World of Action,* Merton as hermit reclaims the constructive role of creative imagination in responding to the question,
"Is the Contemplative Life Finished?" He calls imagination a "discovering faculty, a faculty for seeing relationships, for seeing meanings that
are special and even quite new."[5] He insists that the education and
formation of young monks, or postulants, needs to reverse our culture's
neglect of the imagination. This imaginative development is absolutely
necessary, he exclaims, because the culture has destroyed children's
imaginative response to reality and replaced a liberal education with
twenty years of overstimulated vegetation.[6] What distressed him even
more in monastic culture was the preponderance of "juridical contemplatives," men who live in a contemplative monastery, follow its rule
and exercises, but cultivate the one great defect: a failure of imagination. Such a life discourages imagination and mires the contemplative
life in banality, triviality, and pettiness, Merton confesses: "The great
thing is to sing loud, observe the rubrics, and beg God seven times
in the day to punish Communists."[7] The problem for Merton lingered
in a prayer life that was poor in imagination.

In a very telling entry near the end of his earlier journal, *Conjec-*

tures of a Guilty Bystander, the monk describes the superficial ego as "this cramp of my imagination." To assume that this charley horse in our creative freedom is the inner self dishonors both the self and reality, he warns. The context for Merton's evolving sense of the intimate connection between spirituality and imagination was his growing consciousness of a post-Christian world. One of Karl Rahner's seminal contributions to the Second Vatican Council was the notion of the church in "diaspora," or dispersed in a world which was no longer culturally, politically, socially, or religiously dominated by Christendom. "The Pastoral Constitution on the Church in the Modern World," *Gaudium et Spes* (1965), radically reoriented Catholic Christianity to this post-Christian ethos. A new situation existed when the official church declared that it was no longer threatened by, or condemning of, the secular world.

Thomas Merton felt vindicated. His own instincts, his reverence for nature and creation, had already been leading him to this openness and dialogue with the world. Merton now enthusiastically embraces Rahner's premise that we are theologically obliged to accept the diaspora as the starting point for all deliberations about our behavior as Christians in the modern world. What Merton intuits is a new task: the demise of triumphalism and clericalism means that the human person becomes all-important as formal church structures change and even collapse.[8] In Rahner's language, theology becomes Christian anthropology. Merton concludes that the council has manifested a wholly new concern: the human person. He delights in the irony, finding it awe-inspiring that while the church's problem was once the denial of the humanity of Christ, now it struggles with a practical, concrete, and existential denial of the elementary freedom and dignity of all human persons.[9] He insists that the church shares this focus of Christian humanism when it promotes personal and spiritual emancipation. Then Merton develops his theology of the human person's self-transcending orientation:

> The human ego, or the individual centre of man's natural being, is not (in Christian thought) the centre of personal freedom. Christian anthropology is not yet fully clear about the person, since what belongs to the whole Christian person has traditionally been ascribed to the soul (part of the person only) and to grace. The Christian theology of grace needs to be reviewed in the light of a new and deeper metaphysic of the person and of love.[10]

It is a declaration of independence for Thomas Merton's own developing existential theology. What is more, it crystalizes his theological
agenda and provides a key to his own creative and critical work in the
last decade of his life. The narrative of grace in the person's life is precisely what Christian spiritual autobiography attempts to make intelligible. It is the voice of Merton's *The Seven Storey Mountain* and of
his poetry and journals. Engagement with other literary artists' imaginative worlds summons the theological critic to the crossroads of grace.
It ignites, for Merton, the most intimate personal dialogue. Not only
are we offered the artist's rendition of experience, but by recreating
the experience in us through the medium of the work of art, the artist
interrogates us about ultimate questions.[11]

Merton found the most unambiguous expression of existentialism
in literature, which was free of technical jargon and formulas. Literature, he repeated, is "an experience and an attitude, rather than a system of thought." He pointed to Flannery O'Connor's devasting existential intuition and irony in her fiction that explores the revelation
of personality under the extremities of violence.[12] In an essay on "The
Church and the 'Godless' World," Merton returns to Rilke, whom he
saw personifying "a certain type of modern religious consciousness"
which "seeks to 'create' a new symbolic language for the things of God."[13]
The fiction writer's art diagnoses our spiritual inertia and makes us aware
of the reality of our crisis. By implication, if not directly, the novelist
proposes an alternative existence, which Merton interprets in terms of
grace, the life of the emergent inner self awakened by this experience.

A new confidence breathed through Merton's appreciation of imaginative fiction writers. He forcefully quoted Paul Tillich's remark that
contemplatives and existentialists are united in the depth and sincerity of their "concern." Both reject easy substitutes for ultimate reality.
Both encounter insecurity and the darkness of spiritual risk.[14] He was
convinced that the artist shares with the contemplative an antipathy
to "adjusting to a whole galaxy of illusions." And so the superficial
ego (false self, mask, illusion, empirical self, Cartesian subject) expresses
itself as a "cramp of the imagination." The fiction writer, along with
the poet and other artists, could expose this "trifling and impertinent
identity," which Merton says we "fabricate" from immediate scraps of
experience, and place it in sharp relief against the authentic self of
the person. He trenchantly describes the kenotic dimension of the spiritual malaise that both the novelist and contemplative diagnose:

we have to *die* to our image of ourselves, our autonomy, our fixation upon our self-willed identity. We have to be able to relax the psychic and spiritual cramp which knots us in the painful, vulnerable, helpless "I" that is all we know as ourselves.

The chronic inability to relax this cramp begets despair. In the end, as we realize more and more that we are knotted upon *nothing,* that the cramp is meaningless, senseless, pointless affirmation of nonentity, and that we must nevertheless continue to affirm our nothingness *over against* everything else—our frustration becomes absolute. We become incapable of existing except as a "no," which we fling in the face of everything. This "no" to everything serves as our pitiful "yes" to ourselves—a makeshift identity which is nothing.[15]

The supreme tragedy resides, for Merton, in a person's cramped freedom becoming knotted up in frustration. A person inverts freedom into a protest that hardens, impoverishes, and eventually destroys. To remain in such a posture of refusal, he intimates, is to refuse faith. It is not necessarily "faith" in the full sense of theological and Christian faith, but faith as belief in life. The remedy Merton offers is to seek faith in God as a gift, grace, and "to suffer great indigence and peril while waiting to receive it." By 1968, Merton was voicing an unmitigated confidence in literary artists' ability to awaken us to the threat of despair and the possibility of choosing new life. He portrays them as the ones most aware of the crisis, but ironically "they are for that very reason the closest to despair."[16]

A DEFINITION OF THE SAPIENTIAL METHOD

In his last years, the hermitage years (1965–68), Merton immersed himself in literary interests and ventured his only formal essay on what he termed "the rather troublesome question of literature and religion today . . . [and] the confusions surrounding it." He had been invited to write an introduction for George Panichas's 1967 critical collection, *Mansions of the Spirit,* which he entitled "'Baptism in the Forest': Wisdom and Initiation in William Faulkner." Early in that exploratory essay he ventures to promote the literary artist: "I might also say at once that creative artists and imaginative criticism provide a privileged place for wisdom in the modern world. At times one feels they do so even more than current philosophy and theology."[17] In a 1966 letter to his publisher, James Laughlin, he had alluded to Jacques Maritain's recent visit to the Abbey of Gethsemani and their agreement that "perhaps the most 'living' way to approach theological and philosophical problems now that theology and philosophy were in such chaos would be in the form of 'creative writing and literary criticism.'"[18]

What Merton refuses to betray, however, is the legitimate autonomy of the artist. Even during the early monastic years, when for nearly a decade he virtually abandoned writing poetry, he had avoided any suggestion of confusion between art and the sacred. In a 1956 essay he declared that the subject of art, even when it represents a "sacred event," does not make it sacred. "It can be said that a secular piece that has life and character is itself more sacred than a religious piece that is without either one."

> Art creates its own forms, and they are significant by reason of their own beauty. The meaning of a picture is not to be sought merely in a "message" or in the "subject," but in the interrelation of forms, colors, lines, etc., in an integrated, living, creative unity. Bad art does not give glory to God.[19]

A corollary to this refusal to prostitute art as propaganda can be found salted throughout Merton's literary essays. In July 1968 he marshals all his literary critical powers to review the James Joyce scholarly industry. His grim verdict is that allegorizing and arbitrary distortions of Joyce were rendered by "stand[ing] Joyce on his head. . . . Evidently the academic eye finds him more intriguing in that position," Merton quips.[20] Merton prefers to read Joyce as "comic art," with ironic and mock heroic figures. "The stasis of the Joycean aesthetic is not a full stop in inertia, an end of living contradictions, but a delicate balance between them." He repudiates the moralizing Joyce critics at both extremes — those who condemn Joyce as "the very paragon of lustiness and abandonment to the flesh," as well as those who interpret Molly Bloom's soliloquy as evidence of his Puritanism! Merton finds in Joyce's conscience "a civilized experience of ambivalence in sex," an ambivalence, he recommends, that achieved "full maturity and self awareness" in the Joyce notebook, *Giacomo Joyce,* which had been published in 1968. He enthusiastically describes the theme of this collection of prose epiphanies as "spiritual seduction" and its ambiguities.[21]

At the same time, Merton interprets the Cyclops episode of Leopold

Bloom in *Ulysses* as Joyce's "ironic moral cosmology" and not the promotion of a heroic character. He focuses on Bloom's noble pacifist sentiments in the novel, only to expose them as "a mask of dishonesty" because mere words do not change the world. Bloom's dilemma reveals for Merton the breakdown of language and communication. For the monk, the irony resides in a "spurious nonviolence" that "falls back on force to defend and to affirm love." This touches a deeper ethos, the nonviolence of the strong which "is not for power but for truth."[22]

Two final examples prove pertinent. First, he comments wryly on J. F. Power's *Morte D'Urban*: "Every satirist is a moralist, but as long as he keeps to his art, the morality is never more than an implication. Nor can it be otherwise."[23] Second, Merton faults William Styron's *The Confessions of Nat Turner* on aesthetic grounds. The historical protagonist, Nat Turner, was deliberately caricatured in the novel, inverted from the "prophetic-revolutionary," and "gratuitously overweighted with sex frustration and sadomasochism." He finds the intended reconciliation in this work of fiction "so completely undeveloped that it is merely a formal and perfunctory gesture. Such gestures, such theoretic afterthoughts only help to discredit Christianity."[24]

This sketch of Merton's claim for the autonomy of literature would be incomplete without acknowledging his two essays from the mid-1960s, "Message to Poets" and "Answers on Art and Freedom." Both were for Latin/South American audiences (Mexico City and Buenos Aires). The opening line of the former breathes Merton's roots in New Criticism: "We who are poets know that the reason for a poem is not discovered until the poem itself exists." He continues to caution poets to resist prostituting their art to political and economic "systems" or any kind of "persuasions."[25] In the latter essay, he warns against all forms of censorship, particularly political. Under the heading of "Art and Ethics," Merton unequivocally declares the autonomy of the artist's existential commitment to truth.

> Certainly the artist has no obligations to promulgate ethical lessons any more than political or economic ones. The artist is not a catechist. Usually moral directives are lost when one attempts to convey them in a medium that is not intended to communicate conceptual formulas. But the artist has a moral obligation to maintain his own freedom and his own truth. His art and his life are separable only in theory. The artist cannot be free in his art if he does not have a conscience that warns him when he is acting like a slave in his everyday life.

The artist should preach nothing — not even his own autonomy. His art should speak its own truth, and in so doing it will be in harmony with every other kind of truth — moral, metaphysical, and mystical.[26]

That "troublesome question" Merton wrestles with in his introduction to the Panichas collection of religion and literature essays ultimately revolves around the ambiguity of the word "religion." He is determined that religious and literary values not be confused. He has broadened the term "religious" beyond confessional or even ecumenical labels and particular dogmatic expressions. "Basic problems of human being are embedded in human nature itself." These "truths about man," he concludes, constitute the religious dimension. Literary artists have a dramatic power of "enchantment," which for Merton is fundamentally religious.

It brings you into living participation with an experience of basic and universal human values on a level which words can point to but cannot fully attain. . . . What the author means to convey is not a system of truths which explain life but a certain depth of awareness in which life itself is lived more intensely and with a more meaningful direction.[27]

Careful not to confuse this "power of imaginative communion" with religious faith, Merton finds the artist "activating the deepest centers of decision which truth calls into play." In this context he finds the terms "religious" and "metaphysical" inadequate to communicate this imaginative awareness of basic meaning. So, he volunteers the term "sapiential," "the highest level of cognition."

Wisdom is not only speculative but also practical: that is to say, it is "lived." And unless one lives it one cannot have it. . . . It proceeds, then, not merely from knowledge about ultimate values, but from an actual possession and awareness of those values as incorporated into one's own existence.[28]

Here is Merton, the quintessential monk, renewing contemporary spirituality with water from Cistercian wells. Yet simultaneously he promotes an appreciation of the literary artist's mimetic ability to communicate a unique knowlege ("depth of awareness") through a work which recreates and interprets human experience. In doing so Merton cultivates new directions in spirituality without breaching the autonomy of art.

To appreciate Merton's "sapiential thinking" as a theological method for religion and literature studies, I suggest that a distinction he makes in "The Inner Experience" can clarify what he means. In Merton's theological anthropology the distinction is simple but revealing. In the Genesis 3 story the fall from paradise resulted in alienation. Redemption thus becomes for Merton a return to the paradisal state, a recovery of lost unity. The soul awakens, now conscious of its alienation, and begins the illuminative way. In this context Merton interprets sin as an ontological lapse, not only a moral lapse. Sin violates the person's very being. The distinction approximates contemporary moral theology's understanding of sin as "fundamental option," engaging the deepest levels of human freedom and personal identity. The contemplative enjoys solitude in which to claim and live this "true self." Merton identifies the contemplative's mission today—"to keep alive a sense of sin" as ontological lapse, not merely the violation of the external code.[29] And it will be in imaginative literature that Merton finds sapientially dramatized the deepest levels of human freedom and the discovery of such human authenticity.

In a 1968 essay, "Why Alienation Is for Everybody," written for a group of black writers in Louisville's West End, Merton says, "alienation begins when culture divides me against myself, puts a mask on me, gives me a role I may or may not want to play." He claims modern literature is by and large a literature of alienation.

> The peculiar pain of "alienation" in its ordinary sense—alienation as a kind of perpetual mental Charley horse of self-conscious frustration—is that nobody really has to look at us or judge us or despise us or hate us. Whether or not they do us this service, we are already there ahead of them. We are doing it for them. . . . [T]o live without any awareness of it at all is death pure and simple. . . . It is not enough to complain about alienation, one must exorcise it. . . . [C]onstant, repeated, compulsive self-annihilation is due to the short circuit which puts a conventional judgment, dictated by culture, fashion, literature, style, art, religion, science, sociology, politics, what have you, IN THE PLACE OF OUR OWN IMMEDIATE RESPONSE however unconscious, irrational, foolish, unacceptable, it may at first appear.[30]

His advice to the writers gathered in the ghetto includes learning to write disciplined prose, and poetry with form. He sends them sections of his own experimental long poem (posthumously published as *The Geography of Lograire*). The form of that poetry intimated that

it had emerged from hidden depths: "Rather than making an intellectual point and then devising a form to express it," Merton suggests,
"we need rather to release the face that is sweating under the mask
and let it sweat out in the open for a change."[31] One of the local poet's
works captured the attention of the monk. "This poet dares to express
the reality of religious alienation—an alienation which I myself know,"
he admits. It is the gravity of this human suffering of alienation (as
ontological lapse) and the possibility of human hope for authenticity
through an exercise of transcendental freedom that attracts Merton to
literary artists whose work aesthetically achieved what he described in
a letter as religion with a "human epiphany in art."[32]

Michael Mott, Merton's biographer, has reconstructed the impact
of correspondence with Polish writer Czeslaw Milosz in the monk's search
for his own voice, a literary voice that would cultivate this sapiential
criticism. The Pole encouraged him to venture into Camus, to seek
what Mott calls "the reality behind cliches: the Problem of Evil and
Suffering in Contemporary Life, the Question of Institutionalized Religion, the Question of Guilt," and as an active contemplative "to grasp
religion again as a personal vision." In a 1962 letter Milosz had challenged Merton, "I do not invite you to write theological treatises but
much can be accomplished, it seems to me, through literary criticism
for instance."[33] Merton was now oriented to his unique niche, from
which he would explore the existential theology of the person and grace
in the method he came to baptize as "sapiential" criticism. His applied criticism of three novelists best charts Merton's development of
that method: we must turn to his essays on the novels of Boris Pasternak, Albert Camus, and William Faulkner for the fruits of that endeavor.

APPLYING THE SAPIENTIAL METHOD TO FICTION

BORIS PASTERNAK

"The Pasternak Affair" is an early essay from *Disputed Questions*
(1960). It recounts Merton's concern over the circumstances surrounding political pressures brought to bear on Boris Pasternak by his win-
ning the Nobel Prize for Literature in 1958. It affords him an acid
test for investigating the exact spiritual and Christian dimensions of
an artist whom he regards as a very kindred spirit.[34] His concern is

to emphasize the "spiritual character" of the Russian novelist's *Doctor Zhivago* in terms of the "person" and humanity as "the image of God"—the foundations of Christian freedom. Pasternak had not relented under the political persecution of the Soviet authorities, who were threatened by the vision communicated in *Doctor Zhivago*. Merton points out that the artist has not attempted a political novel. He singles out the novelist for refusing to prostitute his art to politics, even in the wake of some uncomprehending Western sympathizers who fueled the Cold War rhetoric by heralding a new martyr to the cause. "The protest of *Doctor Zhivago*," writes Merton, "is spiritual . . . religious, aesthetic and mystical."[35] But he hurries to qualify this characterization. Pasternak is not enough of a Christian "officially" to pretend to be a Christian apologist, says Merton. So he has no Christian "message" to be distilled from the novel. Nonetheless, the "depth and clarity of his Christian faith" leavens the novel and demonstrates his witness as "essentially Christian."

> That is the trouble: the problematical quality of Pasternak's "Christianity" lies in the fact that it is reduced to the barest and most elementary essentials: intense awareness of all cosmic and human reality as "life in Christ," and the consequent plunge into love as the only dynamic and creative force which really honors this "Life" by creating itself anew in Life's—Christ's—image.[36]

Merton finds Pasternak's vision to resemble the cosmic liturgy of the book of Genesis.[37] It is spontaneous. It eludes ritual. It is much more primitive. But most significantly, "It . . . is not perfectly at home with dogmatic formulas," Merton emphasizes, "but gropes after revealed truth in its own clumsy way."[38] Conversely, it becomes difficult to translate the artist's overpowering religious feelings into exact theological propositions.

What Merton attempts is a rudimentary sapiential criticism of Pasternak. He is drawn to the paschal pattern in *Doctor Zhivago* and finds life filled with "the mystery of history as passion and resurrection" glimpsed obscurely in the narrative.[39] Pasternak has recreated an awareness of the spiritual ordeal of persons struggling against political totalitarians and has offered an "exit" to contemporary Sartrean humanity. Merton distinguishes this salvation from the unsuccessful efforts to escape from the "blind alley," or the unprofitable beating of one's head against the wall. He interprets Pasternak in kenotic christological cate-

gories: "The exit is into an entirely new dimension—finding ourselves
in others, discovering the inward sources of freedom and love which
God has put in our nature, discovering Christ in the midst of us, as
'one we know not.'"[40] The theme and solution he finds in *Doctor Zhivago* is love as the highest expression of human spirituality and freedom.[41] Merton here defines love as the self-discovery in Christ, through
other persons. He interprets the concluding death scene of the novel,
when the doctor falls on the pavement with a heart attack, as implicitly tinged with the victory of the Resurrection. Any tragedy attached
to this event is relieved of frustration because Merton sees it in the
paradigm of the cross. And he attributes this not only to Pasternak's
belief that Christ is the center of history but because of the Russian
artist's existential dedication to the supreme inner value of the person,
a Christian characteristic of Western humanistic thought.[42]

Not all of Pasternak's expressions of paschal symbolism can be fully
reconciled with a manual of dogmatic formulas, Merton cautions. But
he subscribes to the deeper christology in the novel, Christ as liberator
from death, Christ waiting for authentic human liberty to transform
the world by love.[43] In the final analysis, Merton discovers in Pasternak
that history has the capacity to become a Christian creation when transformed human persons begin to change it. He quotes the electric passage
from the opening pages of *Doctor Zhivago*:

> It was not until after the coming of Christ that time and man could breathe
> freely. Man does not die in a ditch like a dog—but at home in history,
> while the work toward the conquest of death is in full swing; he dies shar-
> ing in this work.[44]

Thomas Merton acclaimed Boris Pasternak as being as dangerous and
revolutionary as the gospel when confronting the totalitarianism of East
or West. Here, in the late 1950s, was a catalyst who helped steer the
world's most celebrated monk back to the world, where he would voice
an unrelenting compassion and protest that choruses with Pasternak
against alienation and for the spiritual transformation of persons.

ALBERT CAMUS

If Merton had broken ground for the sapiential method in his criticism of Pasternak's art, his seven essays on Albert Camus almost a decade
later harvested the mature fruit of sapiential criticism. His insistence

that the artist not prostitute art to economic or political systems now extends to encompass Camus's protest against all social systems that invariably poise to exploit and liquidate persons. The theme of judgment in Camus will magnify the religious alienation imposed when the culture assigns masks. If Pasternak's imagination had reclaimed the arena of history as the locus of Merton's spiritual life, Camus's fiction would nuance the meaning of history for him. The French-Algerian novelist and essayist warns that history harbors revolutions which themselves can become tyranny. Merton's stance toward the world is refined by Camus's ethic of the Rebel and the act of Revolt, leading to solidarity.

The seven essays on Camus stretch chronologically over a year and a half, from August 1966 until March 1968. They evidence an intense immersion in works of a fellow French-born artist who wrote in the language of Merton's native country. By following these essays in chronological order the development in Merton's applied sapiential criticism becomes more apparent. While some of the essays repeat and overlap, Merton's steady progression toward a critique of Camus in christological categories grows throughout the collection.

"Terror and the Absurd: Violence and Nonviolence in Albert Camus" inaugurates Merton's series. As in several of the essays he identifies Camus as a post-Christian writer.[45] He begins with a caution: Camus overestimates his intuition of the absurd—it is not the basis for a logical argument but the occasion for an existential wager.[46] The Rebel, who experiences meaninglessness and the crises of human suffering, refuses, says Merton, to accept the diminishing of authentic possibilities for life.[47] It becomes an "aesthetic refusal."[48] The Rebel has witnessed the scandal of modern revolutions which deteriorate into absolute tyranny, leaving a trail of political victims. The Rebel refuses the alienation exacted by business, money, politics, or political revolutions. Merton points to Camus's Rebel moving from revolt to solidarity with other Rebels. He celebrates the risk, limitations, and vulnerability of the Rebel. Then he identifies the Rebel's Franciscan sense of poverty, a remark reinforced by Camus in his own notebooks. Poverty becomes a liberating force. The framework of the essay focuses attention on Camus's claim that he and his Catholic friends "are fighting for the same things."[49] Where they part is in the solution. Merton quotes the Algerian-born agnostic's convergence with Franciscan spirituality: "I feel clearly that if they are right then it is in the same way that I am." It is a lyric moment in Camus: "Being naked always has associations of physical liberty, of harmony between the hand and the flower it touches, of loving understanding between the earth and men who have been freed from human things. Ah, I should become a convert to this if it were not already my religion."[50]

The real question centers on the historical forms of Christianity which have degraded the human and demanded a futile resignation that leaves us at the mercy of blind social forces. In this regard, Merton can agree with Camus that we must choose either the side of the executioner or the victim in response to the absurd. Camus's scorching criticism of institutional and conventional religion accuses the church of cheapening life and trivializing death. But Merton counters, as he will throughout this series of essays, that Camus's caricature of the God of Christianity yields only an abstract God, not the living God of authentic Christianity. The novelist proposes the paradigm of the Rebel as "the poverty-loving, therefore liberated, Franciscan." In solidarity with others, the Rebel revolts against the decadent, postreligious culture, as well as the totalitarian, godless police state because both "strike at every form of power that relies on blood."[51] Revolt differs radically from revolution, which is abstract and seeks to guarantee itself by the exercise of power, therefore by murder. When revolution calls this "justice," it proves self-canceling and can only be corrected by Revolt.

Merton finds in Camus's notebooks the foundations of the Rebels' struggle against absurdity, in solidarity with one another. Love becomes the direction and meaning of their Revolt. The language used by Camus in an unfinished sentence of the notebooks, cited by Merton, echoes the syllables of Merton's mature christology: "The universal order cannot be built from above, in other words through an idea; but rather *from below,* in other words through the common basis which. . . ."[52] In those same notebooks, Merton cites Camus's remark that it is not possible to live Revolt against the absurd "without reaching at some point or another an experience of love that is still undefined." Further fascinating insights from Camus come at the conclusion of Merton's article. He finds the novelist refusing to believe in the transcendent God because Christians have effectively reduced God to an ideology, and all such social systems and abstract concepts can be exploited to justify mass murder, at least by a conspiracy of silence. On the other hand, Camus refuses to believe in a historical dynamic that promises to wipe away absurdity in the future. The Nazi terror succeeded, Camus reminds us, because it was legitimized murder. Merton ponders the example of Simone Weil, who was for Camus an "authentic Christian," a genuine Rebel, because she refused to join the church. She had remarked that official history is only a matter of believing the self-justifications of murderers.[53] But Merton is quick to credit Camus for not arguing against God. The absurd does not deny God, but disregards God as irrelevant to the modern mind and experience.[54]

A second, more ambitious essay, "Three Saviors in Camus: Lucidity and the Absurd," concentrates on the novelist's humanism, which clarifies our consciousness of our lot in the world. The introductory paragraph resonates with familiar Merton themes: our *anguish* must not be evaded, because it is the "perpetual climate" of lucid persons; *language* must be used to *awaken* us to this "lucid anguish in which alone" we are truly *conscious of our condition* and able to revolt against the absurd.[55] The three short story selections, "The Renegade," "Le Malentendu," and "The Growing Stone," all illustrate Camus's theme of communication and estrangement. They compound the problem of communication with narratives involving different countries, races, and religions. Merton interprets "The Renegade" as a satire on the church. The missionary's love of power distorts and perverts the gospel message. His *hybris* over the primitives manifests itself in his preaching himself over Christ. In the end, he converts to the cult of the idol which he was sent to overturn. "Le Malentendu" portrays Jan as a protagonist incapable of simple, direct speaking. Because he does not reveal his true identity to his mother and sister, whom he wants to surprise, he falls victim. The character of Maria, who encourages him to reveal his identity, personifies for Merton the "wisdom of love."[56] Jan persists in defending his image of himself as "savior": a superior person, with an abstract plan for salvation, who will manipulate other peoples' lives. Maria reminds us that it is not a lack of intelligence but a lack of love which is able to say what it means that is Jan's failure. The ironic "misunderstanding" of the title denotes the misguided reasoning that has ended in Jan's death.

The third story, "The Growing Stone," changes the context for the savior-figure, notes Merton, by providing a simple, warm, open group of Brazilian people for the messenger. The ship's cook is to carry a stone to the church in a penitential procession. When he fails, the French engineer D'Arrast, who has obligated himself by a vow to fulfill the ritual, takes up the task. Merton celebrates the story's primitive, pre-

Christian roots. There are dancing and nature rites enacted by the natives. But for all this attempt at communication in Third World environs, Merton questions whether Camus succeeds artistically with the happy ending he intended. He sees here a residue of Camus's criticism of the church as a "liberal daydream."[57] It is evident in D'Arrast not laying the heavy stone before the meaningless church altar, but setting it on the floor in the middle of the poor cook's cabin, where the blacks gather and invite him to sit with them. Merton combs Camus's notebooks and finds a third alternative ending which had D'Arrast take the rock and disappear into the virgin forest. He sees this as Camus's own denial of humanity, an impulse for primitive, unspoiled nature. The chosen ending, however, leaves a dilemma, the very quandary of communication and estrangement which repeats as Camus's theme. Merton notes that the silent blacks in the *favela* merely look at D'Arrast. He cannot dance with them and he cannot go to Mass. In Merton's eyes, this failed ending merely gives us "a love without metaphysical roots."[58] Sisyphus and the historical Christ merge "strangely" for Merton in this *via dolorosa*.[59] Merton finds the point of all three stories in Camus's discrediting Saviors and Messiahs. The human person, like Sisyphus, needs to take up the absurd task—"or, if you prefer, his Cross." History has demonstrated that past hopes for a heavenly savior have been "perverted into an ideology of power and authority seeking to control the course of history for the advantage of the powerful, at the expense of the weak."[60] Merton is generous in concluding that Camus, while explicitly non-Christian, practices an ethic that approximates authentic Christian charity.

His third essay, "Prophetic Ambiguities: Milton and Camus," mirrors Merton's conviction about the sapiential identity of the literary artist. He applauds poets who construct myths which embody personal struggles with ultimate questions. He sees them anticipating in their solitude and struggles a later generation's general consciousness. What Merton begins to develop is an understanding of Camus's post-Christian humanism as "adopting Christian values in classic disguise."[61] Thus, he finds in Camus's fiction the fatal infestation ("plague") of *hybris,* or a satanic self-assertion. This inevitably leads to *nemesis,* or a fatal retribution in which human power becomes self-destructive, an abdication of moral and personal dignity. For Camus, the choice was one for human persons and against systems, whether the power of the state, money, or weaponry. Merton catalogues the path toward *nemesis*: placing ideologies above human persons, politics above humanity, nation or partisan politics above truth, and power above everything.[62]

Before concluding this essay on Milton and Camus, Merton offers Teilhard's Christ as the antithesis of Milton's Satan in *Paradise Lost.* He brackets the question of whether Teilhard's vision was too optimistic, but points to the Jesuit's "Mass on the World" and its resemblance to the "splendid hymn to light" at the opening of the third book of *Paradise Lost.* The tension between Milton's modern temper and classic worldview left Satan a hero and Christ a dubious figure in his epic. This very mindset made it impossible, says Merton, for Camus to become a Christian. Again, Merton has returned to christology for clarity and to diagnose the source of the modern predicament.[63]

A fourth essay, "Camus and the Church," examines the theme of justice in *The Stranger.* Merton mocks, along with Camus, the "elaborate tissue of fictions" whereby the complicated and dishonest social game neglects persons and values. It is alarmingly clear in the trial of Meursault, the protagonist, that "When bourgeois society speaks, God speaks," and no one, least of all the prison chaplain, questions whether God's justice might be different than society's.[64] What distinguishes this essay is Merton's infatuation with language as a metaphysical problem in Camus. "The great task of man is not to serve the lie," he quotes from Camus, reminding himself of the church's timid and ineffective speech about the horrors of the Holocaust.[65] He evaluates the collection of essays, *The Rebel,* as a failure which nonetheless offers "precious" insights in its survey of two centuries of cultural and political history. "Telling the truth" will come to mean identifying the absurd as such and establishing communication among those who resist by revolt.[66]

"Camus: Journals of the Plague Years" sharpened Merton's appreciation of the French-Algerian's literary corpus. He identifies four cycles that develop through Camus's writing: (1) absurdity; (2) revolt; (3) nemesis; and (4) love. The fourth cycle, in particular, reorients the monk to Camus's enterprise. For one, it lends a larger perspective to the notion of the absurd. The first cycle involves the *beginning* of rebellion against the absurd, once this meaninglessness has been discovered. But Merton exonerates Camus from any preference for the absurd. "Camus is not a 'philosopher of the absurd' in the sense of an *advocate* of the absurd," he warns.[67] At the end of the article he repeats that the absurd has no metaphysical existence of its own.[68] Merton again comments on Camus's response to the mysticism of the early Franciscans. They and their faith are real, not an "explanation" or "justification," the sapiential critic points out. He notes that he finds pages bordering on mysticism in Camus's early essays.[69]

Merton calls Camus a religious thinker in the sense of a person who appeals to "an obscure and ultimate faith." It is not theological faith but a faith in the human person, in Revolt, in the Rebel's "No" to the absurd. At which juncture the monk alludes to Camus's axiom that we "create what we are." "If to 'create what we are' is to 'become God' then the Camusian position is not far removed from a traditional and even religious metaphysic, in which created being is a potential epiphany of the uncreated."[70] The christological pattern, grounded for Merton in kenosis, insists that because of the inevitability of God's love (the Incarnation which he had poetically described as Christ "promised first without scars"), humanity *is* already something definite and oriented toward transformation in Christ. Merton discovers that Camus had intended his last work, unfinished at his death, to be entitled *Le Premier Homme* or *The First Man*.[71] The final cycle of Camus was to deal with "a certain kind of love" and the novelist insisted that with the plague out of his system, he wanted to write about happiness. Like the author himself, Merton prefers to read all of Camus's work, novels, and essays as "one vast novel." He identifies the lucidity of the artist with the lucidity of the free man and sees the depths of the artist's work in the struggle with human crises. He places the artist on the tightrope, where his task is to claim human responsibility instead of evading it or lapsing into silence. The essay concludes with Merton's return to the Christ-consciousness. Camus's lucidity means for him "the fullness which we begin to experience when we realize that 'lucidity' is the light itself—the light we look not *at* but *with*; the light that we not only *have* but in some way *are*; the 'true light that enlightens every man that comes into the world.'" He does not spare Camus the blunt corrective, insisting that the novelist needed to discover that this light "is pure mercy and pure gift," not merely the ironic reward for the artist's ethical concern.[72]

Merton's sixth and lengthiest essay, "The Plague of Albert Camus: A Commentary and Introduction," appeared as a separate publication in booklet form. It comes closest to a systematic interpretation of Camus, although it focuses almost exclusively on the single novel *The Plague.* Camus, he says, comes to grips with the problem of evil and unhappiness and solves it in terms of human freedom. The canvas on which Merton chooses to draw his interpretative portrait of Camus is what he describes as Christianity's introduction of a higher dimension of liberty, grace as divine freedom. He retrieves from Gerard Manley Hopkins the poetic phrase, "the death dance in our blood," to contrast the pestilence of evil with love.[73] Midway through the essay Merton concludes that Camus had found himself examining the old chestnut, the argument of grace versus the law, and unawares found himself on the side of grace. Merton's sapiential method will not permit him to claim Camus as a secret Christian, but to remark that a Christian could "understand Camus in a Christian sense" which the novelist himself did not consciously realize.[74] Merton concedes to Camus that too many Christians have embalmed Christianity with misunderstandings of grace that reduce it to a smug self-assurance of their own election. He calls this an inversion of grace, the attempt to force grace to prove something beyond it, i.e., the individual's justified, or righteous, status.[75] Virtue in the Camusian world of the absurd is reduced to a system of social conformity which disguises hypocrisy, doublethink, conventions, and cliches.[76] Lest we become accomplices of this indifference to persons and authentic values, Camus offers two approved motives: (1) Revolt and (2) love.

This dynamic engages Merton's criticism of *The Plague*. He turns to the Jesuit, Father Paneloux, whose reaction to the town of Oran's plague and quarantine personifies the caricature of Christianity against which Camus revolted. In his first sermons to the stricken populace, Paneloux described the plague as a just punishment for sin. Merton captures his attitude: he is a man whose aim is to prove the correctness of the religious establishment and its doctrines rather than help the victims. So he rehearses the old Augustinian axiom that God permits evil and suffering in order to ennoble us. Merton sees Paneloux as a man without a heart, mired in his abstractions and preferring a God who is stone dead.[77] The physician, Dr. Rieux, however, credits Paneloux with a better attitude. He suggests that Christians can be better than their talk. But experience will change the Jesuit, he suggests, because every country priest's deathbed vigils convert him from "truth with a capital T" to efforts to relieve suffering instead of pointing to its excellence.[78] So Paneloux's second sermon mellows and becomes inclusive with his change of person to "we." It suggests a solidarity. But ambiguity shadows the priest's own ability to love. He joins the voluntary squads and ministers to the dying, but himself dies alone and stubbornly self-sacrificial because he has refused a doctor's care.

Merton relates Camus's typology of the plague to the novel's existential context of Nazism and the absolutisms that were possible because the attitudes and dispositions that enable the dictator are, as Merton analyzes, "already present in the people who submit to them, because in the depths of their hearts they want to submit."[79] Ever alert to a writer's vocabulary, Merton halts on the term "modesty," which means "the capacity to doubt one's wisdom." He describes Paneloux's transformation as such modesty. A person finally hesitates before the doctrines and systems that conveniently explain all things and invert evil into a kind of good.[80] Tarrou, the enigmatic character whose friendship with Rieux presages the kind of solidarity and love which Camus imagines, aspires in the novel to "be a saint without God." He is pivotal in Camus's story because his apparent immunity to the plague is the result of his having been previously exposed. He realizes that his whole history is, metaphorically, a history of plague. We discover that his father was a prosecutor, personifying society's blood lust, when Tarrou rebels and initiates solidarity with victims by organizing the sanitary squads in Oran. Merton finds Dr. Rieux's rebuttal, that what interests him is simply "being a man" and not a saint, as heroic enough.

By contrasting the fictional Paneloux with another Jesuit, Pierre Teilhard de Chardin, Merton concludes this essay with a total acceptance of humanity, a confidence in human transformation and divinization. He still holds reservations about Teilhard's optimism, which seems to overlook the suffering of an innocent child and is echoed in the very ironic claim of Paneloux at the child's deathbed that now he understands what grace means. Nevertheless, for Merton, Teilhard's God is more than a remote judge and creator. Teilhard's and the monk's God seeks with passionate love "to complete his epiphany in the world of man by bringing all humanity to convergence and unity in himself, in the Incarnation." This involves for Merton more than the remission of sin, but the "hominization," indeed Teilhard's "christification" of the entire world.[81]

The seventh and final essay, "The Stranger: Poverty of an Antihero," examines Camus's ironic study of Meursault, a character with no interiority, no choice, no God. Merton concludes that the character is stuck in poverty because he is utterly alone.[82] It is only when the jury condemns him to death that Meursault revolts and rejects the identity of "stranger" that society imposes upon him. The monk describes this reaction as a "vain consolation" because it falls short of a significant, responsible first choice.[83] In Camus's own schema, the realization of absurdity does not in itself justify a person. Meursault may have awakened, but he remains inert. Here is a character who lacks love. As a final statement by Merton on Camus, this essay proves singularly important, because here he quarrels in christological terms with the novelist's retrospective preface to the 1955 American edition of *The Stranger.* He admits that Camus is less moderate in now defining Meursault as "a man poor and naked" who "refuses every mask . . . refuses to lie . . . by saying more than he feels . . . [animated] by a profound passion . . . for the absolute and for truth." He faults Camus for encouraging immoderate critics to take Meursault as a Christ-figure when Camus remarks that Meursault is "the only kind of christ we deserve." For Merton, this antihero's poverty has nothing to do with the kenosis of Christ. He suggests that the preface is colored by a vibrant language that prematurely attributes to *The Stranger* an interiority and justification which came only in later, mature works like *The Plague* and *The Rebel* that took him beyond the limits of the absurd and committed him to the compassion and love of characters like Rieux and Tarrou.[84] Meursault remains in the solipsistic loneliness of his poverty. Christ's poverty, for Merton, was the anthithesis of Meursault, because Christ emptied himself in compassion and solidarity with all human suffering. Merton identifies the ground of Camusian absurdity in the negation of ecstasy.[85] So Meursault contradicts Merton's Christ, who is the *ecstatic* dance of the Lord in time and emptiness of *New Seeds of Contemplation.*

In the final analysis, Thomas Merton's sapiential criticism of Albert Camus demonstrates his conviction that the literary artist offers a unique imaginative awareness of our spiritual crisis. Camus's work called into question the most intimate spiritual ground of our human existence. Camus had unmasked the person's flight from illusion with his explorations of alienation and the inner self's movement from Revolt against the absurd to solidarity with other Rebels. Here Merton encountered an existential theology that dramatized grace through human freedom and love. For all his reservations about Camus's "understandable misunderstanding" of the Christian message, Merton claims the importance of Camus's witness to the human plight in the world. We seek to communicate with such authentically anguishing persons. And

Camus suggests conditions under which such communication may be even more valid.[86]

WILLIAM FAULKNER

By concentrating on this Mississippi novelist, I propose a definitive case study of Merton's sapiential method of criticism. One reason recommending this is that Merton coins this term, "sapiential," in his critical interpretation of Faulkner. Secondly, while his seven Camus essays are more extensive, several are earlier than the Faulkner studies, which concentrate and focus more intentionally on Merton's sapiential method. And Camus's own enthusiasm for Faulkner, discovered by Merton, compounded his enthusiasm and interest in the "Sophocles in Mississippi."[87]

In a rebuttal of mainline Faulkner critics, Merton approvingly quotes Sartre: "A fictional technique always relates back to the novelist's metaphysics. The critic's task is to define the latter before evaluating the former."[88] Merton identifies the great religious mystery in Faulkner as the fall. He discriminates between Faulkner's early despair and the mature works' conscious and positive affirmation which follows upon "the awareness of judgment" which Faulkner's characters experience. "Where the fall is fully realized," he says, "the doors are silently open to eschatology if not to history."[89]

The alienation which Merton finds in Faulkner revolves around his use of time as an existentially dense and complex reality. "Faulknerian time is a monstrous nonprogression dominated by the past event which casts a kind of implacable shadow over the present and paralyzes all action toward a definite future."[90] Merton ridicules the school of critics who read Faulkner as an apocalypticist, as renouncing history and embracing tragedy, because they had failed to comprehend the eschatological and historical possibilities dramatized by his protagonists. The positivistic, rationalist worldview eclipsed the dawn on a sapiential horizon in Faulkner's universe.

Three examples of Merton's sapiential reading in Faulkner will fix our attention: "The Bear" from *Go Down, Moses, The Wild Palms,* and the Easter service in *The Sound and the Fury.* "The natural sapiential outlook," which Merton finds, is not a disguised Christian conversion. The initiatory awakening of characters to a cosmic and mythic deeper meaning of life resembles a stage of pre-evangelization, a natural wisdom which Merton claims as enviable when compared to Christianity's often sterile, dogmatic, and empty routines.

"The Bear" portrays young Ike McCaslin's initiation as a bear hunter as he goes into the wilderness with Sam Fathers. Merton discerns Faulkner's connection of this violation of the wilderness with the southern institution of slavery. The stages of young Ike's initiation and progressive awareness of the bear's presence parallel for Merton the degrees of mystical elevation.[91] The boy recognizes first that he is seen by the bear; his adventure moves to "a crucial moment of religious history" for Merton when Ike plunges into the forest without his gun, watch, or compass — all symbolic of the civilized knowledge he surrenders because it is now obsolete in the face of his discovery in the forest of a whole new dimension of being. Merton compares this action to Kierkegaard's leap of faith. Ike's revelatory vision of the bear, followed by the bear's and Sam's deaths, set the stage for his religious decision of renouncing ownership of land. Merton interprets this as a repudiation of the South's historic curse and judgment under slavery, analogous to a monastic vow of poverty, followed by a symbolic chastity vis-à-vis his wife, whose erotic ecstasy is resisted along with procreation of children. Merton's appropriation[92] of Faulkner's mythic tale intrigues. He refers to Ike's "novitiate" and, in the end, to Ike's having established his identity but "remain[ing] a failed saint and only half a monk" in spite of his initiation. Merton's parenthetical remark, that after twenty-five years in a monastery it is extraordinarily difficult for anyone to be more than that, gauges the intensity of his own participation in Faulkner's evocative experience of meaning and direction, so aesthetically truthful.

In the second example, *The Wild Palms,* a pair of stories are counterpointed. Merton's critical eye finds a revealing "sapiential structure" in the book's diptych, which affords "a whole picture of man, neither of which is complete in itself." One aspect of the paradise/Eden motif of the union of man and woman appears in each story. "Old Man" is the story of a Mississippi River deluge in which a convict who is fleeing the penitentiary and a pregnant woman, both desperate for rescue, find themselves morally responsible for one another. In the title story, "The Wild Palms," Charlotte and Harry Wilbourne, lovers seeking erotic fulfillment and having no intention of marriage, stand in contrast to the characters of the first story. Both Charlotte and her child die because of an abortion she forces Harry to attempt. Merton refuses to interpret the story as a homily or lesson in ethics. Instead he sees the real tragedy as lying in the disoriented passion of their relationship, itself as destructive and death-oriented as the deluge in "Old Man." Two alienated, modern people, vulnerable and wrecked, end in ruin, says Merton.

On the other hand, the more human woods people, the convict and pregnant mother, participate in the renewal of life on an archetypal Indian mound where birth defies the destructive force and threat of the deluge. He reads the convict's ontological awakening to another level of being—when he confronts the river as "being itself"[93] and in his glimpse of the newborn "tiny terra cotta colored creature resembling nothing"—as evidence of God's providence.[94] Harry Wilbourne's "mental tidal wave" outside the hospital operating room shattered his world, in Merton's interpretation. Faulkner's greatest irony in the diptych comes in the fact that the convict and Harry both end up in the same prison, the very point where the story began for the convict. Merton's appropriation of Faulkner's meaning intrigues again, as he interprets Harry's lot as the monastic role of grieving; and the convict's return to "do time" is seen as a comic return to the "last refuge of provisional meaning in an otherwise meaningless world"—the monastery as "escape." Harry's decision to grieve over his and Charlotte's destructive symbiotic relationship, Merton notes, countered a temptation to suicide and found him embracing "the monastic life of a penitentiary." Merton admits this was less than the highest monastic vocation, but it approximated an authentic act of freedom because it responded to an awareness of alienation.[95]

Third, and finally, the character of Dilsey in the Easter service of *The Sound and the Fury* is judged by Merton as "one of [Faulkner's] greatest saints."[96] She personifies for him hearing the Word of God and responding to an eschatological vision of enlightenment. In this sense, she and all who gather at the black church on Easter morning "celebrate" the biblical narrative of "Time and Unburdening and the Recollection of the Lamb," the title of Merton's interpretive essay. The blacks are accompanied by the idiot boy, Benjy Compson, whose disjointed experience of time distances him from his family in the novel; with the exception of his sister Caddy, each Compson is manacled to the present and lacking in the Christian experience of time as *kairos,* the real experience of the divine manifest in history. Only Dilsey, the family's cook, has this sense of fulfillment, the ripening of history, in

Merton's interpretation. His attention to the detail of her announcing "eight o'clock" when the ever-slow clock in the kitchen strikes five, separates her from the linear, dead-end time of the others. Merton applauds Faulkner's "artistic solution"[97] of structuring the novel around various characters' experience of time, climaxing in Dilsey's Easter procession and response to the Resurrection proclamation. She is unburdened of real burdens placed by the Pharonic Compson family. The supreme irony for Merton resides in the sermon of the shrunken visiting black preacher whose delivery "sounded like a white man. His voice was level and cold." The thunderclap, Merton exclaims, came when the preacher changed to the honest black voice and "chanting measures" of black preaching. He moved, said Merton, to announce the story of salvation in terms the chosen (i.e., "elect") congregation was ready for: "Now he is simply saying not only what they know, but what is present among them! Now: he is re-creating in them the realization of the great truth: Jesus lives! And these people realize this. They know that they know this."[98]

His enthusiasm for Faulkner drew Merton to rework the coordinates of his christology for a post-Christian world in his March 1967 conferences for novices at the Abbey of Gethsemani. His reflections on the novel coincided with his existential anticipation of Holy Week and Easter Sunday, the climactic event in *The Sound and the Fury*. The burden of the oppressed blacks and the mentally incompetent white boy, Benjy Compson, will be relieved as they gather for Easter Sunday and the visiting preacher. Merton calls this novel "a great book about the crucifixion." The black minister's "whole attitude [is] that of a serene, tortured crucifix that transcended its shabbiness and insignificance."

There are some very special slants that are not at all our "conventional" Christian theology of expiation and redemption. Rather, there are some different twists in what the Reverend Shegog says: for example, what happens when Christ *dies,* in the Reverend Shegog's sermon? God the Father is spoken of as "de widowed God", who "shet His do'": the One most disconsolate and sad at the crucifixion is God in heaven. *He's* all broken up about it: "*Look what they did!*" ... Nowhere in the Four Gospels do you find anything about God, sitting up in heaven, and waiting for this blood-debt to be paid off. This idea of God waiting to get "paid off" is later theology—a lot of it is German, bringing in their tribal, feudal idea of responsibility incurred, that must be "paid off."[99]

It is this attraction to, and comment on, Faulkner's "widowed God," "the One most sad and disconsolate at the crucifixion," that typifies the mature, kenotic christology of Merton.

Merton claims Dilsey's time a *kairos,* the time of life's maturing "in its own leisurely way. It is the time of love."[100] In Dilsey, Merton finds Faulkner's "only fully and unambiguously Christian character"[101] because she experiences the mystery of the Resurrection and returns to history as redeemed time, presenting new possibilities for those who love and show compassion.

By including madness and the tragic experiences, Faulkner's novel provides Merton the opportunity to reclaim a debt to William Blake, from whom he learned "the total acceptance, if ultimate reversal, of the full reality of fallen history." Distinct christological understandings grounded this confidence in the human world. Merton had discovered in Rilke the same eschatological courage when he called him "the hidden God-seeker," who inspired human persons to "look to the future to find God who would manifest Himself in the history that is to come, not in a new revelation but in a creative effort of man that would make the cosmos once more 'transparent.'"[102]

Merton repeatedly refers to the sapiential literary artists as other solitaries. From their contemplative depths, he claims, they speak to one's deepest self and summon every reader to recognize alienation. With them, he dares imagine an alternative history through human freedom. Even by temperament, Merton wrote in a genuinely existential style. He shied away from dogmatic theology, not because he was suggesting anything unorthodox, but because his spirituality touched the more immediate data of religious experience, prior to the secondary language of theology. So he can celebrate Faulkner and be "willing to tolerate theological discomfort,"[103] just as he had savored Pasternak's art, which also was "not perfectly at home with dogmatic formulas, but grop[ed] after truth in its own clumsy way."[104]

In a 1966 essay entitled "The Other Side of Despair," Merton defended Karl Adam's protest against Catholic faith being presented as an intellectual assent to dogmatic propositions, nothing more. He could berate with equal force the modern church's toying with the "mental snake-handling" that is content to establish a self-righteous oligarchy during a time of crisis and the "religious vaudeville"[105] that trivializes religion and degenerates into salesmanship. Merton laments all these false expressions of faith that fail to call into question the intimate spiritual ground of one's existence:

> If organized religion abdicates its mission to disturb man in the depths of his conscience, and seeks instead simply to "make Converts" that will smilingly adjust to the status quo, then it deserves the most serious and uncompromising criticism. Such criticism is not a disloyalty.[106]

The sapiential literary artists provided Merton with his antidote. Here flourished the "stuff" worthy of his theological reflection. The sublimely kenotic insights he discovered in the creative literature of Pasternak, Camus, Faulkner, and others touched Merton's own imagination. He finally turned his religious sensibilities to the project of communicating the possibilities of love and compassion to a "post-Christian" world through his own voice as an antipoet.

5. A Summa of Offbeat Anthropology:
Merton's Antipoetry

At the climax of the eighty-eight poems comprising the lithe, experimental collection entitled *Cables to the Ace,* Thomas Merton introduces Christ. The scene is a garden in the first stanza. Then, the second shifts to ruins. And finally, in the third stanza, "Christ rises on the cornfields." In all three instances, Christ comes "Slowly slowly." It is Eden; then Gethsemani; then the garden on Easter morning.[1] In Eden, Christ speaks to the sacred trees which bear his light, "unharmed." In Gethsemani, Christ seeks the lost disciple, who is too literate for belief, "So he hides." At the empty tomb, the disciple mistakes Christ for the harvest moon and turns over to sleep, murmuring "My regret." But the poet offers hope. The disciple will awaken, he prompts, when the disciple "knows history." Meanwhile "The Lord of History / Weeps into the fire."

The posthumously published *The Geography of Lograire,* an even more ambitious draft of what Merton promised as "a longer work in progress," rummages in history for the disruptive crises where Christ is revealed in ever new kenotic patterns. In the "North" canto of the poem, which is structured on the four geographical directions, the hermit-monk poses the question of what he calls, in his Faulkner reading notebooks of this same period, a "post-Christian Christology."[2] He parodies how Christ "went down to stay with them Niggers and took his place with them at table." When Christ announces that life and salvation are much simpler than imagined, their reply stuns: "'You have become a white man and it is not so simple at all.'" This final poem's theme of universal exploitation, racism, and dehumanization delivers a piercing knowledge of history. It refuses to idealize. It resists the romantic lure. It starkly retrieves and records what Merton described in

155

a September 1967 letter as "my summa of offbeat anthropology."[4] His
poetry has discovered this new form, antipoetry,[5] which affords a literary analogue for the Christ whose strength abides but who chooses to
be weak—the Christ of kenosis.

The bulk of *Cables to the Ace* is a barrage of parody and irony. Merton declares that his attitudes and ironies are as common as magazine
advertisements: "The soaps, the smells, the liquors, the insurance, the
third, dull, gin-soaked cheer." The poet announces in the Prologue
that he "has changed his address and his poetics are on vacation." He
satirically subtitles the collection, "Familiar Liturgies of Misunderstanding," for in the culture's public *persona* the misunderstanding of the
human person's identity and purpose have been almost fatally compromised. One of the more compelling examples of this antipoetry
occurs midway through *Cables to the Ace*. Merton entitles the antipoem "Newscast." If read literally, the verse is nonsense. No logical
meaning can be deciphered from its collage of juxtaposed images and
chattered sounds. It resembles best what we now call "white noise."
Two excerpts from cable 48 illustrate this antipoetic technique:

> In New Delhi a fatal sport parade
> Involving long mauves and delicate slanders
> Was apprehended and constrained at three P.M.
> By witnesses with evening gestures
> In a menacing place where ten were prohibited
> Many others were found missing in colossal purples
> And numerous raided halls.
>
> .   .   .   .
>
> Atoms are bound to go said Nobel
> Prize-waging Physic swinger
> In an unpacked science stadium announcement Wednesday
> He was clapped into recognition
> When he was discovered
> Suddenly full of crowds.
>
> (*CP,* 427–28)

The cadences and breathless barrage of words brilliantly parody the
evening newscast. The antipoem is acoustically perfect as colloquial
sound. It recreates broadcasting's abuse of words which Merton, who
rarely saw television or heard radio, would have alertly retrieved from
the memory of a Louisville visit. The "static" of feeding back the gar-

bled newscast as antipoetry confronts and shocks readers. By punctu-ating the nonsensical news stories with places and exact hours, and the everyday irony of "numerous raided halls" and a Nobel scientist being "clapped into recognition," Merton compounds the trivialization of words in the culture's sacrosanct newscasts. It also serves to remind read-ers that the so-called "news" chase measured superficial happenings, while we had neglected and eclipsed the deeper identity and mean-ings of human life. As the subtitle of *Cables to the Ace* intimates, we are bombarded by all too "familiar liturgies of misunderstanding" in our culture's elaborate communications industry.

By the time he writes his "Author's Note" for *The Geography of Lograire,* Merton is speaking of the news and advertising industry as "the common areas of nightmare." He promises symbols of the omni-present death, which is structured into society as "guilt, police, and undertakers" (*CP,* 458). Echoes of Camus's alarm about systems invariably giving birth to socially licensed killing reverberate through the anti-poems' imaginative static. John Howard Griffin has quoted from Mer-ton's hermitage journals, reporting how the venturesome monk now read the ribald satire and parables of *The Essential Lenny Bruce:* "Such irony was much more pure than the sinister doubletalk of the 'moral' murderers," Merton interjected.[6] There is similar evidence of Merton's enthusiasm for James Joyce's irony, "an essential element in the Joyce canon" he described it, as he returns to the Irish novelist's work in the last two years at the hermitage.[7]

This chapter sketches a profile of a Thomas Merton who is totally unfamiliar to most of his readers. The distance between the form and spiritual horizon of *The Seven Storey Mountain,* or the familiar lyric poetry of the 1940s, and the mature Merton's antipoetry, or the chris-tology to be quarried from its deep strata can be measured only in light years. Four endeavors are undertaken here: (1) to identify how the ironic imagination delivers literary analogues of a kenotic under-standing of Christ; (2) to examine the possibilities of faith in a post-Christian world, and how Merton's acerbic words about authority and freedom vis-à-vis the church and other institutions led him to new po-etic efforts; (3) to define and to appreciate the phenomenon of anti-poetry as an idiom and the antipoet as a constructive identity; and (4) to analyze *Cables to the Ace* and *The Geography of Lograire* in terms of Merton's post-Christian anthropology and a christology from below, with a particular emphasis on the epiphany of the kenotic Christ in the environs of the disruptive, scarred, and wounded moments of history.

THE IRONIC IMAGINATION

Merton's antipoetry marks a boundary not easily crossed by unwitting readers. He delivers its ironies with a caution, "They find me always upside down / In these reflected glooms" (*CP*, 446). No wonder so many who venture to explore the antipoetry shrug, having stalked its pages with a literalist's lenses. The galvanized Christian faith-myth, with its flow of images that provided the matrix for Merton's early work, does not weather as well in the post-Christian world. Life has become more complex for Merton, especially the ambiguity of modern historical events. Only the poet's irony can now shock the world into the recognition of its peril, or convince readers that a critical reflection on their faith will expose fault lines and flaws. The antipoetry of Thomas Merton might, in fact, best be appreciated as a modern-day thesaurus of parables.

It is no coincidence that the parables of Jesus himself have come to us in the literary form that they do. New Testament scholars compare this form of storytelling with other ancient Near Eastern forms of narrative and discover something foundational about parables for Christianity. Indeed, parables function as a paradigm of the Jesus tradition. We can quickly examine the spectrum of storytelling forms, from myth through parable, and determine the precise nature of the form which would have been most familiar to Jesus' listeners. John D. Crossan has provided a succinct description of each. On the spectrum of storytelling, we can describe each of the following:

(1) *Myth:* establishes the world, creates a structured, ordered, meaningful world, a habitable world in which we can live securely.

(2) *Apologue:* defends the world established by the myth; this is often the type of storytelling found in moralizing tales for young people.

(3) *Action stories:* narrate a complication and the characters' resolution in a "neutral" form of storytelling; action stories investigate the world of the myth.

(4) *Satire:* attacks the world of the myth by exposing one or more of its flaws, then exaggerating and ridiculing it. Satire makes the myth vulnerable.

(5) *Parable:* dismantles the world established by myth. It not only

ridicules the weaknesses of the myth, it subverts the myth. It reveals that the reigning myth is bankrupt.

Crossan is quick to nuance two facts about parable: (1) It is not anti-myth because it ultimately anticipates the establishment of a new myth. What parable gives us, in Crossan's words, is a "dark interval" between the death of one myth and the birth of a new myth; but (2) in subverting the mythic paradigm of a culture, the parable does not specify the particulars of the new myth. Parables are, in some sense, indeterminate in meaning. They discredit an old myth, point to a new horizon, but do not exhaust the possibilities that reside in the future. So parables also continue to exercise judgment and critical function vis-à-vis all contemporary and future myths and paradigms.[8]

The simplest literary definition of irony is "a figure of speech by which one thing is said, and another is meant." Crossan describes the ironic imagination of the parabler in terms of its reversal of expectations. The very opposite of the hearer's expectation repeatedly comes out in the biblical story: the first shall be last; the barren are with child; the blind see; the dead rise to new life; outsiders become the new insiders.

Irony affords not only Christ-the-parabler but also the modern imagination its most natural ally. In his seminal *Anatomy of Criticism*, Northrop Frye ranges the fictional modes across a spectrum ranging from: myth, romance, high mimetic, and low mimetic, to irony. This description remarkably parallels Crossan's spectrum of biblical types of story. Frye defines the antihero of the ironic imagination as "inferior in power or intelligence to ourselves, so that we [the reader] have the sense of looking down on the sense of bondage, frustration, or absurdity."[9] Whether comic or tragic, irony seeks a return to the mode of myth, but a critically revised myth. In both *Cables to the Ace* and *The Geography of Lograire*, Merton returns at key junctures to the Christ, but only in order to reverse the expectations of his hearers by confronting us with the epiphany of Christ in emptiness, in poverty, in weakness, in defeat. This Christ of kenosis is never the Christ expected by Merton's audience, nor even the mythologized Christ of later layers of the gospel narrative and tradition. Now, history itself manifests Christ in surprising new eruptions, in unexpected and parabolic developments of historical discontinuity. These repeatedly stand on its head the establishment's dominant myth, the meanings and inherited order that have, in effect, endorsed the exploitation and indignities which the monk mocks in these antipoems.

William F. Lynch has examined the aptness of irony for the Christian imagination in his interdisciplinary exploration *Images of Faith.* "The irony of Christ," he notes, "relies on the simultaneous presence of contraries: we express this classically in christology as 'truly God and truly man.'" "Love," says Merton in this kenotic manner, "is the epiphany of God in our poverty."[10] This sense of contraries testifies to Lynch's affirmation, that "faith loves its own interior and poor humanity."[11] Christianity means by this more than a coexistence of the low and the high. In Lynch's words, "The lowliness is the very instrument to be passed through in order to reach the high." In that sense, for Lynch, christology's "low" is the "high." It involves more than paradox or brilliant irony; in fact, the actual transformation of being.[12]

The purpose of this chapter is to reflect on how irony serves this christological understanding—and is reflected in the new paradigm or pattern of Merton's attention to the human poverty and emptiness where God's epiphany is uniquely manifest. The irony found in these late renderings of Gethsemani's antipoet becomes a literary analogue to his christological understanding of kenosis. He resists remythologizing Christ in *The Geography of Lograire* because the dense historicity of the American South's racism, the genocide of Mayan culture, the exploitation lamented in the New Guinea cargo cults, and the ghost dance of the southwest United States, all continue to ambush us with God's hidden mercy and compassion. *Lograire* reveals a pattern of kenosis which eludes systems or precise order. It is enough for Merton to live intensely amid the tension of these dark intervals, in the recognition that the reigning myth has been broken and exposed for distorting God's mercy in Christ.[13]

FAITH IN A POST-CHRISTIAN WORLD: AUTHORITY AND FREEDOM

For an age that Merton diagnosed as "suicidal" and badgered by propaganda,[14] he had been inclined to prescribe the antidote of a "belief that order is possible." He became more and more chaste about the nature of that order in his final years, especially in the antipoetry. This commitment to reorient the needy contemporary world challenged the poet-monk to explore the precincts of a hitherto unprecedented irony in his poetry. The instinct was to follow in the direction of myth, but myth[15] in a sense other than the "evasion" which only troubles a society into further illusions, such as "America is an earthly paradise," Merton chided.[16] Such a myth evades both history's discontinuities and sin. In a March 1967 letter to pacifist James Douglass, the monk wonders: "If we are in the post-Christian era (and we are) are we not also perhaps in the post-political era and post-historic era? Or soon about to be?" He mourns the politics that had led to the Vietnam war and asks if history and politics are being slipped into "the old base position once occupied by metaphysics." He points to a danger of accepting a provisional historicism because it would contribute to "the big slide into technical totalism." "Will we not soon have to face the fact," he asks, "that *all* of it has to die on us and is one big embarrassing corpse?"[17]

We should first acknowledge Merton's early and effective use of the classical secular and Christian mythic matrix throughout his work. Dante's seven terraces of the Mount of Purgatory—the ascending path of purification—were imaginatively wrought in the autobiographical odyssey of faith, *The Seven Storey Mountain* of 1948. In the earlier and no longer extant novel, *The Man in the Sycamore Tree*, the young secular intellectual identified with Zachaeus's conversion (Lk. 19:1–9). In 1953 *The Sign of Jonas* appropriated the identity of the mythic reluctant prophet from Hebrew scriptures. Five years later Merton imaginatively recast the biblical myth in a verse-drama, *The Tower of Babel*. Similarly, we find his use of the Prometheus myth in the 1961 volume *The New Man* and its warning that even theology hazards false power in imitating this hero's hubris. Blake's mythos nurtures apocalyptic images both in Merton's early poems, where the city recurs as a symbol of depravity, and in segments of the antipoetry. Pauline images and the Greek Fathers' mythos of re-creation and transformation are integrated in the metaphors of the true self throughout the range of Merton's poetry.

One of Merton's most revealing uses of myth comes with the 1961 volume *The Behavior of Titans*. It is a book written in the new voice Merton claimed in his pivotal years of transition, 1958–62. What intrigues a reader is the distinction he makes between the Prometheus of Hesiod and the Prometheus of Aeschylus. Hesiod's hero, says Merton, is Cain; and Aeschylus's Prometheus is Christ on the Cross. It is the latter who gives us courage to face the terror, the "abyss of nothingness," and helps us to realize our divinization in Christ. The fire that Hesiod's Prometheus would steal is nothing other than our own identity and our spiritual freedom. Merton concludes that "The one who loves Christ is not allowed to be [Hesiod's] Prometheus."[18]

He also describes the historical figure of Herakleitos as one who awakens us to our destiny, to the fire that is within us. His fire is the key, says Merton, to the spiritual enigma of the human person. His protest is that of the Dionysian mystic. "True peace is the 'hidden attunement of opposite tensions'—a paradox and a mystery transcending both sense and will, like the ecstasy of the mystic."[19] He relates Herakleitos' effort to the Logos, God's Wisdom manifest in creation. God's Wisdom is "not so much at work in nature but rather at play there," Merton suggests.[20] Wisdom seeks to awaken the disciple "by paradox without mercy." Merton describes Herakleitos' protest as "the protest of love . . . against power." So Herakleitos has rebelled against the Olympian order. "He preferred loneliness to the warm security of the collective illusion."[21] Herakleitos' "parables" speak to us because they are closer to the spiritual and intellectual climate of the gospels than much that pretends to be spiritual. So he points to the appropriation of Herakleitos' intuition of patterns and harmonies in a famous poem of Gerard Manley Hopkins, "That Nature Is a Herakleitian Fire and the Comfort of the Resurrection," in which Hopkins celebrated this "clearest-selved" spark of the divine self in the human person. The monk interprets Hopkins as wrestling with the angel of tribulation to reach resurrection, and "I am all at once what Christ is . . . immortal diamond." Merton concludes that while Herakleitos could not yet know Christ, he already had an intimation of immortality and of resurrection.[22]

The envelope in which this essay on Herakleitos was written is the monk's "Letter to an Innocent Bystander," from Part Two of *The Behavior of Titans,* entitled "The Guilty Bystander." The title's irony presages the title of the journals of this period, *Conjectures of a Guilty Bystander.* Merton directs his remarks to fellow intellectuals, the ones who claim to be innocent and without responsibility by virtue of their identity as intellectuals. The fact of the matter is that they are actually "power-seekers" over others. Merton confesses that his own and other intellectuals' emptiness is activated in their exploitation of others.[23]

Finally, in 1962, at the height of his transition to a new affirmation of the world, Merton published another myth-centered "Letter." This one, addressed to South American fellow-poet Pablo Antonio Cuadra,[24] describes the "cold war" battle in the West as the mythic Gog and Magog apocalypse of Ezechiel 39–40. Turning his attention to the future of the southern hemisphere, the Third World peoples of Latin America, South Africa, and Australia, he characterizes their spiritual outlook on life as uniquely concrete, hieratic, intuitive, and affective, as distinct from the West's abstract, pragmatic, rationalistic, and aggressive manner. The great sin of the West, he claims, is an *"unmitigated arrogance towards the rest of the human race."*[25] Conquering missionaries and colonizers had claimed undue superiority when their victims were humanly equal, and in some important ways superior. Merton echoes Karl Rahner's provocative insight on the "anonymous Christian" when he speaks of these Third World cultures as being an opportunity to encounter Christ. "It is my belief," says Merton, "that we should not be too sure of having found Christ in ourselves until we have found him also in the part of humanity that is most remote from our own."[26] Pointing to the ignored and suppressed message of cultures in India and China, the cultures of the Maya and of the Inca, he remarks, "No one considered that the children of the Sun might, after all, hold in their hearts a spiritual secret."[27] Five years later Thomas Merton's poetry returned to these spiritual secrets to awaken the post-Christian Western culture.

How did Thomas Merton come to rework the coordinates of faith in a post-Christian world? What possessed him to subvert the domesticated images of an all-powerful Christ through his parables of the kenotic Christ? The twin essays "The Unbelief of Believers" and "Apologies to an Unbeliever" in *Faith and Violence* capture something of his irony in their very titles. But they also orient Merton's readers to the disturbing new direction of his antipoetry. These two essays reflect a debt Merton felt and which he had recorded in the preface to *New Seeds of Contemplation*—a debt to what he there called the spirituality of people without formal religious affiliations. He now redefines the context for his prose and poetry in these frank and provocative writings, first published in 1965 and 1966. Martin E. Marty's *Varieties of Unbelief* precipitated the meditations of "The Unbelief of Believers." What Merton alerts his readers to, however, is not the dangers of nineteenth-century liberal atheism but to an indifferent, complacent pathology within modern secularity. He complains that apparent believers are being lured into institutionalized unbelief. Theologians have since dubbed this phenomenon of American belief in success, prosperity, individualism, the Puritan ethic, nationalism, and capitalist progress as "civil religion." The monk protests the pragmatism, sentimentality, and "tepid reassurances" which the marketing techniques of an affluent society invite. By contrast, he shares Marty's respect for the concerned atheist "whose unbelief implies the courageous assumption of loneliness, dread and risk." Much of supposed Christian faith, he finds, is merely "a deplorable cult of idols," with nationalism and the absolute authority of the state assuming the functions of a church. He ends this essay with the hallmark of his mature spirituality, a summons to dialogue. True dissent from civil religion means, for Thomas Merton, to show "the need for spiritual awakening and constructive analysis."[28]

"Apologies to an Unbeliever" is among the most important of Merton's essays. He rarely, if ever, published a more engaging or exploratory reflection on faith in the post-Christian world. Intending the essay to "scandalize" some Christians, he confesses embarrassment for the inadequate and impertinent falsifications of religion which have been inflicted upon people, and is grateful they have refused its arrogance. But, more significantly, Merton apologizes for those who exaggerate the difference between him and unbelievers. His new attitude shies from patronizing, and corrects the label of "unbeliever," claiming that "*Non*-Believer" more accurately describes modern persons who neither reject nor accept religious belief.

The single purpose of "Apologies to an Unbeliever" is to beg pardon for the affront to the conscience of sincere nonbelievers. Merton finds in his own faith a duty to love and to respect the nonbeliever's frailty and perplexity. To do otherwise betrays, for him, only self-justification and inadequate faith. He refuses the salesmanship that trivializes religion into "religious vaudeville." Then, he turns to Rahner's diaspora model for the survival of Christianity in a secular, nonbelieving world. Mentioning Christians' illusions about ecclesial institutions continuing to play dominant roles in society, "I very much doubt it!" Merton apprises, and predicts a "more and more marginal" existence for Christianity. Merton shifts to a higher gear with the admission that some theologians say nonbelievers may be "closer to God" and possibly more believing than many believers. "One must first be able to listen to the inscrutable ground of his own being, and who am I to say that your reservations about religious commitment do not protect, in you, this kind of listening?"[29]

The relevance of Merton's apology to his venture into antipoetry is found in his concern for language and metaphors of God's silence and absence. Familiar communication between God and human persons has broken down. Merton finds that this makes our attempts to reveal God to nonbelievers "border on blasphemous idiocy." Our language, he confesses, hides rather than reveals God. He points to the Second Vatican Council's "Pastoral Constitution on the Church in the Modern World" (*Lumen Gentium,* 19) for an explicit admission of our deficiencies in communicating God. The complexity of our dilemma is magnified for Merton when the very conventional religious routines do not celebrate God's presence in the world, but "only make the spiritual void all the more embarrassing." To admit this failure is to accept "an existential religious fact"— that the silence of God in human experience reveals to us something about God "in new and disconcerting ways" that we have yet to learn "to decode." Now, in the antipoetry's ironies, Merton could find an analogue for this silence of God in the Christ of kenosis. He concludes his apology with an appeal for dialogue, a dialogue which implies an intelligent communication: "Half of talking is listening." But, more importantly, it is a conversation of equals who listen with "compassionate respect" because they share a "common predicament." He is now both lyric and lucid in his statement of identity:

> My own peculiar task in my Church and in my world has been that of the solitary explorer who . . . is bound to search the existential depths of faith in its silences, its ambiguities, and in the certainties which lie deeper than the bottom of anxiety. In these depths there are no easy answers, no pat solutions to anything. It is a kind of submarine life in which faith sometimes mysteriously takes on the aspect of doubt when, in fact, one has to doubt and reject conventional and superstitious surrogates that have taken the place of faith. On this level, the division between Believer and Unbeliever ceases to be so crystal clear. It is not that some are all right and others are all wrong: all are bound to seek in honest perplexity. Everybody is an Unbeliever more or less! Only when this fact is fully experienced, accepted, and lived with, does one become fit to hear the simple message of the Gospel—or of any other religious teaching.[30]

For Merton, our twentieth-century religious problem remains a problem about believers, not about unbelievers or atheists. Faith grown cold, rigid, sentimental, becomes, for him, lost in "pontifical and organizational routines, or evaporated in activism and loose talk." Here brewed the imagery and irony of Merton's antipoetry.[31]

The monk-turned-hermit indeed roared in a new tunnel. This newly defined context for the dialogue between believers and nonbelievers proved a fertile matrix for reimagining faith in the hidden Christ. The author of *The Seven Storey Mountain* could never again be completely uncritical of authority in the church or in secular society. "Conscience is a bronco well-busted," he complained in *The Geography of Lograire* (*CP*, 516). Now Merton used a prophet's words to question the institutional church's complicity in evil, its contributing to the maintenance of systems that liquidated persons in the name of seemingly higher values. The custodians of the Christian myths and symbols stood with clay feet. Small wonder that Merton could sarcastically quip in *Cables to the Ace,* "Consult your ordinary delay / Or wait for the clergy" (*CP*, 428).

An essay written in 1963 but only published in 1981 is indicative of the evolution in Merton's questioning of ecclesial authority. The immediate object of "The Trial of Pope Pius XII: Rolf Hochhuth's *The Deputy,*" is Hochhuth's new drama, which Merton the monk panned as ponderous, crude, a labored melodrama, complete with naive stage directions that become interminable sermons.[32] He finds it nowhere equal to the critique of the church in Dostoevsky's Grand Inquisitor, or the works of Berthold Brecht, or even Sartre's *The Flies.* He claims its appearance significant because it coincided with eruptions of racism in the United States, the Cuban missile crisis, and the struggle of the Curia to retain power during the Second Vatican Council's revolutionary deliberations. The crux of the matter is the portrayal of Pope Pius XII as indifferent and unwilling to protest Hitler's Holocaust of Europe's Jews. What Merton does acknowledge is that the issue of the church's use of power is both momentous and serious. He refuses to accept Hochhuth's interpretation of the pope as a politically expedient authority whose expediency hid behind the "spiritual" character of the church. He charges that the dramatist crudely states the legitimate question: When faced with the critical choice between the law of love of God and human persons, and the practical, immediate dictates of power politics, is the church so accustomed to choose the latter that it is no longer able even to see the former? Does the church so consume itself with self-preservation and power that the appeal to blind obedience impedes the dictates of personal conscience?

Merton laments the fact that the image of a "super-Pope" and the official authorities of the church remain a stumbling block for contemporaries. He coyly forms the question: "Is it not the habit both of some who can speak officially in the name of the Church, and even of some who cannot, to evoke this image in support of interests and projects which are not, to put it mildly, those of God and of the Church?"[33]

Merton's correspondence during this period is more straightforward in addressing the underlying questions about authority conjured up by Hochhuth's play. To W. H. "Ping" Ferry he writes on July 1, 1964, about the nonachievements of the second session of the Second Vatican Council under Pope Paul VI. He parallels it with *The Deputy's* baroque image of the papacy. His diagnosis is that curial power is an essential element of such an idol. He claims that the machinery (read, system) of the Holy Office abrogates the powers of the papacy and becomes "in the end the real seat of infallibility." Merton was never more critical of church authority abused than in the prophetic lines that follow:

> This means of course that infallibility becomes organized and to some extent anonymous (no longer a charism but an institution) and of course that means one thing: totalism and the monolith. But if that is it, then what happens to the guys down the line? Do they suddenly acquire rather frightening obligations to dissent? There is going to be quite a crisis one of these days. . . .[34]

He writes to E. I. Watkins in December 1963 that the Catholic notion of obedience and authority has come to depend on a concept of papal political advantage and power. Merton describes the "grim" picture of the Curia's "shocked exasperation" about the bishops at the council daring to question curial procedures. He turns the tables by accusing the curial officials of practicing obedience in the context of their own power, obeying a pope "as long as he plays their game." With stinging sarcasm he notes that the First Vatican Council's definition of papal authority apparently was understood "as a definition of curial omnipotence."[35] He writes a more sanguine January 1964 letter to Bishop John J. Wright, but speaks directly of the "temptation" of confusing church policy in diplomatic affairs with obedience in faith.[36] To Gordon Zahn, the pacifist historian of German Catholic opposition to the Nazi regime, he writes bluntly on December 13, 1963, about the Vatican and the hierarchy's "abominable and moss-grown concept of authority and obedience." He concludes by again remarking the awful literary quality of Hochhuth's play, but wisely questions whether it is to the church's advantage to attempt to keep it off the stage.[37]

A muted facet of Merton's enthusiasm for church reforms is found in his comments on the Tübingen theologian, Hans Küng. Merton reviewed Küng's book, *The Church, Reunion, and Reform,* a volume that won the Roman-educated Swiss theologian a wide hearing and celebrity among moderate and progressive bishops at the council.[38] Merton has just lamented the promulgation of the 1962 apostolic constitution, *Veterum Sapientia,* restoring Latin as the language for teaching theology, in a March 1962 letter to John Tracy Ellis. "Poor Bride of Christ, and poor Bridegroom of the Bride," he moans. "We all contribute something to her wrinkles." Then he turns immediately to Küng's book, promising that it will "gladden your heart." He lionizes it as "one of the most forthright, direct and powerful statements of our actual condition and problem that I have ever seen." He calls it a portent, predicting that it will have "a terrific impact." Yet Merton was hardly naive about Küng's controversial theology. In an April 1963 letter to Gordon Zahn he mentions that Küng did not show up for a visit to the abbey, as planned, during Holy Week. He wonders if the coincidence of the apostolic delegate's plans for a visit (which did not happen) at the same time affected Küng's decision.[39] One could imagine fewer more volatile personifications of the authority question than the scene of Küng and the apostolic delegate, together on the abbey doorstep.

Meanwhile, Merton weathered the trials and indignities of ecclesial and religious superiors' censorship of his writings on the issue of war and peacemaking. He had pressed and won his two-decades-long case to live the eremetic life as an authentic Cistercian charism. The Second Vatican Council had burst open the confines of a reactionary, integralist self-understanding of the church. And Christian America's Vietnam War wreaked havoc with aerial assaults in southeast Asian countries where Buddhists were expendable, just as Merton prepared finally to travel east and to draw a wealth of wisdom from their monastic traditions. In a rare interview in 1967 with Thomas McDonnell, Merton pronounced that the great crisis in the church is a crisis of authority precipitated because the church, as institution and organization, has overshadowed the reality of the church as a community of persons united in love and in Christ. He now charged that obedience and conformity with the impersonal corporation-church are a fact in the life of Christians. "The Church is preached as a communion, but is run in fact as a collectivity, and even as a totalitarian collectivity."[40] In January 1967 he wrote to W. H. Ferry about the celebrated case of Charles Davis's leaving the priesthood and the Roman Catholic Church. He regretted this extreme solution, but even more complained about the real problem of reforming the church people who remain inside. He found Davis's points unassailable. "Authority has simply been abused too long in the Catholic Church and for many people it just becomes utterly stupid and intolerable to have to put up with the kind of jackassing around that is imposed in God's name," Merton concluded. Three months later he wrote about a warm letter from Brazil's Archbishop Helder Camara, whom he described by contrast, as "a live Bishop and not a rack for episcopal robes."[41] The irony and questioning of authority combined to evidence the mature freedom and a faithfulness to the depths of his religious experience which Thomas Merton now dared to voice in the syllables of antipoetry.

ANTIPOETRY

As early as 1957 Merton was teaching a novice who is the now-famous Nicaraguan poet, Ernesto Cardenal, who had joined the Abbey of Gethsemani for a time and then returned to his native Central America to write and to pursue a contemplative spiritual ministry at Solentiname. He proved for Merton a conduit to emerging new currents in Latin American poetry circles. With the abbey's new daughter-house in Chile, direct contacts began to multiply. Merton's publisher, James Laughlin of New Directions Corporation, also kept him well supplied with this avant-garde literature. He began not only to read but to translate an entire network of poets from the southern hemisphere, poets whose spiritual vigor and warm humanity aroused his own poetic instincts: César Vallejo and Pablo Neruda (Peru); Pablo Antonio Cuadra, Enesto Mejia Sanches, José Coronel Urtecho, Angel Martinez, Alfonso Cortes, Azarias Pallais, and Ernesto Cardenal (Nicaragua); Jorge Carrera Andradé (Ecuador); Nicanor Parra (Chile); Manuel Bandeira and Jorge de Lima (Brazil); Octavio Pas (Mexico); Esther de Caceres and Susana Soca (Uruguay); and Victoria Ocampo and Miguel Grinberg (Argentina).[42]

In 1966 he was visited by Chilean Nicanor Parra, whose "antipoems" heralded a significant new development in the realm of contemporary poetry. Merton had already translated some five poems from Parra's *Versos de Salon* (1953–62) that appeared in the major English edition of Parra by Miller Williams.[43] They were contemporaries, Merton being only a year older than Parra. Merton's fascination with antipoetry was excited.

What did Merton read in this movement of antipoetry? By way of retrospect, he offered two illuminating comments in the context of his 1968 Asian journal. What proves striking about antipoetry for Merton is the very positive effort on the part of the poet to reclaim the purity of poetic language. In that sense, despite the forbidding first impressions, it remains a humanistic, affirmative project. He saw the convergence of the contemplative life and the poet's art in creating "a new experience of time" that was not a "stopgap" but a *temps vierge,* "a space which can enjoy its own potentialities and hopes—and its own presence to itself," he wrote. It would be a *"compassionate* time, rooted in the sense of common illusion and in criticism of it." He referred to the anticulture precipitated by a mass culture that stifles creative work "by the sheer volume of what is 'produced'":

> In which case, poetry, for example must start with awareness of this contradiction and *use* it—as antipoetry—which freely draws on the material of superabundant nonsense at its disposal. One no longer has to parody, it is enough to quote—and feed back quotations into the mass consumption of pseudo-culture.[44]

Feeding back the culture's nonsense created a definite "static" which was enough to show inner contradictions in the system. Merton compared it to the Madhyamika ("middle path") school of Buddhism, forerunner of the Mahayana Buddhist tradition, which showed an opponent the absurdity of his position through principles and arguments already accepted by him. He repeated this sense of antipoetry later in the journal-notebook of complementary readings which he undertook on the Asian trip.

> The antipoet "suggests" a tertiary meaning which is *not* "creative" and "original" but a deliberate ironic feedback of cliche, a further referential meaning, alluding by its tone, banality, etc., to a *customary and abused context,* that of an impoverished and routine sensibility, and of the "mass-mind," the stereotyped creation of quantitative preordained response by "mass-culture."[45]

It proves helpful to return to Merton's 1966 essay on "Camus and the Church" to gain further insight into his experiments with antipoetry. As we have already examined, this article is typical of his efforts to address the problem of "belief" and illusions in the contemporary world. In the middle of the article he addresses the dilemma of a child's loss of innocence as she is educated into the environment of a criminal system's values: oppression, massacre, torture, humiliation, exploitation. He names these the structured axes of a world "penetrated and informed by sin." We are not born in paradise, so holiness must begin with a breach: thus, Camus's "Rebel." Merton concludes this article by identifying the most intimate and profound level of Camus's dialogue with Catholicism—"an appreciation of language as ultimately a metaphysical problem." Camus looked above all to the writer and artist to carry out the prophetic task of his "Rebel." Language occupied a pivotal role in the process of revolt against the absurd. Bruce Parain, Camus's friend who studied extensively the phenomenology of language (and converted to Catholicism in the late forties), had helped the French-Algerian author come to this insight. Camus posed the question: Can language make sense if there is no God? The alternative, he saw, was "a series of more or less arbitrary noises in the solitude of a mute world." With the possibility of language, communication arises as a possibility, and with it the possibility of a community of persons. Merton admired how Camus seized Parain's respect for words: "the great task for man is not to serve the lie." And so he admired the declaration, "To name a thing wrong is to add to the miseries of the world." He quotes Camus's remark, in a review-article of a Parain book, that our age needs not gods but a dictionary!

> Our task is not to burst out into the dazzle of utter unadulterated truth but laboriously to reshape an accurate and honest language that will permit communication between men on all social and intellectual levels, instead of multiplying a Babel of esoteric and technical tongues which isolate men in the specialities.[46]

Here was a sober attempt to give the world back its language, to rescue us from the tyranny of logical positivism's absurdities and to open us to communication and community. It cues us to the driving force behind Merton's late antipoetry. *Cables to the Ace* and *The Geography of Lograire* attack the "complex, unclear, evasive and bureaucratic language" of society and the church that timidly obscures and manacles the truth. He speaks of "the sheer quantity of printed and broadcast doubletalk" that must be confronted by human consciousness. The simplicity and austerity of this new language would not degrade, but return words to common use, "bringing them to the

honesty that is required for them to be purified of lies and hatred."[47]
We are tugged back to the environs of the true, or inner, self.

Michael Mott has excavated from Merton's simultaneous critiques
of the peace and liturgical movements a trenchant revelation about
the monk's use of language. It sheds much light on the antipoetry.
Merton had cautioned in a 1963 essay that we must guard against "a
kind of blind and immature zeal . . . which represents precisely a frantic compensation for the deeply personal qualities which are lacking
to us." He immediately defines the zealot as a person who loses the
self in a cause, only, paradoxically, to immerse the self in one's own
willfulness. This is hardly the self-forgetfulness of the inner self "in
Christ." The zealot, says Merton, is "alienated by the violence of his
own enthusiasm: and by that very violence he tends to produce the
same kind of alienation in others."[48] "The giveaway was language," Mott
cues. Both the progressive zealot and the entrenched conservative used
language as "unreal rhetoric — the rhetoric of sounding abstractions,
of violence, of evasions." Mott contrasts the language of the free and
unobsessed persons as *parrhesia,* or "prophetic speech." It was the Greek
patristic term Merton had employed in *The New Man* to describe the
discourse between God and humans: Adam, Job, and the mature contemplative. But Merton enlarges the circle of those who use such free,
prophetic speech until it includes even those outside the church. His
1967 essay, "War and the Crisis of Language," addresses in prose form
the same issues as the antipoetry. Language can unite or divide human
persons. It can be used well or badly.[49]

Merton wrote as a poet "sensitive to the sickness of language" that
prompted a declaration of war on conventional language. His complaint
began with official Washington statements about the Vietnam War.
They were symptomatic, for him, of a deeper illness, what he called
"an antilanguage, a concrete expression of something that is uttered
in fire and bullets rather than in words." Violence had replaced civilized communication. He quoted from a Swedish poet, Gunnar Eke-
lof's "Sonata for Denatured Prose":

> crush the alphabet between your teeth yawn
> vowels, the fire is burning in hell vomit and
> spit now or never I and dizziness you or never
> dizziness now or never.
>
> we will begin over.[50]

The monk found the "God is Dead" theology infected with the same "spastic upheaval of language." But he turned his attention to the language of advertisements which hypnotized and drowned all but the deaf. An *Arpege* perfume ad proved a case in point, with its "foolproof tautology" posturing as a definitive statement that has nothing to do with reality: the perfume coifs you with a new identity, an experience of "self-enclosed narcissism woven of misty confusion." The *you* made imminently lovable by *Arpege* usurps, for Merton, the ultimate conceptions of theology and metaphysics. He laments the distorted, denatured language which results. It was the language and logic of Hitler with his "final solution," a logic of power and absurd conclusions that Merton found in all war makers. He hauntingly quotes one example of Hitler's weeping over the ruins of Warsaw: "How wicked these people must have been to make me do this to them."[51]

THE ANTIPOETRY AS A THEOLOGICAL ANTHROPOLOGY

Merton maintains a dominant poetic vision throughout *Cables to the Ace* and *The Geography of Lograire:* by a transformation of consciousness, we human persons can come to recover our essential dignity as persons, created in the image of God. The problem of the person vis-à-vis the deluding social organization magnifies in these elusive poems. They continue the themes struck in poignant prose poems found two years earlier in *Raids on the Unspeakable.* The world is even more damaged and depraved in the antipoems than in the early poems, where the monk had scorned cities and society. But Merton's perception of God's mercy and compassion erupts in sublime new images of the capacity for human wholeness in the wake of sin, tragedy, terror, and evil.

Both poems open with descriptions of themselves as "mosaics." The word aptly names the form Merton employs in these lengthy, sometimes sprawling collections. Readers may recall Merton's enthusiasm for the early Cuban poem "Song for Our Lady of Cobre," in which he wrote, "all the pieces of the mosaic earth / Get up and fly away like birds." Even more compelling is his recollection in *The Seven Storey Mountain* of the mosaics in Rome, before his conversion, where the artists first touched his mind and heart with a knowledge of "who this Christ was." In the "Author's Note" introducing *Lograire* he speaks of "the first opening up of the dream" and recollects how a poet repeatedly undertakes to build his dream, which is "experienced as yours and mine as well as 'theirs.'" He concludes this introduction to what he envisioned as "a longer work in progress" with an affirmation that marks both poems. The living and the dead participate, he says, "in the work of constructing a world and a viable culture." But the route now will be through satire and irony.

CABLES TO THE ACE

The depth of Thomas Merton's literary gift reveals itself in *Cables*. Merton repeatedly alludes to T. S. Eliot's *The Waste Land*, the axis of modern poetry, and evokes Shakespeare's *The Tempest* by introducing the persona of Caliban, antipoet and slave. The eighty-eight "cablegrams" of varying length and form include colloquial language, French poems, excerpts from writers as varied as Ortega y Gasset and Meister Eckhart. Some are slang-riddled, or laden with surrealistic images. Others are highly esoteric, delving into Zen philosophy. When the poet tells us in the prologue that he "has changed his address and his poetics are on vacation," he forewarns us that, "He is not roaring in the old tunnel." Any interpretation of these works therefore resembles an asymptote, stalking after meaning in endless nuances and allusions. Concentrating in particular on Merton's efforts to approximate a theological anthropology and a kenotic christology, our study will focus on three controlling symbols: (1) cables; (2) the ace; and (3) the identity of the human person.

Cables

The poem opens with an italicized epigraph: *"Lament of Ortega. The crowd has revolted. Now there are bathrooms everywhere. Life is exempt from every restriction."* Most telling in this indelicate satire is the parody on authentic "lamentation," a word that integrates grief and sorrow within a larger hope. It proves an important cue. The echoes of Camus's "Rebel" in the revolt of the crowd plays ironically on the fact that authentic rebellion comes not through mass culture but through the solitary and heroic struggle of conscience. The specter of the fascist state's tyranny, through the Ortega y Gasset reference, contrasts with the love that impels Camus's revolt.

The first cable, which speaks of "Edifying cables," of "societies doomed to an electric war," brings to mind Søren Kierkegaard's title, *Edifying Discourses*. But because "Cables are never causes," Merton cautions us against reading them as imperatives. He elaborates in cable 22: "Over the door of Hell is written: '*Therefore!*'" Anthony Padovano has suggested that cables recall for Merton the cablegrams that announced his father's imminent death of a brain tumor and his brother's death at sea during World War II. The letter from his mother announcing her death to the six-year-old boy was like such a cable.[52] In each instance, cables are associated with an unresolved lamentation in Merton's autobiography. They connote emotional distancing, a cold, antiseptic announcement of separation. And the final, startling cablegram had yet to come from Bangkok, announcing the sudden, accidental death of Merton himself. At a more general level, cables are a means of communication. They are thin, cryptic, ambiguous, but the typical means of interpersonal language in a deteriorating culture. From the opening "vroom vroom vroom of the electric guitars" in *Cables,* Merton mocks the electric gadgetry that gives a pseudo-animation to the "electric jungle" world. He had termed it the "Faustian tendencies" of the modern world's scientific-technological culture in *Redeeming the Time.*[53] By satirizing, he conjures up an underlying positive vision, a summons to reclaim a deeper identity.

At another level "cables" connote connections, such as the cables stretched to support a bridge. The image suggests linkage, an important metaphor to reverse alienation. There is journey, search, transport, and motion associated with the bridge. The cables of the bridge's structure support by distributing stress and tension.

Finally, since cables are frequently coded, Merton plays with the symbol to suggest the necessity of "decoding" or unscrambling the codes to make them intelligible. This occurs throughout the poem with the metaphor of a moral code or duty. In cable 18 a character parodying Eliot's J. Alfred Prufrock "worries about the code." The guards in cable 22 revere "the GREAT MEANING" and come down upon "Another one who has shirked his duty." "All their disciplines will *speak!*" Merton warns. In cable 52 he mocks "the comedy of orders" of the ants, each with "his appointed task" in the anthill. Finally, in cables 67 and 69, Merton satirizes the "imperatives" that characterize the banalities of our culture. These social conventions mask an underlying identity for Merton. It is reminiscent of his interpretation of the Genesis 3 story: sin is not so much a matter of moral evil as a more pervasive, deeper ontological lapse.

The imaginative use of Shakespeare's *The Tempest* serves to unify the *Cables*. Throughout his own last poetic testament published before his death Merton alludes to elements of the Bard's final play. The character of Caliban, candidate for antipoet *par excellence,* provides Merton a persona who intricately and dramatically integrates the poem's themes.⁵⁴ In cables 6, 22, 24, 44, and 88, this abuser of language figures directly. His symbolic value proves threefold: (1) a figure of transgression in cable 44, "Future of transgression. It is in the homes of Caliban. A splendid confusion of cries";⁵⁵ (2) a figure of unnurtured nature harking back to Prospero's words in *The Tempest,* "A devil, a born devil, on whose nature / Nurture can never stick! on whom my pains, / Humanely taken, all, all lost, quite lost!" (IV.i. 215–17); and (3) a figure of the perversion of human language, the medium of communication and the symbol of interpersonal relationships and community.

Caliban offers Merton an ideal antihero for the poem. As a symbol of unredeemed earth (whom Prospero announced as "thou earth" [II. ii.382]), Caliban personifies the inhabitant of the wasteland world of humanity that the monk confronts in *Cables.* Like Shakespeare, the poet here looses his own tempest, "the wide rain's foundering accelerations" (cable 77), imaged in the likes of autobiographical memory by "the banging old tempest in the rooms of Tenth Street" (cable 55). Having entranced his readers in cable 2, "two lids: the petals of sleep," he releases them from the antipoetic nightmare in the final cable, 88, as "the public sender of this island shuts down its trance."

It is worth wondering how much Mark Van Doren's Shakespeare course, some thirty years earlier at Columbia University, influenced *Cables.* Merton's imagination never let go of his mentor's analyses of the Shakespeare canon. Van Doren's 1939 study, *Shakespeare,* included a comment that almost anticipated Merton's use of this matrix, as well as the very symbols the monk would employ: "Any set of symbols, moved close to this play, lights up as in an electric field. Its meaning, in other words, is precisely as rich as the human mind, and it says the world is what it is."⁵⁶

Caliban fits easily into this "electric world" (cable 14) and jungle of the herd mentality, which allows the totalitarian state of Ortega y Gasset to thrive. Caliban's abuse of language connects the two foci of the poem: (1) the problem of communication; and (2) the problem of illusion. We have seen how effectively Merton mocks communication in the "Newscast" antipoem. In cable 3 he declares the antipoet's task, "Some of the better informed have declared war on language." After sustained attention to the problems of communication in the post-Christian modern environs, in cable 78 Merton delivers a description of his own antipoetry, strikingly distinct from his earlier lyrics:

> Love's wreckage is then left to die
> All around the breathless shores
> Of my voice
> Which on the coasts of larking meadows
> Invented all these children and their mischievous noises.
>
> (*CP*, 448)

The imagery of illusion focuses our interpretation of Merton's anthropology and kenotic christology. The obvious irony of Caliban as the antithesis of human dignity is evident from his inability to communicate. Merton creates an apocalyptic, mechanical, Hieronymus Bosch vision in cable 22: "Twelve smoky gates flame with mass-demonstrations. Power of Caliban. Mitres of blood and salt. Buildings as well-run machines with eyes and teeth. (Bosch)." A by-product of decadence is the human search for identity in objects, a search which proves illusory. The advertisements in magazine ads short-circuit the pilgrim in *Cables*. Cable 61 mocks the familiar Marlboro cigarette romanticism:

> I will get up and go to Marble country
> Where deadly smokes grow out of moderate heat
> And all the cowboys look for fortunate slogans
> Among horses asses.
>
> (*CP*, 434)

All contact on a fulfilling personal level is precluded in the Eliot-like wasteland of *Cables* because, as cable 3 alerts us, "Each one travels alone in a small blue capsule of indignation." Such solitary drivers in automobiles image for Merton a spiritual isolation and emotional sterility.

"Ace"

The symbol of the "ace" in *Cables to the Ace* proves the poet's center of gravity. He refers to his poet-classmate, Bob Lax, as the "ace" in *A Catch of Anti-Letters*.[57] One might find a sad reference to his pilot brother, whose aircraft crashed in the sea during World War II.

The poet himself might be imaged as such a daredevil of heights, with the imagery of cable 87:

> I am about to make my home
> In the bell's summit
> Set my mind a thousand feet high
> On the ace of songs
>
> .   .   .   .
>
> But birds fly uncorrected across burnt lands
> the surest home is pointless:
> We learn by the cables of orioles
>
> (*CP,* 453–54)

What is universally overlooked in analyses of *Cables* is the "ace" of a deck of playing cards. In various card games, the ace plays "high" or "low." The sequence can find the ace as the first card ("one" before the "deuce"), or as the last card, after the hierarchy of queen and king. The concluding stanza of cable 87 lends itself to this interpretation by identifying the ace with freedom.

> I am about to build my nest
> In the misdirected and unpaid express
> As I walk away from this poem
>
> Hiding the ace of freedoms
>
> (*CP,* 454)

As we will discover upon examining Merton's anthropology in *Cables,* the ironic imagination indeed introduces Christ in a mythic environs in the climactic cable 80 — but it will now, ironically, be Merton's familiar Christ of kenosis. If Christ is the "ace of freedoms," it is Christ-the-ace as "low," or empty of power and strength which abides, who again identifies with the wounded and seemingly bankrupt moments of human life. Even the world of *Cables* is not abandoned by Christ, but he comes "Slowly slowly" as the manifestation of God's unfailing, and inevitable, compassion and love. As William F. Lynch has reminded us, the low is indeed the high in such an understanding of christology.

The Identity of the Human Person

Five separate cables integrate Merton's thematic interest in theological anthropology in terms of the human fall from Paradise by sin. The resulting "human condition," as presented in *Cables,* is deprived of the nurture of grace needed to elevate and transform it. This foreshadows the poem's denouement, a parallel to *The Tempest's* theme of reconciliation. Cable 7, "Original Sin (A Memorial Anthem For Father's Day)," advises, "Weep, weep, little day / For the Father of the lame . . ." in two repeating refrains. Weeping occurs in the fact of antipoetry in the same cable, "Weep weep little day / for his walking and talking. . . ." We are told further:

> Weep little history
> For the words he offended
> One by one
> Beating them grievously
> With a shin bone
>   (*CP,* 399)

Cable 27 offers an ironic exclamation from a midget, "Hats off to the human condition!" This truncated person's saltue to Adam's progeny is sustained in the following cable's parody:

> The wounded football hero
> Is nominated to share
> In the human condition
> Which he smilingly calls
> "Straight fact."
>   (*CP,* 412–13)

Perhaps Merton's intention is to parody Eliot's "wounded surgeon" of *Four Quartets,*[58] who operates as a figure of Christ, healing us from "Adam's curse," for "The whole earth is our hospital / Endowed by the ruined millionaire."[59] The great irony of Merton's "wounded football hero" resides in the bankrupt culture's acclaiming "hero" status for an athlete, and a wounded one, at that. There is irony in his wound advancing his candidacy: "Now gains at last / A prizewinner's compassion." Despite the fact that his celebrity pose is "at home," "Smiling out of all the groggy news prints," his alien status is cryptically rendered: *"He is coming to investigate."*

In cable 32 Merton compounds the hero imagery with "a squad car / Full of heroes," whom he portrays as "Stand[ing] around / In good condition." Finally, in cable 42 we view again the wounded gridiron athlete whose response to the aero captain's cries, "Try harder!" pro-

duces "an artificial twelve mile gain" for "the undaunted martial am-
putee." The allusion in the earlier "Original Sin" poem to "the Father
of the lame," and "He went on one leg / Or maybe four," knits these
cables closely. "Do it harder and go further" pushes "The basketface
hero" to the limit. The captain responds with ambiguous, mocking
lines about the human condition: "I nominate your lost member / This
year's leader in profit and loss."

The football hero's mechanical, Pavlovian motions on the field remind a reader of Eliot's personality, Prufrock, in cable 18. Both characters share a cramped allegiance to their respective "codes." In Prufrock's
case, the stagnation arrests him from venturing "the overwhelming question": "Do I dare / disturb the universe?"[60] Merton has imaged blind
submission to a dehumanizing "code" with the indignity of the "rush-
hour" flight in cable 13 ("The Planet Over Eastern Parkway"):

> We expect 8 A.M.
> With cries of racers
> "Here is the entrance
> To the start"
> . . . .
> He sees executives
> Begin to run
> Over fresh cut graves
> The whole civic order
> Of salads
> (*CP,* 402)

The same preoccupation with thoughtless "imperatives / I mean
models" repeats in cable 67.

> If you act
> Act HOW
>
> Do this
> When you are missing
> Your home address
> HUSTLE!
> Because ours is a culture of bare-
> Faced literal commands:
>
> Go, Buster, GO!
> (*CP,* 436–37)

A chart of "Vital imperatives for Chester," lifted from advertisement pages, adds a layer of irony and specifics to cable 69.

Several of the cables address specific perversions of human potential. The monk parodies the exploits of modern Calibans who engage in a drunken pleasure frenzy of absurd behavior. Cable 17 presents the "urgency" of "sheer fascination," the "ambitious men" who mimic the stereotypes of advertisements in an exploitative *Esquire* magazine: "With friendliness and sex / At instant command." It is reminiscent of the same empty, recreational sex of Eliot's "typist" and the "young man carbuncular" in their sad wasteland. Merton returns to this illusion in cable 44: "Loose minds love the public muscles of death."

In cable 19, Merton parodies the experimental laboratory of behavioral scientists who seek "methods" to wire "the pleasure center" with cables and buttons to direct "the pencils of control." The height of irony is delivered by "Man's friendly rat the competitor," when the mad scientist "Found fifty persons all with wires in the pleasure center / They were being moved by rats." Humans can be reduced to performing by laboratory stimulus, a haunting premonition of the drug culture: "A long distance call / Via your own brain / . . . Split second doses of motivation." Merton sees the greatest threat when, "Political man must learn / To work the pleasure button." The inversion of human dignity reaches an apex in his sarcastic description:

> Ringing the septal region
> That earthly
> Paradise in the head
> Two millimeters away
> From my sinus infection.
>
> (*CP,* 409)

Here resound Eliot's lines: "I think we are in rats' alley / Where the dead men lost their bones."[61]

As early as cable 55 the poet has foreshadowed references to the resolution of the poem through an Advent scene. There he says:

> The bare tree. The faithless vow. We make the best of bad beginnings and hope the end will do better. Come, Dark-Haired Dawn!
>
> (*CP,* 432)

Christian overtones of the "bare" tree of Eden and the tree of the crucifixion juxtapose the fall with resurrection. The Advent prayer,

"Come," teases hope out of the "bad beginning." In cable 72 Merton announces a similar "Morning" that inaugurates a sudden reversal in the imaginative patterns of *Cables.* Springtime nature imagery unfolds, even when lightly parodied in the Wordsworth-Coleridge cable 74. A signal image triggers the entry into these last cables, which are more reminiscent of Merton's poetry of the forest; "The sound of the earth gets up to embrace the constant sky. My own center is the teeming heart of natural families." This contact with the transcendent, imaged as the symbolic sky, sparks the poet's imagination. He populates cables 75, 76, 82, and 87 with birds and their pirouetting (cable 73), only to end by building his nest in the last of these cables. The transition is marked in the opening of cable 77, a complex of nature images:

> Angels again
> Farmers of the mind
> In its flowers and fevers
> Fishers in the blue revolutions of oil.
> (*CP,* 446)

These angels escort the poet through the tempest ("Lost in the wide rain's / Foundering acceleration") and find the poem under the anti-poem ("They find me always upside down / In these reflected glooms"). There is an echo in this cable of Ariel's song of "sea change" in *The Tempest*[62] with his lines: "Clearly show me how to cross / The dubious and elastic / Rail way" of these "salt water flights." He delivers us into a new moment, out of the vortex of *Cables'* tempest, in cable 78, "The Harmonies of Excess." An abundance of earth imagery, the symbolic scene of the climactic garden of cable 80, "the hidden lovers in the soil" and life-giving "rain" ("the wet sun's poem"), all converge to offer a scene of springtime restoration and resurrection. The life force of these hidden lovers in the soil testifies to an indefatigable creative force. Merton reorients us from "Love's wreckage," which echoes the poem written on the occasion of his brother's death, to a higher spiritual principle at the heart of life. There is faith and hope in the mystery of germination.

> So those lovers teach April stars
> To riot rebel and follow faithless courses
> And it doesn't matter
> The seed is not afraid
> Of winter or the terrible sweetness

Of spring's convivial nightmare
Or the hot surprise and dizzy spark
Of their electric promise

For the lovers in the sleeping nerve
Are the hope and the address
Where I send you this burning garden
My talkative morning-glory
My climbing germ of poems.
                    (*CP*, 448)

Christ's appearance in cable 80 marks a return to the three gardens, Eden, Gethsemane, and Easter morning. His presence in the "ruins" of *Cables* parallels Christ in the ruins of his own Gethsemane. He is no stranger to desolation. Or to the rejection of the disciple who murmurs, "My regret!" in the third stanza. Easter's new horizon has been eclipsed for the disciple. Cable 69, "The Prospects of Nostradamus," presages this antipoetic irony of the empty tomb:

The Eighties open with a twotime Easter
Day of a monster clam
No decision and no sound
From the hermetic tomb
                    (*CP*, 439)

Merton's concluding lines of this cable reach back to cable 7, "Original Sin," where the poet has reflected on Adam's sin, humanity's sinfulness: "Weep, weep little history." The chronicle of our failures, our dehumanization of self and culture, resists the "ace of freedoms" which is manifest in Christ. We slumber. The antipoet struggles to shock and awaken us to a new consciousness.

The disciple will awaken
When he knows history
But slowly slowly
The Lord of History
Weeps into the fire
                    (*CP*, 449)

Thomas Merton has begun to struggle with a knowledge of history that does not fit easily into the myth of Christianity's "Lord of History." There is an unresolved tension in this climactic cable. It is a kenotic

Christ who weeps, unnoticed and himself "a pilgrim in exile,"[63] in this post-Christian crater of the spirit toured through *Cables to the Ace.* A final affirmation of the Christ manifest in historical poverty, emptiness, and rejection remains to be spoken in Merton's antipoetry with *The Geography of Lograire.* Midway through *Lograire,* Merton's personal reflections would echo this kenotic christology with a line that echoes *Cables to the Ace:* "Poles apart sighs ace in the cradle" (*CP,* 507).

THE GEOGRAPHY OF LOGRAIRE

When Merton set about writing the posthumously published *The Geography of Lograire,* the scope of his imaginative venture promised "a longer work in progress" ("Author's Note," *CP,* 457). This map of his consciousness was "only a beginning of patterns, the first opening up of the dream" that his poetic ambition could continue to enlarge. Upon first encounter with *Lograire* one thinks of the epic proportions of Walt Whitman's *Song of Myself,* William Carlos Williams's *Paterson,* or the career project of Ezra Pound's *Cantos.* Structured in terms of the four-directional mapping of human experience, Merton encompasses the universal by integrating mythic materials from the Mexican and Central American religious culture, seventeenth-century English Protestant dissenters, New Guinea cargo cults, native American ghost dances, and records of anthropological expeditions. The "North" canto of the poem brims with childhood and family autobiographical allusions, woven into a stream-of-consciousness design. In numerous prose sections of the poem he freely paraphrases or directly quotes lengthy excerpts of anthropological texts and myths. His "Author's Note" disclaims any "explicitly theological or even metaphysical" interests in the poem. But here, as throughout Merton's poetry, rich veins of a kenotic christology await.

The title of the poem has been clarified by Thérèse Lentfoehr's explanation that the real name of the French lyric poet François Villon was François Des Loges. From that surname, Merton created his own imaginary country of "Lograire." "Loges" also designates the cabins or huts occupied by foresters and woodcutters. In addition to Merton's being one-time chief forester of Gethsemani Abbey, Lentfoehr saw "an immediate relevance" to his hermitage on a rising, wooded knob near the monastery ("Notes," *CP,* 596–97).

The theological anthropology of *Lograire,* like *Cables,* comes through

Merton's lacerating irony. To focus upon this interpretative key to the poem, this analysis will investigate: (1) a résumé of the myriad episodes of human exploitation which Merton recapitulates in the poem and a vision of the implicit dignity of the human person that he finds, ironically, in the lamentation of exploited victims; and (2) the horizon of Merton's christology articulated through Christ's coming in weakness, poverty, and exile to the marginalized victims who have suffered history's abuses.

Lograire's panorama of human exploitation, portraying persons robbed of their innate dignity, is distinct from *Cables'* preoccupation with Western culture's inability to communicate. His attention has shifted to the saga of historical moments of degradation. His perspective comes from the resilient hopes of the weak, the abused, and damaged of the earth, whom we have come to call Third World peoples. He grounds this fact of sin in the Creation story's Cain-Abel conflict.[64] Then, from exploitations he moves to the lamentations and aspirations for a savior in each specific historical and cultural context. At this juncture Merton's christology matures to a final kenotic moment. In the process, his affirmation of a theological anthropology alerts us to the extent of human exploitation. It promises hope in the Christ whose epiphany surprises the victors when he empties himself in solidarity with the brokenness of their victims.

The Prologue of *Lograire* opens with the figure of a "Tarhead unshaven" captain of a slave ship. In section 9 of the Prologue he is "selling the sables / To Cain and Abel by design." Section 10 picks up the primordial "blood fight" between the mythic brothers, and God's consequent anger, with puns on the word "desire" and "ira," or anger.

> Desire desire O sign of ire
> O Ira Dei
> Wrath late will run a rush under the
> Funnel come snow or deadly sin
> Design of ire rather I'd dare it not dare
>
> (*CP,* 461)

In section 12 of the Prologue these separate symbols converge. The poet identifies the sacrificial black slave, "Jim Son Crow's" with the "Lamb Son's Blood," a paschal image identifying Christ with the dehumanized victim. The primordial Cain and Abel conflict is now played out in racial violence. God's wrath flares, unplacated.

Ira water Ira will not wash in blood
Dear slain son lies only capable
Pain and Abel lay down red designs
Civil is slain brother sacred wall wood pine
Sacred black brother is beaten to the wall
The other gone down star's spaces home way plain
                    (*CP,* 461–62)

In section 13, Merton recreates the angry sin of this murder with
Genesis imagery of the serpent in the garden: "Under shadow there
wait snake / There coil ire design father of Africa pattern." The sacrificial
motif continues in section 14: "And blood and ram and Isaac done
in a dare." The Prologue resolves in section 17, when Merton returns
to the fratricide with a prayer, "Hallow my Savior the workless spar-
row / Closes my old gate on dead tar's ira slam." The image of the
heel grinding down to destroy the cotton-head snake raises an ironic
question: "When will they all go where those white Cains are dead?"

In the first canto, "South," the contemporary black descendents of
the original African slaves are exploited. Merton begins with the question, "Will a narrow lane / Save Cain?" He records the abuse of blacks
by white racists. The unmistakable venom of the mitred Ku Klux Klansmen strikes in the predatory scene: "A raw Lamb coming from the hollow / Tied to killer Bishops for the feast." The first poem in this "South"
canto ends with a redemptive note to answer the opening question:
"One narrow lane saved Lamb's friend Paschal Cain."[65]

By the fourth poem of the "South" canto we arrive at the poem's
explicit confrontation with the false self, the source of fratricide and
all forms of dehumanization. In no one section of the poem does a
single, self-contained poem so articulate Merton's express design for
Lograire as in "Miami You Are about to Be Surprised." The point of
the poem is to alert us to the recesses of Cain in our own person. The
first half of the poem catalogues images and antipoetic jargon phrases
associated with the artificial holiday world of Miami: "make expensive
waves"; "You can't control so many / Wonderful people." The poet's
irony begins with the promise, "You are going to be pleasantly surprised by this," only to turn immediately to admit that the reader will
find himself "sweetly insulted." The epitome of antipoetry blares in
the capitalized lines:

IF YOU HAVE HEART FAILURE WHILE READING THIS
THE POET IS NOT RESPONSIBLE

(*CP,* 473)

The last lines of the first half of the Miami poem invite the reader to
the deeper central event: self-discovery. "Well you wanted to stay in
focus / But did you?" the poet asks sarcastically. A caution lurks in
the poet's imagery. "You are going to be warned / By a gourmet with
a mouthful of seaweed." The water imagery suggests again a Tempest-
like sea-change, as in *Cables.* The true, or inner, self can only be discovered by wrestling with identity. The poet promises to assist.

> He will try to help you decode
> Your own scrambled message
> Teach you your own way
> As if you wanted that
> Will you please try?
> (*CP,* 474)

The invitation is to accept the new being, a self congruent with the
freedom of Christ. "Our new method takes you out of the stream / Of
cold function," he promises. But it demands flexibility, the transformation of grace building on nature.

> But you have to bend
> Like all our other gamebirds
> While you are gently made over
> All the way down to the jawline
> (*CP,* 474)

The poet-dreamer warns, finally, of the cost of this new staying in focus,
the inner self's discovery. You will be charged "With more than the
usual bill"—"Unless you are pregnant," or already nurturing the new
life that will be the birth of the inner self.

The second historic irruption of the Cain and Abel conflict which
Merton selects is focused on African exploitation in "Thonga Lament"
and "Notes for a New Liturgy." In the latter, he satirizes the "big Zulu"
who "runs the congregation" by corrupting native patterns with Western pomposity. He styles himself with the credentials and authority
of exploitative missionaries:

I dreamt this Church I dreamt
Seven precious mitres over my head
My word is final.

(*CP,* 478)

The final four poems of the "South" canto turn to Mexico and the Yucatan civilization, where exploitation wreaks havoc on a third culture. In the poem, "Chilam Balam (Yucatan)," named after the native religious leader whose prophetic books are burned by conquering Westerners, the intrusion of white society brings domination and the dissolution of native identity.

Then the Lords
Rich in cotton
Meet Gods
Equal in voice to Gods
And those whose voices
Were not equal to God's voices
Were thrown into the well
To cry louder.

(*CP,* 487)

Stanza 7 of this poem announces "Lamentation" by the native priests. In the two previous stanzas Merton has described the new name of "Maya men" who brought laws and high pyramids and has recounted the unfolding chaos, "The plain smoked / All the way to the sea." The prophet Chilam Balam announces the new slavery imposed upon the natives, and the monk-poet plumbs the depth of their despair:

"But now we carry the sons of Itza on our backs like boulders."
And the priests have come to the end of submission. The end
    of desire.
They are about to destroy themselves because of the injuries
    done to our people.

(*CP,* 489)

He quotes from Chilam Balam a poetic description of exploitation in a poem, "Dzules (Yucatan)": "TO MAKE THEIR OWN FLOWER OPEN THEY SACKED AND SMASHED THE FLOWER OF OTHERS." The catastrophe eventuates in stanza 12's lament:

With brimming tears
We mourn our lost writings
The burned books
The flaming harvests
Holy maize destroyed
Teachings of heaven and earth
Destroyed.

(*CP,* 492)

An ironic equation is framed by Merton in stanza 18: "*Justitia* = vex Christians." He proceeds to describe the mushrooming degradation of aristocrats' wives prostituting themselves for their enemies. Stanza 23 climaxes the humiliation with the overt complicity of the church in the exploitation of natives.

Friars behind every rock every tree
Doing business
Bargaining for our souls
Book burners and hangmen
Sling the high rope
They stretch the necks
Lift the heads
Of priest and noble
Our calendar is lost
Days are forgotten

.   .   .   .

We count the pebbles of the years
In hiding:
Nothing but misfortune.

(*CP,* 493–94)[66]

In the "North" canto, the poem "The Ranters and Their Pleads (London)" rehearses a third scenario of exploitation in the seventeenth-century Calvinists' persecution of the fanatical English sect known as Ranters. Because these antinomians attacked the established church, the Bible, and the clergy in favor of the mystical Christ within the person, they aroused interest among the poor. Parliament quickly suppressed them, and charges of sexual license and unorthodox doctrine — such as a belief in a universal salvific will of God and "generall Restauration" (*CP,* 520)—shadowed the Ranters. Merton exposes the puritanical and pharisaic Christianity that condemned and oppressed them. He quotes the accusations against "An Abominable Ranter, Jacob Bauthemly," who wrote "that the Devil and Hell were 'the Dark Side of God'" (*CP,* 522). Sin becomes, for the Ranters, "the dark side of God but God is not the author of Sin / Nor does he will it." Echoes of Merton's own spirituality of the true, or inner self, are mirrored in the Ranters' aversion to a God of power and wrath.

> And my heaven is to have my earthly and dark
> Apprehensions of God to cease
> And to live no other life than what Christ
> Spiritually lives in me . . .
>
> (*CP,* 523)

The violent reaction to these belivers without doctrine or systems, a sect who discredit "the whistling, multifarious fancies and foolish fragments of thine own aiery brain and inconstant spirit," sears the reader's conscience.

> I saw a letter that one of them writ to a friend of his
> And at the bottom of the letter he writ thus:
> "From Heaven and Hell or from Deptford
> In the first yeare of my reconciliation to my Selfe."
>
> Then God does not hate? Not even sin?
> So heaven and hell are in Deptford, Woolwich,
>   Battersea and Lambeth?
>
> Burn him through the tongue!
>
> (*CP,* 524)[67]

A fourth illustration of exploitation, the most detailed in *Lograire,* chronicles events in Melanesia at the end of the nineteenth century. The cultural upheaval occasioned by the advent of white colonialists led to "cargo cults." Merton defined these moments of social crisis as messianic or apocalyptic movements which attempted to change injustices and perceptions of inferiority by magical and religious responses. The "cargo," or manufactured goods, which occupying whites easily procured, represented not just a desire for material possessions but for a respectable identity, an equality and fundamental human worth otherwise denied to the natives. Their efforts to have access to the same cargo tapped a spiritual and anthropological interpretation of the nature of the human person. Our antipoet charges that the native myth reflects a concept of rights that is at odds with our pragmatism. While we say that people have a right to what they are smart enough to acquire, the natives' "concept is that you have a right to the necessities of life *because you are a human being.*"[68] Merton indicts our myth-dream as "racist." Our arrogance, self-complacency, and exploitation of the Third World native means that we treat her or him as a "nonperson." The social and interpersonal relationships symbolized in the cargo natives' sharing their meal table encounters a line of resistance by the white man: You do not enter my home or eat at my table. The monk halts and reminds us of the "disturbing truth" about this fact. "This great human gesture has been raised to the highest religious dignity in the Eucharist by Jesus."[69] The exploiters resist the natives' invitation to share in a future in which both oppressor and oppressed are emancipated in a whole new order of social life.[70]

Merton records a telling example from anthropologist Bronislaw Malinowski's South Sea Island journal in "Cargo Songs": "I gave them portions of tobacco and they all walked away without posing long enough for a time exposure. My feelings toward them: exterminate the brutes." (*CP,* 551.) In the poem, "Sewende (Seven Day)," a parody about Seventh Day Adventist missionaries, he includes "Prayer of Kaum." The crux of the cargo cults is central to this scene of the native prophet's intercessory prayer, recollecting the theft and injustices of white exploiters:

> "O Father Consel you are so sorry
> You are so sorry for us Kanakas.
> You can help us we have nothing no planes
> No jeeps no ships not even hammers not even pants
> Nothing at all because Whiteman
> Steals everything and you are so sorry
> O Father Consel
> Now you send
> Something."
>
> (So sorry!)
>
> (*CP,* 557)

"Cargo Catechism" follows with nine prose paragraphs. It opens Genesis-like, "Here is how it all began." The New Guinea story about

Anut's creation and the paradise myth is followed by the native version of Noah, who builds a steamer which lands in Australia after the deluge. The racism theme unfolds when Noah's son Ham "watches and laughs when the old boy takes off his pants" after drinking whiskey. Ham is deprived of cargo "and sent to New Guinea to be a black man," while his brothers Shem and Japheth remain in Sydney. The fifth paragraph of the native catechism identifies the trouble with the Bible—it is incomplete. Instructions about cargo, "the best parts," have been torn out of the Bible, which natives claim has been rewritten by the Jews. Their corrected version reveals that their ancestors are alive and well, and, under God and the Catholics' supervision, are preparing cargo now labeled for New Guinea natives. "The problem now is how to get Cargo direct without recourse to ships and planes belonging to white men?" (*CP,* 558–59)

But natives resist the oppression. Merton's poem, "John the Volcano," recreates the action of natives against white merchants. In preparation for the apocalyptic and eschatological reversals of their plight, natives take price tags from all merchandise in the stores. When they also begin burying coconuts, Presbyterian missionaries interpret this as a subversive activity and authorities order them dug up. In "Dialog with Mister Clapcott," Merton reworks details of the 1923 murder of a British planter in New Hebrides when a cargo cult prophet incited natives to kill Europeans so that their ancestors would return in ships filled with cargo.

> Our dead shall rise
> Black shall be white
> Cargo shall come to Santo
> Ancestors come home in white ship
> From where you sent them you sonofabitch
> With all your papers.
>
> (*CP,* 569)

But even before this account of the natives' resistance, Merton has placed an emphasis on the key christological aspect. "Cargo Songs," the third section of the East canto's nine sections, provides an overture to his reworking of the cargo cults. Only after journeying through the later poems' saga of exploitation, however, is it apparent how the prospect of cargo introduces hope into the lives of the natives. The awaited steamer even bears a devotional name of Christ:

> Be ready for big Blackfela Catholic Steamer:
> Most Sacred Heart of Jesus Ltd
> Turns brown man white
> In a quaking boat
> Full of ancestors
> Speaking in tongues.

(CP, 550)

The christological connection with cargo cults becomes more direct in "Cargo Catechism."

> Jesus Christ is now in Sydney waiting to deliver Cargo to na-
> tives without the intervention of white men. He has a
> steamer and it is all loaded. But he does not yet have the
> proper clothing. Jesus Christ is waiting in a hotel room
> for someone to bring him a suit.

(CP, 560)

The advent of Christ into the world of natives deprived of human dignity becomes an expression of supreme hope. The impediment of his lacking "proper clothing" resonates with the cargo cult's constellation of metaphors of identity. Merton provides a poignant cameo of the welcome the natives prepare for "the Advent of the King" (who was not to be mistaken for conquering Germans or any other alien power in Melanesia). Natives had observed that whites kept flowers on their tables. So they begin to imitate the gesture as an expression of cargo theology. They are jailed because of the appearance of bouquets, a reaction reminiscent of the whites' paranoia over natives burying coconuts. There is a paradise consciousness in this symbolic resistance of the wounded, oppressed victims of white domination. Merton ends the catechism with echoes familiar to "Night-Flowering Cactus" and "Song for Nobody": "When those who displayed flowers were arrested, bouquets were made in secret and hidden under baskets. As soon as Jesus appeared with Cargo they would lift up the baskets. Their world would be all flowers" (*CP,* 560).

The poet concludes "John the Volcano" with a fundamental axiom of his theological anthropology. The speaker in the poem announces, "we two fit like the two halves of a cockle shell." The congruity of human persons, despite racial, ethnic, economic, religious, social, or any other difference, grounds Merton's vision. He appropriates this truth from below, from the experience of the violated, damaged natives. This attention to their expectation of Christ's coming fathoms the depths of his own kenotic christology and gauges the resiliency of authentic Christian faith that regenerates in disruptive historic moments.

The sixth and final illustration of exploitation drawn by Merton in *Lograire* occurs in the "West" canto. Poems 3 and 4 rehearse the 1869–90 ghost dance phenomenon of native Americans in Nevada and South Dakota. The parallels with cargo cults are extraordinary. The broken treaties and broken promises on the part of the United States government unleashed a wave of oppression and indignities perpetrated by whites which is even today being further exposed. Merton captures the tragedy of a Sioux leader's lament: "We are told if we do as white men do we will be better off but we are getting worse off every year" (*CP*, 587).

The hunger for human dignity, equality, and eschatological hope reverberates throughout the poem. Merton recreates the natives' indefatigable hope in a new order of justice: "Dr. Frank said that when the dead returned all the white people would disappear and half breed children would drop dead. There would be no more race conflict" (*CP*, 589). In *Ishi Means Man*, a contemporaneous collection of essays, Merton addresses the "alienated helplessness" of aboriginals. He describes the victims' sad pilgrimage. They are deprived of identity and reduced to inarticulate silence. He interprets the dances on the reservation as expressions of the natives' essential identity, as distinct from an identity derived solely from their relationship with white culture. The latter he names "systematic violence" and points out how this violence defines the limits of our white society and betrays our own inhumanity. Merton protests the demand that native Americans, Asians, blacks, and other peoples of color assume these "invented identities" which place them in subservient and helpless roles. He compares the ghost dance with Negro spirituals, the songs that voice a desperate appeal to supernatural power. Both are forms of an appeal for a religious liberator. He identifies structural flaws in the systems that manipulate and coerce the powerless who are excluded by our systems. Poverty, he says, is a symptom of those "deprived of the experience and responsibility as individuals and as communities."[71]

The global cry echoing through Merton's final testament, *The Geography of Lograire*, warns that "geography is in trouble all over Lograire" (*CP*, 516). In the second poem of the "West" canto, "At This Precise

Moment of History," his sarcasm turns on the political charades of the Vietnam War era. The "Shirley Temple" persona is forcefully parodied as the "voice of a sexy ventriloquist mignonne" to ridicule our violence. The doublespeak compounds in an auspicious premonition on Merton's part, delivered in 1968: "Governor Reagan thinks that nuclear wampums are a last resort that ought not to be resorted." He follows with a haunting intuition, learned from the lessons of *Lograire*'s historical rummaging: "All historians die of the same events at least twice" (*CP,* 585). The universality of sin, distorting human persons by violence and exploitation, throughout *Lograire*'s compass of cantos has reoriented Thomas Merton to the presence of the kenotic Christ in the crises of history.

ANTIPOETRY: ANTIDOTE FOR THE "DEATH OF HISTORY"

In *Raids on the Unspeakable,* a meditation on the Christmas mystery, Merton turned instinctively to the profound hopes aroused by a genuinely biblical eschatology. The vicissitudes of history had by now proved too stubborn for him to ignore, or to allow him to indulge in a Pollyannish version of Christianity. Recoiling from the "unutterable void" of armies, missiles, weaponry, bombs, concentration camps, race riots, and genocide, he asks, "Is it pessimism to diagnose cancer as cancer?" He recommends a vision of joy inseparable from tribulation, because human tribulation becomes joy when seen in paschal perspective as the victory of life over death. Merton resists a sense of eschatology that deteriorates into resignation to the apocalyptic, violent end of history by God's judgment and punishment. Rather, Christian eschatology draws us to God's future, which for Merton is "the final beginning, the definitive birth into a new creation," not the "last gasp of exhausted possibilities."[72]

The prologue to *Raids* orients the monk's audience to that book's intuition that poetry and irony are preferred paths to the "difficult insights at a moment of human crisis." His quarrel centers on the void underlying the much-heralded programs, good intentions, and public or official declarations that simultaneously "ring dead with the hollowness of the abyss." To transfigure the evil of our stricken world he points to the disruptive miracle of the coming of God in the paradigm of Christ. The christological core of *Cables* and *Lograire* radiates his con-

viction, voiced unequivocally in this prologue to the book about which
he confessed, "I think I love you more than the rest": "Christian hope
begins where every other hope stands frozen stiff before the face of
the Unspeakable."[73]

By 1966, when *Raids* was published, Merton's compassion in the wake
of mounting inhumanities expressed itself in in a new kenotic declaration. "[Christ] dwells in the solitude, the poverty, the indigence of every
man," he attested.[74] The overwhelming question with which he wrestled in these hermitage years remained, How do we communicate with
the modern world? His antipoetry, particularly *Cables*, eviscerates the
"pseudo-communication" that fabricates "pseudo-events" in history.
He calls our culture's hype about "making history" a grotesque illusion, leaving us with nothing more than the banalities of television
and advertising. The real events that concern the church are "saving
events," "the encounter of man and Christ in the reconciliation of man
with man." Merton deplores the church's complicity in reducing the
proclamation of the Good News of Christ to a convert-making effort
centered on pseudo-events and image-making.[75]

"The Death of God and the End of History," a 1967 essay later integrated in *Faith and Violence,* affords a unique insight into Merton's
mindset at the very threshold of his antipoems. He generally discredits
the "radical theology" of the "Death of God," which flashed across the
horizon of the mid-1960s like a meteor. His critique proves apprecia-
tive of the movement's roots in Bonhoeffer's embrace of worldliness,
a theological shift paralleled by the Second Vatican Council. But Merton faults the Death-of-God advocates on two accounts: (1) their anemic
conviction that the concept of sin is dead in the post-Christian, secular
world; and (2) their uncritical acceptance of the new secular myths,
which are historical, political, and pseudo-scientific, and their evacua-
tion of the religious and spiritual myths. Merton argues that this merely
substitutes history and politics for metaphysics and revelation. His underlying question again borrows from Camus's fear that the logic of history, manipulated by political lies, justifies murderous illusions. Have
we so fabricated our idea of "history" that we are poised for the "death
of history" and the "post-historic" and "post-political" era? he wonders. "Are we deluding ourselves in fabricating a new Christian myth
by which we reassure ourselves that this great political mosaic is in fact
a kind of jigsaw puzzle in which we (the initiates) know that what is
really being formed is the face of Christ?" He refuses to accept such

a gnostic "new system" from the technological world because its dictates compromise human freedom and are "impervious to revolutionary change." The only freedoms it offers are the choice of advertisements and what he once called the "cramp of the imagination," which hurls a "no" at the world in protests taking the form of "nihilism, dope, riot, crime or something else equally destructive and futile." The antipoet glimpses a more positive alternative. He can regret "the world" when it means militarism, greed, or exploitation—the web in which the false self, the ego becomes hopelessly entangled. He can embrace "the world" when it means solidarity with "those who are concretely victims of these demonic abstractions."[76]

Merton becomes pellucid at the conclusion of his essay on "The Death of God and the End of History" when he retrieves Thomas J. J. Altizer's *The New Apocalypse* from the shelf of God-is-dead theology. Because Altizer grounds his reflections on William Blake's prophetic acceptance of history, Merton perceives his creative iconoclasm as an attack upon the real idols of our time, which are not religious but secular idols: power, mystification, and super-control. Merton sees Altizer's attack upon such idols as a radical one because it does not merely reiterate Christendom's cozy compromises with the secular establishment's tyrannies. In the wake of such secularization, there is the temptation to one of two actions: to retreat from history, or to call the Lord of History to come and to damn everything. Altizer follows Blake's lead to meet the temptation "with the faith that a totally fallen history is finally the redemptive epiphany of Christ." Merton finds the God-is-dead theologian's phrasing "arresting" because it is a sophisticated "dialectical acceptance and reversal of 'fallen history.'" By saying "yes" to history, the poet-monk sees reversal of the exploitation mapped in *Lograire*. To situate Christ as liberator in both *Cables'* and *Lograire*'s climactic passages means to find there the kenotic Christ, empty of power and vulnerable as the exploited victims themselves. But it is this Christ from below, his unfailing epiphany made manifest in human poverty and indigence, who continues to convert us to the authentic responsibility we share for history. The trip through *Lograire*'s ironic cantos finds a prelude on the concluding page of "The Death of God and the End of History."

> [T]he reversal [of history] is not a rejection of history in favor of something else that is totally outside history. The reversal comes from within history

accepted, in its often shattering reality, as the focus of salvation and epiphany. It is not that the world of Auschwitz, Vietnam and the Bomb has
to be cursed and repudiated as the devil's own territory. That very world
has to be accepted as the terrain of the triumph of love not in the con-
demnation of evil but in its forgiveness: and this is certainly not an easy
truth when we confront the enormity of the evil![77]

Such disruptive crises of history have become privileged moments
in which Thomas Merton recognizes the presence of the kenotic Christ.
He discovers the mystery of the freedom of the divine mercy, which
alone empowers the damaged of the earth to reclaim their human dignity. Now history proves for our antipoet that, "Law is consistent. Grace
is 'inconsistent.'"[78]

6. A Common Spiritual Climate:
Merton's Christology in Interreligious Dialogue

Just hours before his accidental death in Bangkok, Thailand, on December 10, 1968, Thomas Merton made a telling remark to another participant at the conference of Benedictine and Cistercian monastic leaders in Asia. She expressed her bewilderment at the content of conference papers and talks during the first two days with a question: "Why are we now asked not to speak of Christ to people, when we have been sent precisely for this purpose?" Merton's immediate, direct reply orients us to the ultimate horizon of his christology: "What we are now asked to do," he said, "is not so much to speak any more of Christ as to let him live within us, so that people may feel him by the way he is living in us."[1]

The conversation confirms Merton's consistent preference for the sapiential tradition of theology, a theology grounded in experience. The monk prefers an immediate personal experience of Christ, rather than relying upon the dogmatic formulas, concepts, and abstract theories of speculative theology. His passion is for the simple imitation of Christ and is not first directed to the cognition of Christian truth. This chapter explores the final frontier of Merton's christological reflections, his dialogue with other religious traditions. In this context we will find new dimensions of his understanding of Christ's kenosis, or self-emptying of the power which abides in him, so that in weakness he might be newly manifest to us. The dangers of distorting the image of Christ in interreligious dialogue loomed large for the Abbey of Gethsemani's celebrity-hermit. Yet his sense of the possibilities for deeper contemplative and mystical experience of the true self "in Christ" converged with his appreciation of the spirituality of other world religions. As a case study, this chapter will evaluate Merton's christology of the "true

199

self" vis-à-vis Zen Buddhist experience of awakening to "emptiness,"
"no-mind," the ontological awareness of pure being, beyond subject
and object. Without our confusing Merton's Catholic Christian identity with Zen Buddhism, we can avoid a facile syncretism and discern
how his own christology developed through the dialogue.

The range of Merton's interreligious dialogue embraces not only Zen
Buddhism but also Judaism, Islam, Sufism, Taoism, Hinduism, and
Confucianism. In each instance, he looks at the problematic issue of
Christ for non-Christians. He writes to Zalman Schacter in February
1962 about the unconscious antinomy and complacency which Chris-
tians have placed between themselves and Jews:

> The suffering servant is One: Christ, Israel. There is one wedding and
> one feast, not two or five or six. There is one bride. There is one mystery,
> and the mystery of Israel and of the Church is ultimately to be revealed
> as One. As one great scandal maybe to a lot of people on both sides who
> have better things to do than come to the wedding.

Merton goes on to diagnose the Christian fault in imaging Christ as
Prometheus. This image had justified war, pogroms, crusades, Auschwitz, the atomic bomb. He describes Michelangelo's Christ in the Sis-
tine Chapel, "whipping sinners with his great Greek muscles." This
Promethean type "blow[s] the door wide open" for the poor, the helpless, the maimed, the blind. But Merton laments the inversion of the
authentic Christ of faith.[2]

Likewise, in dialogue with Islam, Merton probes deeper for a convergence of Christ and the Sufis' extinction of the false self:

> In Islam, too, the Sufis sought *Fana,* the extinction of that social and
> cultural self which was determined by the structural forms of religious cus-
> toms. This extinction is a breakthrough into a realm of mystical liberty
> in which the "self" is lost and then reconstituted in *Baqa*—something like
> the "New Man of Christianity," as understood by the Christian mystics
> (including the Apostles). "I live," said Paul, "now not I but Christ lives
> in me."[3]

While Judaism and Islam enjoy a special dialogue with Christianity
because they share a common religious root in Abraham and Sarah's
faith, Merton the sapiential theologian did not sustain or develop a
dialogue with either of them equal to the intensity of his study of Zen
Buddhism. Five texts provide a unique matrix for exploration of that

dialogue: (1) *Gandhi on Non–Violence* (1965); (2) *The Way of Chuang Tzu* (1965); (3) *Mystics and Zen Masters* (1967); (4) *Zen and the Birds of Appetite* (1968); and *The Asian Journal* (1973). By way of method, this chapter will examine in chronological order various essays in these volumes, keeping in mind three particular questions: (a) What does Merton see as the nature of the Christian-Buddhist dialogue? (b) How does he understand the analogous religious *experience* common to the wisdom theology of Christianity and Buddhism? and (c) in what way does the "true self" in Christ, particularly the kenotic Christ's poverty and weakness, converge with the Zen Buddhist experience of "emptiness," the dissolution of the empirical ego-self? After surveying this material, the chapter will conclude with a brief critique analyzing Merton's interreligious dialogue with Zen Buddhism specifically along these lines.

"WISDOM IN EMPTINESS":
DIALOGUE WITH D. T. SUZUKI (1959)

Chapter three of this book has pointed to the late 1950s as a pivotal epoch in Merton's return to the world to cultivate contact with other solitaries, most notably Boris Pasternak. What is often overlooked is his simultaneous turn to Asian interests. Because his Zen studies were published only in the last three years of his life, many readers have the impression that this interest arose only in the monk's final, hermitage years. The arrangement of chapters in *Zen and the Birds of Appetite* suggests that the dialogue with Zen scholar D. T. Suzuki is the climax of Merton's interest in Zen, although the author's "postface" and the footnote indicating the previous 1961 publication of this "Wisdom and Emptiness" essay clarify the fact. In March of 1959 Merton sent Suzuki excerpts from his manuscript for *The Wisdom of the Desert,* a translation of sayings of the Western desert fathers. He remarks on the kinship between the teachings of his own monastic ancestors and Zen Buddhist masters' aphorisms. He confesses already a great debt to Zen, saying that without breathing Zen he "would probably die of spiritual asphyxiation." "Zen is the very atmosphere of the Gospels, and the Gospels are bursting with it," he writes. "It is the proper climate for any monk, no matter what kind of monk he may be."[4] The following month he wrote to Suzuki that their identity as

Zen Buddhist and Christian monk, "far from separating us, makes us most like one another." This time he sent the entire manuscript for *The Wisdom of the Desert* with a request that Suzuki consider writing an introduction to the book. In this April 11, 1959, correspondence he applauds the Zen Buddhist monk for his intuitive grasp of Christianity. And then his attention homes toward christology:

> In your phrase "God wanted to know Himself, hence the creation," you touch upon a most interesting theological idea that has been developed by some Russian Orthodox thinkers and which has deep consequences and ramifications. Writers with this perspective are S. Bulgakov and N. Berdyaev. The Russian view pushes very far the idea of God "emptying Himself" (kenosis) to go over into His creation, while creation passes over into a divine world—precisely a new paradise. Your intuition about paradise is profoundly correct and patristic. In Christ the world and the whole cosmos has been created anew (which means to say restored to its original perfection and beyond that made divine, totally transfigured). The whole world has risen in Christ, say the Fathers. If God is "all in all," then everything is in fact paradise, because it is filled with the glory and presence of God, and nothing is any more separated from God. Then comes the question whether or not the Resurrection of Christ shows that we had never really been separated from Him in the first place. Was it only that we *thought* we were separated from Him? . . . Each one slaved in the service of his own idol—his consciously fabricated social self. Each one then pushed all the others away from himself, and down, beneath himself: or tried to. This is Original Sin. In this sense, Original Sin and paradise are directly opposed. . . . [O]nce we break free from the false image, we find ourselves what we are: and we are "in Christ."[5]

He asks what this christocentric spirituality means: "Does it mean conformity to a social and conventional image of Christ?" Merton cautions Suzuki on the alienation lurking in such a distortion. Such a Christ is not Christ, he contests, but the projected image of a social sector, a certain group, class, or culture. "Fatal," Merton declares. The Christ we seek is within, "*is* our inmost self, and yet infintely transcends ourselves." "We have to be 'found in Him' and yet be perfectly ourselves and free from the domination of any image of Him other than Himself." Merton anticipates Suzuki's understanding of Christ "in us as unknown and unseen. . . . *He is ourself*," he writes, intimating the theology of the "true self." This remarkable early letter concludes with advice to Suzuki to avoid challenging the "theological watchdogs" by expressing his intuitions as definitive statements about the nature of Christianity. He goes on to describe the Christian's finding of the "true self" in Christ as "a free gift from God." He stresses God's freedom, "the indeterminateness of salvation," as what most corresponds to Zen. The nature of the analogy between Christianity and Zen at this early point in Merton's dialogue integrates his understanding of grace and salvation as the epitome of Christianity, when God's freedom breaks through into the person's life: "The breakthrough that comes with the realization of what the finger of a koan [one of Zen's paradoxical sayings] is pointing to is like the breakthrough of the realization that a sacrament, for instance, is a finger pointing to the completely spontaneous Gift of Himself to us on the part of God — beyond and above all images, outside of every idea, every law, every right or wrong, everything high or low." The bridge to Zen is built through Merton's preferring the apophatic way of "knowing by unknowing" and seeing God's freedom work "outside of all set forms, all rites, all theology, all contemplation," while he carefully backpedals and asserts that these have their place and are "most important."[6]

The joint essay, "Wisdom in Emptiness," includes both Suzuki's article, "Knowledge and Innocence," and Merton's article, "The Recovery of Paradise," and brief final remarks by way of response from each. Merton prefaces the essay with a complaint about "verbalistic ideologies" that substitute for religion, philosophy, and spirituality in the West. He finds that Zen stories "almost exactly reproduce" the sayings of desert fathers which he translated for *The Wisdom of the Desert.* In fact, he finds that the same stories occur when persons seek and realize poverty, solitude, and emptiness.[7] He is attracted to Bernard's spirituality, recovering the lost likeness to God in pure simplicity, to communicate the union with God as not an object but as the "divine poverty."[8] The Merton article emphasizes Cassian's "purity of heart" to center the desert fathers' quest for paradise in the present, as a state or place on earth, not in the future. Like Suzuki, he faults the ego as the source of illusion which shatters our original unity with God. Suzuki describes it as polluting us with ignorance and knowledge (in the sense of limited "science," and therefore the opposite of wisdom). Merton puts it in the Pauline language of dying with Christ to the "old man" of our egotistical self and rising to the "new man" who is the One Christ. At this point he contrasts Buddhism's emptiness as

the complete negation of all personality and Christianity's "purity of
heart" and "unity of spirit" as a supreme and transcendent fulfillment
of personality.[9]

When Merton turns to grace, he offers a theological insight. He insists that grace is not the work of our self, or some Pelagian enterprise.
Scientia, or knowledge, only deludes and alienates us from the true
self, enslaving us to the power of illusion. He warns against narcissism
in the love of one's spiritualized, purified, "empty" self that could turn
out false mystics and pseudo-saints. His language now integrates familiar images of this theology of the false self, "the disfigured image,
the caricature, the emptiness that has swelled up to become full of
itself, so as to create a kind of fictional substantiality for itself."[10] His
concluding response to Suzuki points to Christianity's distinctness from
Zen, by "dependence upon God as Savior and giver of grace." He points
out that grace is not a quantitative reality, a reified substance, but emptiness, liberality, and gift. God's freedom prevails in the Christian's
recovery of paradise as this graced "true self" in Christ which, all along,
has been a radical possibility.[11]

GANDHI ON NON-VIOLENCE (1965)

When Merton edited his selections from Mohandas Gandhi's writings, his introduction, "Gandhi and the One-Eyed Giant," began by
scorning the "laughable syncretisms" of publicity-seeking contemporaries, more often in the East than in the West. In Gandhi, *satyagraha,*
or "holding on to the truth," and non-violence were not a means to
achieving unity but the fruit of an inner unity already achieved. Merton found here a universally valid spiritual tradition which he claimed
was neither syncretism nor indifferentism. One of the beauties of
Gandhi's story is that he discovered the East via the West, or as Merton
put it, "Gandhi discovered India in discovering himself," and his inclusive mind was awakened.[12]

When Merton surveys the Western ethos he finds masters of concepts and abstractions, people pursuing quantitative knowledge, a
myopic "one-eyed" giant who had science without wisdom. He recalls
how the West exploited the ancient civilizations of the East, which had
wisdom without modern technological science. Premonitions of *The
Geography of Lograire*'s imaginative antipoems can be found in this

essay. There is likewise the ethos of *Cables to the Ace* in Merton's assertion here that "violence is essentially wordless," beginning where thought and rational communication have broken down. "Any society which is geared for violent action is by that very fact systematically unreasonable and inarticulate." The systematic greed, terrorism, and oppression of modern industrial society evoked a response of "non-cooperation" from Gandhi, a response which Merton heartily endorses. He describes *satyagraha's* first task in familiar imagery, "to unmask the injustice."[13]

Merton touches the theological fulcrum of christology when he engages the question of whether evil is irreversible. Tyrannies, he says, are built upon that premise. It was Hitler's central dogma, used to launch the "final solution." By contrast, the monk points to the insistence of the Christian tradition that evil is reversible and that the motive of mercy overcomes and changes evil into good. The obstacle erupts when tyranny eliminates conscience's appeal to reverse forms of oppression and violence. The monk finds Jesus' and Gandhi's "triumph of love" in resisting and overcoming evil day by day, in the midst of constant needs, sufferings, sins, and failures. He cites Christ's admonition to Peter that forgiveness is endless. The fabric of society's change is "in becoming," or in Gandhi's terms, "on the loom."[14] What is involved, however, for this forgiveness is "the immolation of one's empirical self, by mercy and sacrifice." The result can be the liberation of the person and the other, the oppressed and the oppressor. Such forgiveness, for Merton, becomes a christological mystery: "To forgive others and to forget their offense is to enter with them into the healing mystery of death and resurrection in Christ, to return to the source of the Spirit which is the Heart of Christ." It was this very mystery that Gandhi, ironically, proposed anew for Western Christianity. Merton says that the Indian martyr never ceased to believe in the possibility of "a love of truth so strong and so pure that it would . . . awaken in [the most recalcitrant enemy] a response of love and truth." What matters for the monk and Gandhi is not pragmatic effects but the devotion to the truth it implies. In the end Merton sees the Third World nations of Asia and Africa harboring a predicament as new nations. He describes it as the inherited guilt legacy of colonializing powers, a tenfold self-hatred, incapacity to understand themselves, and limitless fear of themselves and others. He calls this the barbarism of "post-historic" humanity and prescribes the principles of Gandhi and Pope John XXIII as the only antidote.[15]

THE WAY OF CHUANG TZU (1965)

Five years after his translations of the Western desert fathers' sayings, Merton turned to the East and rendered into poetry the sublime paradoxes of the Chinese Taoist monk of the fourth and third centuries B.C.E., Chuang Tzu. Merton described the book, which was five years in the making, as "my intuitive approach to a thinker." His thesis, the fruit of twenty-five years as a monk, and by his own admission a disputable thesis, was that "all monasticism, Christian or non-Christian, is essentially one." This was not to deny obvious characteristics peculiar to Christian monasticism. Merton found a "monastic outlook" common to those persons who question a total submission to "arbitrary secular presuppositions, dictated by social convention, and dedicated to the pursuit of temporal satisfactions which are perhaps only a mirage."[16]

The experience of Chuang Tzu is not concerned with words, formulas, or abstract analysis. Merton finds in him a sapiential approach, a "taste" for simplicity, humility, and self-effacement, the refusal to be self-important or aggressive in order to climb in society. The Chinese sage is concerned "with the direct existential grasp of reality in itself."[17] Merton finds that the heirs of Chuang Tzu are the seventh-to tenth-century Zen Buddhists. The contemporary West recovers spontaneity and depth from this heritage. It is a heritage that relaxes the rigid, artificial, and spiritually void world of technology. A key to Merton's interpreting Chuang Tzu is an appreciation of his approach to "seeking 'the good.'" Merton cautions that when we analyze "the good" objectively we treat it as something to attain by special virtuous techniques. Then "the good" becomes less real, it recedes into abstraction. The danger is that persons concentrate on complex means to attain ends and forget "the good" itself. In Chuang Tzu, Merton finds *wu wei,* the non-doing or non-action, which is divine and spontaneous. It contrasts with the self-conscious, deliberate accumulation of virtue or merit. It is not intent to achieve results, carry out elaborate plans, or deliberately organize endeavors.[18]

In a theological comparison, Merton strikes an analogy between St. Paul and Chuang Tzu. While he finds that the Chinese Taoist philosopher lacks the apostle's theological mysticism, his teaching about spiritual liberty (*wu wei*) is analogous for Merton to Paul's teaching on faith and grace, contrasted with the "works" of the Old Law. This analogy is less directly christological than in some of the monk's other comparisons with Eastern spirituality. But he gravitates again to the "true self," who is unmistakably congruent with Christ. The illusion, for Merton, is to be so obsessed with interior progress that a person mistakes giving up self-conscious virtuousness to immerse in a more exaggerated self-conscious contemplation. There is an ironic motif of kenosis in Chuang Tzu's preaching of humility. It is not, says Merton, the "unctuous" humility of "virtuousness and conscious self-abasement." It is an ontological, cosmic humility, a self-forgetfulness which can "manifest itself everywhere by a Franciscan simplicity and connaturality with all living creatures." Society complicates and confuses human existence because it makes us forget our identity, our paradise "true self," and obsesses us with "who we are not." In the same way, Merton cautions against a passion for a social "system" that tends to situate our happiness in a single kind of action, to the exclusion of all other ways.

It is no wonder that Merton revels in Chuang Tzu. He celebrates his instruments of irony and parable. Here is a sage who avoids preaching and recognizes the uselessness of dogmatizing. But perhaps most of all, here is a kindred spirit for Merton's spirituality, one who simply lives his relatedness and union with others. He delights in the fact that Chuang Tzu does not set himself apart from other persons. He is not elitist. "And yet there is a difference," says Merton; "he differs 'in his heart' from other men, since he is centered on Tao and not on himself."[19] So Merton, indeed every Christian, differs in his or her heart when centered in the Pauline Christ of kenosis and abandoning a false self's works for the spiritual liberty of grace.

MYSTICS AND ZEN MASTERS (1967)

When Thomas Merton wrote the preface to *Mystics and Zen Masters* in Advent of 1966, he began explicitly implementing the Second Vatican Council's openness (formally announced less than a year earlier) to other mystical traditions' striving to penetrate "that ultimate mystery which engulfs our being, and whence we take our rise, and whither our journey leads us" (*Nostra Aetate* [Declaration on Non-Christian Religions], 1.) In both East and West he found a renunciation of an aggrandized false self. This book, he states, typically aims to be "practical rather than speculative" because now he shares the values and the experience embodied in other traditions. He can no longer take the stance of a "cold, objective, outsider's look."[20]

He launches the book by questioning the caricature of Zen as a rest in "individual essence," abolishing the interest in social and historical realities. The Zen tea ceremony provides him an illustration of a contemplative exercise whose discipline of communal simplicity, silence, and self-effacement leads to convergence. It is a liturgy "not without certain spiritual features in common with the Eucharistic repast" for Merton. What intrigues him is the necessity of participants to "put off" their artificial social, external *persona* to enter the "poverty" of oneness and communion. He describes it as a Franciscan simplicity.[21]

Merton's sketch of Zen catalogues familiar characteristics: the refusal to tolerate abstract or theoretical answers; an aversion to logical analysis; Suzuki's insistence that Zen is not mysticism; the inability to communicate its insight in doctrinal formulas or precise phenomenological descriptions; the frustration of writing about the "experience" because it is not an experience which a "subject" can "have"; an abhorrence of the dualisms of subject/object, and matter/spirit. Merton describes Zen as beyond reason or speculation, non-verbal, and having nothing of system about it.[22]

When Merton diagnoses the West's failure to distinguish between the empirical ego of Descartes and the "person," he discovers the absence of any concept of "person" in Zen because it tends to be equated with the "individual," who cultivates an external, false self. "Zen insight is not *our* awareness," he remarks, "but Being's awareness of itself in us." He alertly discredits the popular image of Zen as "mirror-wiping," because the resulting "emptiness" itself comes to be regarded as a possession, an attainment, which Merton calls narcissism under the guise of experience and contemplation. Zen is attained by self-forgetfulness in the existential present. Merton cautiously suggests that Christianity's "light that enlightens every one who comes into the world" (Jn. 1:9) "seems to correspond pretty closely" to the Zen Buddhist *prajna*, or wisdom that grasps our primordial emptiness, which is destined to manifest the light of Being.[23]

In his essay on "Classic Chinese Thought," Merton compares Christian *metanoia*, or conversion, with the Zen *satori*, "the explosive rediscovery of the hidden reality within us." Both traditions deal with the problem of recovering an original transcendent union by complete transformation: Christianity, by an affective change of heart; and Zen, by an ontological grasp of being itself. He concludes this particular essay with an ambiguous challenge to the Christian scholar. On the one hand, Merton insists that we understand and preserve the heritage of all great mystical traditions "insofar as they contain truths that cannot be neglected and that offer precious insights into Christianity itself." On the other hand, he suggests a superiority of Christianity because there is "the sapiential awareness of the hidden patterns of life which, in Taoism, foreshadowed their fulfillment in the Gospel of Christ."[24]

"The Jesuits in China" affords perhaps Merton's most important reflection on the natural and supernatural, or nature and grace, in his dialogue with Asia. He combs the strands of experience engaged by the sixteenth-century missionaries. In a telling remark, the monk observes that the Jesuits not only appraised the unfamiliar cultural conditions of the Chinese, but also those of Western civilization. The result was their sacrifice of all that was secondary and accidental in Christianity. Merton implements the kenotic motif: "Far from being a shrewd 'natural' tactic, this was a supernatural and Christian sacrifice, a stripping of [the missionary] in imitation of Christ, who 'emptied Himself, taking the form of a servant' (Phil. 2:5–11), and of St. Paul becoming 'all things to all men.'" This was not, Merton insists, a betrayal of the gospel or the cross of Christ. Rather, in Merton's eyes, the usual "supernatural" solution of contradicting the "natural" in a culture only alienates indigenous peoples from Christianity. He laments the ways that the nature and grace distinction "has sometimes been sadly confused by prejudice and ignorant generalizations," preferring Paul's missionary style, with Christ as the natural fulfillment of the aspirations of the human heart. Thus, Merton can conclude his discription of the Jesuit missions in China in pure christological language: "It is the story of Christ in China: a kind of brief epiphany of the Son of Man as a Chinese scholar."[25]

"Contemplation and Dialogue" integrates more methodically than other essays in *Mystics and Zen Masters* the questions of the nature of interreligious dialogue, the common "experience" of a wisdom theology, and the kenotic christology. Merton opens with the realization that contemplation as the direct intuition of reality is a gift, but he grieves that it has also become a lost art. He locates "genuine ecumenism" beneath "surface differences," exterior worship, and "information and doctrine which are totally and irrevocably divergent." He suggests that religious intuitions and truths "may turn out to have something in common" at a deeper level of dialogue, the higher and personal knowledge of God which contemplatives enjoy.[26] The crux of Merton's insistence on the "momentous" role of Christian contemplatives in future interreligious dialogue is his desire to dismantle the poles of a superficial caricature that denies, on the one hand, non-Catholic claims to the validity of contemplative religious experiences and asserts, on the other hand, a loose and irresponsible syncretism that holds that all religious traditions are equally true and supernatural in all respects. Merton does not suggest abandoning Catholicism's claim to announce the definitive message of salvation in Christ, but he insists that supernatural contemplation is a possibility in other religions.[27]

The monk shifts from this level of doctrine to the experience of contemplation. He combats a false and insufficient notion of contemplation as "consecrated narcissism" and "esoteric and quasi-magic technique." Again he turns to the cross of Christ and kenosis (Is. 52 and Phil. 2:5–10) for the fullest expression of "the dialectic of fullness and emptiness, *todo y nada* [John of the Cross], void and infinity, which appears at the heart of all the great traditional forms of contemplative wisdom." It is here that Merton finds "the emptying of all human wisdoms (I Cor. 1:18–25)" and reverses the common usage of this passage to destroy "pagan mysticisms." Rather, Merton suggests that this kenotic theme at the heart of Christianity will be seen as "Christian answers to the profound questions raised by all these ancient traditions, which seem to have been grasping at the central truths in their own way." Because Christian contemplatives afford unique access to this insight, Merton finds their participation in interreligious dialogue an imperative for the future.[28]

The particular ethos of Zen Buddhism radiates from Merton's essay, "The Zen Koan." He describes the "non-method" of these paradoxical sayings as liquidating the false self. The Zen student seeks to "immolate" the superficial empirical consciousness, the ego identity, with the *koan*. The false self is described by Merton as an identity built on happiness as a conscious certitude that attains or possesses a sought object. He describes such a false self as an "illusory fire . . . kindled by craving," a self with no metaphysical status. There is a decidedly sapiential note to the koan for Merton, because one "taste[s] the heart and kernel of the koan" when it liberates a whole new consciousness. It dissolves individuality, he says, which is imaged as knotted into an autonomous self.[29]

Merton describes the experience of the koan as an active, *"personal response"* which involves the whole being and freedom of the person in the capacity "to 'see' and 'move on.'" This existential character of the koan as an event coincides with Merton's theology of the "true self" in Christ as an encounter and awakening, the *metanoia* of ongoing conversion. His comparison of Zen's resulting "no-mind" with the mystical night of St. John of the Cross leads him to claim "an exact correspondence" at the psychological level, but a profound theological difference in the two traditions. Merton differentiates Zen as a "way of insight rather than a way of 'salvation'": Christianity is a salvific religion because it is the gift of love, God's Christ. Zen, on the other hand, says Merton, comes from the ground of one's being.[30]

The closing essay of *Mystics and Zen Masters,* "Buddhism and the Modern World," emphasizes the awakening of the true self, "the Buddha which one is," in *Sunyata,* or "emptiness." Merton describes the basic aim of Buddhism as the search for an answer to the urgent question of how to cope with suffering. The source of our alienation is individual and collective illusions which are rooted in the ignorance of distorted, false selves. Merton finds that Buddhism offers a transformation of consciousness that restores unity and solidarity. It returns us to touch human experience itself. In both East and West, he concludes, a sclerosis of ideas and forms have alienated us from our true selves by substituting for authentically experienced realities.[31] Here, in the transformation of consciousness — the domain of Western mystics and Zen masters — is the future meeting ground of global interreligious convergence envisioned by Merton.

ZEN AND THE BIRDS OF APPETITE (1968)

The new material which Thomas Merton incorporated with the 1961 "Wisdom in Emptiness" essay to comprise *Zen and the Birds of Appetite* confirms the fact that the monk's books invariably were amalgamated as loose volumes of eclectic interests. Four of the new essays, published previously in other journals or books, shed particularly important light on Merton's developing christology. He addresses there the question of the nature of the Christian-Buddhist dialogue, the analogous understanding of religious experience common to the wisdom theology of Christianity and Buddhism, and the "true self" in Christ, particularly the kenotic Christ's poverty and weakness, converging with the Zen Buddhist experience of "emptiness," the dissolution of the empirical ego-self.

In 1966 he published "Transcendent Experience," comparing the Zen no-self or void with the Christian mystic's annihilation of the ego-identity in order to become the "person" who is identified with Christ, one with Christ. "I live now not I but Christ lives in me" (Gal. 2:20). Again he gravitates to Philippians 2:5–10 to appreciate the Christian's transcendent experience as a participation in "the mind of Christ"— "Let this mind be in you which was also in Christ Jesus . . . *who emptied himself* . . . obedient unto death. . . . Therefore God raised him and conferred upon him a name above all names." Merton calls the transformation of Christian consciousness by the dynamic of emptying and transcendence "a kenotic transformation," an emptying of the ego-consciousness's contents in order to become the void in which God's light and glory radiate and manifest his Being and Love. He describes the Buddhist experience of identification with the enlightened Buddha mind with the emptying of the individual ego. Merton parallels the Buddhist entry into the self-emptying and enlightenment of Buddha to the Christian entrance into the self-emptying (crucifixion) and glorification (resurrection and ascension) of Christ. He differentiates the two, however, by pointing out that the Buddhist experience is "existential and ontological"; and the Christian experience is "theological and personal."[32]

With his 1967 essay, "New Consciousness," Merton expressly welcomed the Second Vatican Council's new explorations in christology. He appraises the static metaphysics by which Hellenistic philosophy had domesticated the dynamic truths of Christian belief. "The existential sense of Christian encounter with God in Christ and in the Church as a *happening* (marked by divine freedom and pure gift)," he complains, "became more and more an experience of stabilized *being.*" When we began to experience not an event, but "a new ontological status" and a "new nature," Merton observes, grace became experienced not as God's action but as God's nature shared by divine sonship and ultimately in "divinization." What perplexes Merton most in this drift of the mystical nuptials with Christ toward "ontological mysticism" is the resulting caricature of Christian contemplation and mysticism. Contemporary Christianity had come to distort the mystical experience as "an individualistic escape from community." Merton quarrels with both the new, radical Catholicism and the broader "new consciousness" because he finds them cavalierly repudiating personal contemplative union with God and deep mystical experience. Merton attributes the "new consciousness" of secular, post-Christian, activist Christianity to the antimystical bias of Karl Barth and neo-orthodox theology.[33]

The heart of Merton's resistance to the "new consciousness" exposes the Cartesian *cogito* as the culprit of Western philosophy. He describes the "subject" in Descartes's dualism of subject versus object as a "solipsistic bubble of awareness," or an ego imprisoned in the false self's consciousness. One result of this mindset is that God soon is reduced to an object, opposite the thinking subject. Merton declares that sooner or later God-as-object dies because he is unthinkable as an object. The antidote to this poison of the Cartesian *cogito* is still available to modern persons, he reminds us. This metaphysical consciousness "starts not with a thinking and self-aware subject but from Being, ontologically seen to be beyond and prior to the subject-object division." In such *"pure consciousness"* the subject disappears. Merton points out that both Oriental religions and Christian mysticism stress that the self-aware subject is "a provisional self-construction." This self is ultimately not its own center "and does not orbit around itself" but centers on God, who is grace and presence. The monk confirms the relevance of the mystic's experience to contemporary culture by emphasizing that the true self of this mystical consciousness is disposed to encounter with other persons because it is already united "in God."[34]

In the midst of his critical analysis of the "new consciousness," Merton cautions us about its natural turn toward history, event, movements, and progress. This new consciousness, he says, "seeks its own identity in action toward historic political or critical goods." The question Merton asks is subtle. While the new consciousness experiences God's presence as "an inscrutable word summoning to community," he asks, "But what community and what other men?" There is a vague, even subjective community that "happens" in such a church or other community. Merton sees it ambiguously, as both "excitingly charismatic" and "strangely capricious." At its worst, he fears it could degenerate into temporary political agreements or "the mild confabulation of clerical hippies." Echoes of *Cables to the Ace* and *The Geography of Lograire* resound through this essay's prodding reminders. While the self becomes a center of decision making with "elephantitis of self-will," and while commitments are publicly worn on political buttons, Merton ponders whether such "new consciousness" merely inverts the mystic's true self and leaves "simply a new, more fluid, less doctrinal kind of conformism."[35] Gethsemani's antipoet once again has struck gold!

The essay which introduces *Zen and the Birds of Appetite,* "The Study of Zen," was first published only six months before Merton's death. In many respects it recapitulates and summarizes insights from previous essays and articles. He first distinguishes Zen as offering a metaphysical insight and Christianity offering a theological salvation. He concludes that the study of their diverse structures and systems finds that they mix no better than oil and water, alien to each other. He sees both Buddhism and Christianity as promoting life-affirming liberation, but to compare them on the level of doctrine, with a Westerner's intellectual or theological chip on the shoulder, is for him like trying to compare mathematics and tennis. He remarks that the mystic's experience of the mystery of Christ transcends the individual psychological level in the sense that the mystic "experiences theologically with the Church." Merton identifies the genius of Christianity as reducing the mystic's experience to a theological form that is shared by the rest of the church. Thus Christianity has a natural tendency toward language and symbols. Zen, on the other hand, he describes as "resolutely resist[ing] any temptation to be easily communicable," and as preferring paradox and blasting away explanations and symbols. What draws Merton to interreligious dialogue is the fact that "they all end up with the simplest and most baffling thing of all: direct confrontation with Absolute Being, Absolute Love, Absolute Mercy or Absolute Void, by an immediate and fully awakened engagement in the living of everyday life." He concludes this comment from a sketch of Daisetz Suzuki with the ultimate distinction: In Christianity the confrontation is "theological and affective, through word and love"; in Zen it is "metaphysical and intellectual, through insight and emptiness."[36]

Recognizing in "The Study of Zen" that the nature of the dialogue lies beyond comparative doctrines, Merton insists again that "the mind of Christ" found in Philippians 2:5–11 "may be theologically worlds apart from the 'mind of Buddha.'" Nonetheless, he finds that the self-emptying of Christ and the self-emptying of the disciple which makes the disciple one with Christ "in *His* kenosis" can be understood "in a very Zen-like sense as far as psychology and experience are concerned." Again, Merton refuses to confuse the Christian vision of God and Buddhist enlightenment, but he finds in both "this psychic 'limitlessness'" in the sense of Eckhart's poverty, John of the Cross's dark night, and the emptiness, perfect freedom, and no-mind of the two traditions. For Merton, the convergence of the two distinct traditions comes through Eckhart's statement: "A man should be so poor that he is not and has not a place for God to act in. To reserve a place would be to maintain distinctions." But in that poverty where the false self is dissolved and "no self" is left, both Buddhist and Christian recover the "true self." For Eckhart, "This true identity is the 'birth of Christ in us.'" Merton concludes that whatever Zen is, or however defined, "it is somehow there in Eckhart." He renders the sapiential nature of this convergence between the two traditions by an arresting metaphor of the mystical experience: "penetrate the outer shell and taste the inner kernel which cannot be defined."[37]

Merton had earlier prefaced his friend John C. H. Wu's book, *The Golden Age of Zen,* with the essay "A Christian Looks at Zen." What most recommends this study is the monk's exegesis of the Pauline theme of kenosis in looking for analogies and correspondences between Zen and Christianity. Moreover, Merton concludes this article by affirming the importance of the dogma of the Trinity for interreligious dialogue. He is optimistic that theology, rather than psychology or asceticism, will be the area for future ecumenical investigation. Merton finds two distinct kinds of wisdom in Paul's first two chapters of the letter to the Corinthians: (1) a rational, dialectical wisdom, which comes through knowledge of words and statements; and (2) spiritual wisdom, which is a matter of paradox and of experience. So Merton finds in the "word of the Cross" a stark, existential union with Christ in death, in order to share resurrection. Being "nailed to the cross" means the death of the ego-self as the principle of our deepest actions; now they proceed from Christ's life in us. "To receive the word of the Cross means the acceptance of a complete self-emptying, a *Kenosis,*" says Merton, "in union with the self-emptying of Christ 'obedient unto death' (Phil. 2: 5–11)." He quotes Gabriel Marcel's comment that there are thresholds which thought alone does not permit us to cross. They require "an experience of poverty and sickness."[38]

ASIAN JOURNAL (1968/1973)

The posthumously published *Asian Journal of Thomas Merton* is composed of vignettes and reflections he recorded from October 15 through December 8, 1968, while traveling to and in Asia. The very genre of this final journal precluded the possibility of the sort of retrospective or reworking of impressions and insights that was typical of Merton's various reading notes and successive drafts and which eventuated in the familiar, cogent essays. Nonetheless, it affords a perspective, though it is certainly not preoccupied with or even particularly attentive to christology. The immersion in Asia demanded that Merton experience its traditions on their own terms. As he points out in an October 1968 talk in Calcutta, he was seeking a *"lingua franca* of religious experience," a "communion" which could be encountered on both pre-verbal and post-verbal levels.[39]

What perdures for Merton is his own identity as a Cistercian Christian monk. He signs a September 1968 circular letter to friends with the salutation, "With all affection in Christ." Two months later, in another circular letter from New Delhi, he remarks how, in his contact with new Asian friends, "I also feel consolation in my own faith in Christ and His indwelling presence." His notes for an October paper in Calcutta touch upon christology as he delineates carefully on "a wholeness which is described in various ways by the different religions": the self-realization of *atman;* the void; life in Christ; *fana; baqa,* or annihilation and reintegration according to Sufism.[40]

He repeats time and again how the nature of the dialogue in Asia centers on experience, not dogmatic theology. He emphasizes the "similarities and analogies" between East and West at the level of religious experience. He carefully distinguishes them from "cultural and doctrinal differences," without dismissing that dimension. On the one hand, he describes learning more information and facts, a quantitative approach to Asian traditions; he prefers, on the other hand, the qualitative enlightenment that comes from drinking "from ancient [Asian] sources of monastic vision and experience."[41] Merton insists that he can remain faithful to his Christian commitment and yet learn from the Buddhist and Hindu experience. The unity he seeks is not a newly invented syncretism. "We discover an older unity," he writes. This "original unity" means for him that "what we have to be is what we are." He emphasizes in his notes for the Calcutta paper the necessity of a "scrupulous respect for important differences." When understanding and agreement fail, he cautions, "this must be kept clear—without useless debate." In other words, Merton finds "differences that are not debatable."[42]

His Bangkok address on December 10, 1968, entitled "Marxism and Monastic Perspectives," identifies a common starting point in Buddhist and Christian monasticism. Both traditions "start from the problem inside man himself" and attempt a transformation of consciousness from the ego-centered consciousness to Christianity's "true self" in Christ, or Zen's "emptiness" of "no-mind." Merton expresses this dynamic in the monastic fathers and Christian patristic teaching as the dissolving of the illusory individual ego. The resulting "person" is "Christ dwelling in each one." But the ramifications of this transformation of consciousness are broader for Merton. They converge with his own interreligious dialogue: "So in each one of us the Christian person is that which is fully open to all other persons, because ultimately all other persons are Christ."[43]

CRITICAL ANALYSIS

Having surveyed Merton's writings about the spiritual insights of Zen Buddhism, with a particular emphasis on its convergence with the monk's theology of the "true self" or "inner self," we can now appraise the three underlying questions addressed in this case study.

(1) *What does Merton see as the nature of the Christian-Buddhist dialogue?*

The preeminent concern of Thomas Merton is to avoid any syncretism or glossing over of differences between distinct religious traditions. He admits freely that there are irreconcilable doctrinal differences. For example, he can bluntly and categorically affirm that the kenotic "mind of Christ" and "the mind of Buddha" are "theologically worlds apart." Yet this does not preclude for him the possibility of understanding Christ's kenosis "in a very Zen-like sense as far as psychology and experience are concerned." The integral role of the Christian contemplative in dialogue with the Zen monk guarantees for Merton the fruitfulness of interreligious dialogue because it must be grounded in religious experience, not dogmas. At Bangkok he speaks passionately of monasticism, both East and West, as an imperishable charism, an instinct of the human heart, transcending cultural, sociological, and psychological factors. Both traditions need the dialogue in order to promote their very identity and survival, he warns.[44]

Despite the clarity of Merton's definition of the nature of interreligious dialogue, he repeatedly retreats from a necessary theological project. In one sense, he consistently avoids reducing the dialogue to theological investigations. But in another sense, one might question whether, in the process, he confines theology to an unnecessarily narrow definition and thus "bails out" of legitimate questions. Examples abound in his Zen studies. In the *Mystics and Zen Masters* preface, he remarks, "In writing of Zen, needless to say, it is Zen I am trying to explain, not Catholic dogma." He insists, correctly, that Zen is not theology.[45] But as he admits in *Zen and the Birds of Appetite,* Catholicism (and all Christianity) tends toward the forms of theological and symbolic language. He points to "personality," whether human or divine, requiring considerable clarification before real East-West dialogue can flourish.[46] Yet he does not attempt to deliver this projected clarification. When he confronts Buddhist "emptiness" as the negation of personality and Christian "purity of heart" as a supreme and transcendent fulfillment of personality, he abdicates any critical assessment with the comment, "This is an extremely complex and difficult question which I am not prepared to discuss."[47] Merton's readers come away with occasional disappointment. For example, he merely records for us, without any resolution, a theological quandary: "The fact that Zen Buddhism does not deal with a personal God is of enormous theological consequence." In response to Suzuki's objection to the distinction which Merton makes between "God and Godhead," the monk admits to avoiding "a thorny theological problem."[48] To an embarrassing degree, Merton fails to explain to his readers the rich traditional theology of created and uncreated grace as a Western means of approaching the mystery of God. Along these same lines, he asks if the Zen experience is "perhaps already grace?"[49] The question cannot remain rhetorical. His insistence on the distinction between the "theologically worlds apart" "mind of Christ" and "the mind of Buddha" goes nowhere when he volunteers, "this I am not prepared to discuss."[50] He points to the need for "a great deal of study and investigation" over the question of whether various philosophies and theologies become irrelevant when we see they are merely "equally efficacious means" for arriving at the same end. His own inclination is to reverence the unique beliefs as constitutive of the mystic's very experience, not a disposable "suit of clothes."[51] In a letter to Abdul Aziz, he suggests an analogy between Christ and the Muslim prophet, Mohammed, but skirts the issue with an all too typical "I must leave this to future consideration."[52]

It is certainly unfair to expect Merton to resolve such questions. But a critical evaluation of his contribution must note his occasional lapses of a fuller theological effort.

(2) *How does he understand the analogous religious experience common to the wisdom theology of Christianity and Buddhism?*

In both Christianity and Buddhism, Merton identifies the dynamic of the false self versus the true self. He states directly at Bangkok that both traditions address this transformation of consciousness. They seek to liberate by emptying the ego-consciousness, which is a provisional self-construction. This awakening comes by a personal response either to the existential call to *metanoia*, or conversion, of the gospel, or to the *satori*, or enlightenment, summoned by the Zen koan. Merton finds the Christian myth of original sin analogous to Zen Buddhism's teaching of *avidja*, or ignorance. Whether following Paul's theology of grace versus "the Law," or Zen's *wu wei* of non-doing, or non-action, divine and spontaneous, he finds the same dynamic. In the end, Merton sees the convergence of plural religious traditions in the direct confrontation of Absolute Being, Absolute Love, Absolute Mercy, or Absolute Void. The unique route to such a confrontation, however, is by way of the Christian kenosis, or emptying, of the ego's false self and the birth of Christ in our poverty as the "true self"; and by the emptying of any center of self in Zen to experience "Being's awareness of itself in us." Merton's preference for the apophatic tradition of Christian mysticism makes his attraction to Zen all the more persuasive. For all the analogies he draws between the two traditions at the level of psychology and experience, it is important to note that Merton pointed to the doctrine of the Trinity, and a genuine dialogue of theology, as the promise of the future.[53]

(3) *In what way does the "true self" in Christ, particularly the kenotic Christ's poverty and weakness, converge with the Zen Buddhist experience of "emptiness," the dissolution of the ego-self?*

Merton proves less than precise in his suggestion that the Light of Christ that enlightens everyone who comes into the world "seems to correspond pretty closely" to Zen Buddhism's *prajna*, or wisdom, that grasps our primordial emptiness, which is destined to manifest the light of Being. His distinction between Christianity as a salvation experience and Zen as a way of metaphysical insight should not be confused or overlooked. He describes the experience of Christ as an experience of God's grace and love; it is both personal and theological. The Zen enlightenment, by contrast, comes from the ground of one's being; it is ontological and existential. Merton has carefully attributed grace to the contemplative religious experiences of other traditions. But in dialogue with Zen Buddhism he shares Daisetz Suzuki's dichotomy of two mindsets: (1) Christianity as theological and affective, through Word and love, and (2) Zen Buddhism as metaphysical and intellectual, through insight and emptiness.[54]

While the "no-mind" of Zen "emptiness" can alert us to the natural techniques as well as graces of this dynamic tradition, it does not reveal Christ. And if both Zen "emptiness" and the kenotic Christ summon us to liquidate the false self or fictitious ego as the center of consciousness, the Christian person lives "in Christ" with a unique affective and spiritual abundance, an abundance of the heart.

Conclusion

Thomas Merton exercised an uncanny ability to see around corners. How better to describe his untiring struggle to recognize the hidden Christ of kenosis, as manifested in the myriad parables and ambushes of autobiography, self-identity, and a post-Christian history's discontinuities? This book has attempted to focus Merton's sprawling, sometimes scattered, and temperamentally unsystematic prose and poetry through the master lens of his sustained Christocentric spirituality. Whether he wrote popular classics of the spiritual life, essays on contemporary social issues, lyric poetry, antipoems, journals, or well-researched monastic and mystical treatises, the "hidden wholeness" of his life and work radiates from his distinctively kenotic christology. Merton's sustained reflections on the Christ whose strength abides, yet who chooses to be weak, gained extraordinary momentum and clarity over the course of his twenty-seven years as a Cistercian monk and poet.

In February of 1967, the celebrated hermit wrote to theologian Rosemary Reuther a revealing comment about his early christology as a convert. He resists arguing with her about her work and confesses that his entry into the church was "marked by a pretty strong and dazzled belief in the Christ of the Nicene Creed." His context, he explains, was "a strong reaction against the fogginess and subjectivity and messedupedness of the ideas about Christ that I had met with up and down in various kinds of Protestantism. I was tired of a Christ who had evaporated," he reminisces. Then Merton turns in this letter to an immediate "bother," the fact that in church history "you run into a bigger and bigger hole of unconscious bad faith." He admits that he cannot reconcile this with the church's dictating to other religions "that we are the one authentic outfit that has the real goods."[1]

Four months later, in June of 1967, Merton wrote to Jan Yungblut, "I am still hung up in a very traditional Christology myself." He had been asked to comment on a chapter of the Quaker theologian's book, *Rediscovering the Christ.* The reason for his self-described hang-up, he explains, is that in the end "you are always dealing with some kind of authority anyhow: whether the councils of Nicaea and Chalcedon or the works of Renan, Loisy, and the rest." He questions the comprehensibility of some of these authorities, but the letter quickly shifts to Merton's disclaimer that, for him, "Christ is not simply 'a mystic' among others," as Yungblut has apparently suggested. Merton cannot adjust to Christ "just receiving a little flash of light like the rest of them," but says he prefers the Christ of Byzantine ikons or Mt. Athos's transfiguration mysticism.[2]

These two voluntary self-appraisals of Merton's christology might give one pause. Is he so "traditional" that it proves wrong-headed to attempt to trace a creative, contemporary christology in his poetry and existential prose? He alludes in the Yungblut letter to his not having much of a historical Christ, in the sense of historico-critical biblical studies. Then, in a March 1968 letter to June Yungblut, Jan Yungblut's spouse, he returns to the discussion about his "[d]isjointed ideas" and by now "serious reservations" about the Christ of the ikons. He freely admits, in retrospect, the absurdity and misconception of limiting himself to the Christ of Byzantine theology. The earlier remark he explains as an exaggerated reaction to the Christ of historical criticism, but then he inquires: On what grounds is the Christ of the ikons "'my' Christ"? His example of ikon painting relates to the *experience* of the ikon painter as a person of prayer. The hieratic rules for ikon painting are not just rigid and formal, but a "guarantee of the authentic possibility of this experience" of "the illumination and awareness of the glory of Christ within us (by faith)." It is not the external representation of Christ, a historical person, "seen" in prayer before an ikon, he insists, "but an interior presence in light, which is the glory of the transfigured Christ, the experience of which is transmitted in faith from generation to generation of those who have 'seen,' from the Apostles on down." Merton echoes the primacy of experience as the source of his theology, the existential and autobiographical refrain chorused throughout his literary corpus. He concludes that when he claims the Christ of the ikons as "'my' Christ," he means that Christ can not be reached by any scientific study but must be mediated through liturgy, art, prayer, and a theology of light. As an afterthought he remarks that he is not "hung up on" orthodoxy as he ventures this explanation.

Merton's reservations about claiming the Christ of the Russian and Greek ikon traditions present, as it were, a compelling last testament of his christology to parallel the insights and kenotic motifs of *The Geography of Lograire*. He hesitates over the culturally bound misdirections of Byzantine theocratic imperialism as a political and social oppression. "Christ as imperial ruler" or the emperor as a locus of the divine manifestation, he emphasizes, "I certainly don't buy." He records a bald "No" to "Christ as a ruler of a history" in which the royal figure or any other figure has a central and decisive "Christian" role. This particular reflection distills the essence of Merton's mature kenotic christology and so it deserves a lengthy excerpt to encounter the Christ to whom he confesses an unequivocal "Yes":

> So one would have to multiply other examples to say what I mean. Like the Christ born in us in poverty, as Eckhart; but also the Christ of Julian of Norwich; the Christ of immediate experience all down through the mystical tradition, but in each case detached from special historical and cultural residues. I don't know if you get what I mean. The point is that I don't think the historical Christ can be known in a way that is as relevant as this, and this is the kind of knowledge of Christ that St. John talks about in the Gospel and in his Epistles. In comparison with this "knowledge" of Christ, the knowledge of Jesus as a man who "was" a Jewish mystic is to me somewhat irrelevant. That is knowledge "about" Christ, not knowledge "of" Christ, and not (what interests me more) knowledge "in" Christ. Christ not as object of seeing or study, but Christ as center in whom and by whom one is illuminated. I will be the first to admit that all this may be extremely ambiguous. And I am questioning it much more now than I would have, say, ten years ago. The ambiguities are of course those of monasticism itself, and the Christ I am talking about is essentially the "monastic" Christ. *The real problem comes in when early monasticism lost its truly kenotic and eschatological character, and became dogmatic imperial shock troops in the service of a Christian social order (so called).* To what extent is the Christ of monastic worship, with all the purity and refinement of ikon painting, Greek liturgy, theology of light, Hesychasm, etc., the justification of a certain "order"? To what extent is the experience of that Christ the experience of an inner security that came from supporting a "divine" social order? Hm. That calls for some thinking.[3]

Thomas Merton's honest and compelling synthesis of his own christology in this correspondence, written only eight months before his death, exhibits the same kenotic motif reflected through autobiography when he quips that "monks have tended to be mavericks, if only interiorly," as distinct from "the most static and established kinds of Christendom." He points especially to the hermits who literally broke away, only to be reincorporated and canonized like the Russians St. Nil Sorsky and St. Joseph of Volokolansk.[4]

This "provisional" synthesis, which the Abbey of Gethsemani's hermit admits leaves him with more thinking and revising to do, concludes with a careful distinction about monastic ambivalence toward "the world." In retrospect, it maps Merton's own phases of world denial and world affirmation analyzed thoughout the chapters of this book. He credits monastic world denial as originally a denial of the world not yet penetrated by Resurrection light. Its purpose is to awaken the world "to see that the world *has* been transformed and illuminated." Unfortunately, he confesses, monastic spirituality collapsed into pure world denial and affirmation of the Resurrection as "a proof of pure transcendence." Merton finds the problem to lie in a tendency toward the "light" of theophany repudiating the world rather than becoming an epiphany transfiguring the world. His final comment on "my Christ" turns to the kenotic expression of emptiness, a preference for the paradoxical apophatic Christ, "light that is not light and not confinable within any known category of light, and not communicable in any light that is not not-light: yet in all things, in their ground, not by nature but by gift, grace, death and resurrection."[5]

Jean Leclercq's 1980 introduction to *Thomas Merton on St. Bernard* ventures one of the rare christological assessments of Merton. Without referring to these then-unpublished letters of 1968, where Merton avoids the christological extremes, this Benedictine monk and Bernard scholar from Clairvaux, Luxembourg, delicately balances the positive elements of a christology "from below" with a christology "from above" in Merton. He describes the foundation of Merton's reflection on contemplation as an act of faith in Christ the contemplator of God, *Abba,* and the possibility of our participation in Christ's contemplation, uniting us with the God experienced as a Trinity of divine persons.[6]

The image of Christ as the contemplator of *Abba* evokes the affective "abundance of the heart" which Merton's spirituality and poetry celebrates—from the nativity of the incarnate Christ, through the agony of the Garden of Gethsemani, and the abandonment on the cross. But this contemplative experience and desire for transforming union came

to encompass for Merton something altogether different from the rare-
fied "special and unique experiences"[7] of success-and-happiness-seeking
Western Christian culture. The Christ of kenosis subverts for Merton
any complacency in his own spirituality. He discovers the epiphany of
Christ in the human experience of poverty, in historical discontinuities, at the margins of Christendom, and in the rejection and vulnerability of the world's scarred victims and despised outcasts.

In what I treasure as the most sublime and lyric of his essays, "Rain
and the Rhinoceros," introducing *Raids on the Unspeakable*, Merton
exposed the pretense of what masquerades as Christian spirituality when
the "true self" of Christ's kenosis is domesticated, or worse, denied:
"The problem today is that there are no deserts, only dude ranches."[8]
At the heart of this acerbic critique stirs Merton's spirituality of an
awakened "true self" or "inner self," which inevitably leads him to Christ.
Whenever he coaxed the discovery of this true self, Merton clamored
for us to recognize the laws and illusions of collective existence, the
stampeding herd mentality which is alien to our deeper truth. We fabricate fictitious identities and hide behind masks in order to suppress
our awareness of contingency and radical need that only faith can complement. Merton always nudges us toward solitude and the interior
desert to confront our poverty and to renounce the empirical self. Then
our encounter with "emptiness" flowers in the birth and awakening
of the true self, the very self who "imitates Christ."

> It is in the desert of loneliness and emptiness that the fear of death and
> the need for self-affirmation are seen to be illusory. When this is faced,
> then anguish is not necessarily overcome, but it can be accepted and
> understood. Thus, in the heart of anguish are found the gifts of peace and
> understanding: not simply in personal illumination and liberation, but
> by commitment and empathy, for the contemplative must assume the uni-
> versal anguish and the inescapable condition of mortal man. The solitary,
> far from enclosing himself in himself, becomes every man. He dwells in
> the solitude, the poverty, the indigence of every man.[9]

Without this transformation of consciousness to our true self, Merton finds that "our freedom remains abortive." The cruelest irony in
this Cistercian's optimistic spiritual vision resides in the "satanic theology" which he finds "hides Christ from us altogether, and makes Him
so impossibly beautiful that He must remain infinitely remote from
our wretchedness." The poet Rimbaud personifies for Merton such a

"satanic theology." He quotes the French poet's warped christology, speaking of God cheating by giving Christ the beatific vision even in his suffering. Merton finds in Rimbaud the denial of Christ's human- ity: "He knew He was God. He knew He was *not like you.* . . . He thought: I am God, I am *not like them.*" The monk asks how to recon- cile this with the parable of the Pharisee and the publican. "It is Satan's theology," he declares, "to make Christ the most perfect of all the Phari- sees, so that the publicans will all despair while the Pharisees will come to Him and be confirmed in their self-righteousness."

Merton's meditation on the kenotic Christ reorients:

> "There is in Him no comeliness." Christ came on earth, not to wear the awful cold beauty of a holy statue, but to be numbered among the wicked, to die as one of them, condemned by the pure, He Who was be- yond purity and impurity. If Christ is not really my brother, with all my sorrows, with all my burdens on His shoulder and all my poverty and sad- ness in His heart, then there has been no redemption. Then what hap- pened on the Cross was only magic, and the miracles were magic without purpose.[10]

He prompts a haunting, lingering question about those who have misunderstood this Christ of kenosis: "Whose fault, I wonder?"

Merton faults Rimbaud for the "contempt" on his lips. It is the same word he juxtaposes with Flannery O'Connor's fiction. In this instance, he eulogizes her and points to "respect" as the key word in her stories. Merton finds that her art enacts the "anatomy of the word": "respect." He ponders her portrait of the ambiguity and decay of respect that finally dies of contempt but keeps calling itself respect. O'Connor's "great slashing, dry-eyed innocence of that irony" recorded for him the South's despair. He finds her fiction peopled with characters of self- contempt: (1) the contempt of primitives who admit they would hate to be saved; and (2) the "great contempt of primitives whose salvation was an elaborately contrived possibility always being brought back into question." What the monk admires in her drama of the human fall and dishonor is her respect for all these people, her suspending judg- ment on them. To condemn them, he argues, would be to connive in their demonic imagination, to get tangled in their contempt.[11]

Early in "The Inner Experience" Merton describes the end of the journey of faith and love bringing us to a depth of being and releasing us to "voyage beyond ourselves to God." We are awakened and transformed in the mystical life that experiences the presence of God "beyond all description." He quotes John of the Cross's description of the soul's belief that God has moved and awakened, but in reality it is the soul which has moved and awakened. This inner self paradoxically seems to be a single "I," God and the soul. Our exile from God and alienation from the "inner self" are reversed in Christ's call that awakens us from sleep. Merton describes our return and discovery in Gregory the Great's symbols, as the "end of the prodigal's homecoming journey," entry into the "Father's House."[12]

Thomas Merton borrowed from the dramatist Ionesco a quotation that provides a hermeneutical key to his own autobiography, self-identity, and christology: "[A] country where art is not understood is a country of slaves and robots." Merton's own art, his poetry canon, proves indispensable in his spirituality to the discovery and liberation of the true self in Christ. The false self can ultimately be liberated only by the "ace of freedoms," the Christ of kenosis. It is this Christ we have tried to quarry from the strata of the monk's poetry and antipoetry, his journals, his correspondence, his literary essays.[13] He identified the artist as peculiarly aware of our spiritual crisis and therefore alert to the epiphanies of Christ in human poverty, emptiness, and the inviolable transcendental freedom of every human person. Here, in the artist's epiphanies of the true self, we experience Merton's homecoming. It is patterned on the personifications of the inner self in his poetry — the transformations of a "landscape of disaster," such as he lamented in the April wreckage of his "poor traveller"–brother's death, into a haunting but welcome summons: "they call you home."[14]

Abbreviations

AJ	*The Asian Journal of Thomas Merton.* Edited by Naomi Burton, Patrick Hart and James Laughlin. New York: New Directions, 1973.
AT	*The Ascent to Truth.* New York: Harcourt, Brace and Company, 1951.
BW	*Bread in the Wilderness.* New York: New Directions, 1953.
CGB	*Conjectures of a Guilty Bystander.* Garden City, N.Y.: Doubleday, 1966.
CP	*The Collected Poems of Thomas Merton.* New York: New Directions, 1977.
CWA	*Contemplation in a World of Action.* Garden City, N.Y.: Image Books, 1973.
DQ	*Disputed Questions.* New York: Farrar, Straus & Cudahy, 1960.
FV	*Faith and Violence: Christian Teaching and Christian Practice.* Notre Dame, Ind.: University of Notre Dame Press, 1968.
HGL	*The Hidden Ground of Love: The Letters of Thomas Merton on Religious Experience and Social Concerns.* Selected and edited by William H. Shannon. New York: New Directions, 1985.
LE	*The Literary Essays of Thomas Merton.* Edited by Patrick Hart. New York: New Directions, 1981.
LF	*The Last of the Fathers.* New York: Harcourt, Brace and Company, 1954.

MAWG	*My Argument with the Gestapo: A Macaronic Journal.* New York: New Directions, 1975.
MJ	*The Monastic Journey.* Edited by Patrick Hart. Kansas City: Sheed, Andrews & McMeel, 1977.
MZM	*Mystics and Zen Masters.* New York: Farrar, Straus & Giroux, 1967.
NM	*The New Man.* New York: Farrar, Straus & Cudahy, 1961.
NSC	*New Seeds of Contemplation.* New York: New Directions, 1962.
RT	*Redeeming the Time.* London: Burns & Oates, 1962.
SC	*Seeds of Contemplation.* New York: New Directions, 1949.
SJ	*The Sign of Jonas.* New York: Harcourt, Brace and Company, 1953.
SSM	*The Seven Storey Mountain.* New York: Harcourt, Brace and Company, 1948.
TMR	*A Thomas Merton Reader.* Revised edition. Edited by Thomas P. McDonnell. Garden City, N.Y.: Image Books, 1974.
TMSB	*Thomas Merton on Saint Bernard.* Kalamazoo, Mich.: Cistercian Publications, 1980.
VOC	*A Vow of Conversation: Journals, 1964–65.* New York: Farrar, Straus & Giroux, 1988.
WTW	*What Are These Wounds?* Milwaukee: Bruce Publishing Company, 1950.
ZBA	*Zen and the Birds of Appetite.* New York: New Directions, 1968.

Notes

INTRODUCTION: THE EPIPHANY OF GOD IN WEAKNESS AND DEFENCELESSNESS

1. Karl Barth, quoted in Thomas Merton's "Reflections on Some Recent Studies of St. Anselm," *Monastic Studies* 3 (1965).

2. *SJ*, 323.

3. *CGB*, v.

4. *Night* (New York: Farrar, Straus & Giroux, 1960), 2.

5. *CGB*, v.

6. *LE*, 128–33.

7. *FV*, 156, 208. Cf. "The Other Side of Despair," *MZM*, 255–80.

8. See David Tracy, *The Analogical Imagination: Christian Theology and the Culture of Pluralism* (New York: Crossroad, 1981) for this specific sense of the term "classic": "We all find ourselves compelled both to recognize and on occasion to articulate our reasons for the recognition that certain expressions of the human spirit so disclose a compelling truth about our lives that we cannot deny them some kind of normative status. Thus do we name these expressions and these alone, 'classics.' Thus do we recognize, whether we name it so or not, a normative element in our cultural experience, experienced as a realized truth" (108). Tracy goes on to being "caught up" in the world of "the authentic experience of art": "[W]e are shocked, surprised, challenged by its startling beauty *and* its recognizable truth, its instinct for the essential. In the actual experience of art we do not experience the artist *behind* the work of art. Rather, we recognize the truth of the work's disclosure of a world of reality transforming, if only for a moment, ourselves: our lives, our sense for possibilities and actuality, our destiny" (110).

9. Elizabeth A. Johnson, *Consider Jesus: Waves of Renewal in Christology* (New York: Crossroad, 1990).

10. Rahner, "On the Theology of the Incarnation," *Theological Investigations IV* (Baltimore: Helicon, 1966), 105–20; *Foundations of Christian Faith* (New York: Crossroad, 1978), 285–305.

11. Cf. Jean-Marc Laporte, *Patience and Power: Grace for the First World* (New York: Paulist, 1988), 158.

12. Merton, "Baptism in the Forest: Wisdom and Initiation in William Faulkner," in George A. Panichas, ed., *Mansions of the Spirit* (New York: Hawthorn, 1967), 41.

13. *NSC,* 294.

14. One of the most influential sources for such a contemporary christology is Edward Schillebeeckx's *Church: The Human Story of God* (New York: Crossroad, 1990). He summarizes this thesis: "[W]e cannot detach the defencelessness of Jesus on the cross from the free power and the positivity which revealed itself in his actual career of solidarity with oppressed men and women on the basis of an absolute trust in God" (127). He goes on, "God was not powerless when Jesus hung on the cross, but he was defenceless and vulnerable as Jesus was vulnerable" (128). And, "In this defencelessness, however, at the same time God uses his superior power because his defencelessness is the consequence of his fight against evil in a wicked world. The messianic 'must suffer' of Jesus is not a 'divine' must. It is forced on God through Jesus by human beings, yet God and Jesus are not thwarted by it . . . because his 'going around Palestine doing good' was itself already the beginning of the kingdom of God" (128–29).

15. *SC,* 14.

16. *AT,* ix, emphasis mine.

17. *HR,* 137 (graph).

18. Cf. *SJ,* 9 where Merton declares "perhaps the scandal of my own obvious mediocrity" in his prologue, while explaining his protecting fellow monks' privacy and anonymity throughout the book.

19. *WTW,* 74.

20. *SJ,* 182.

21. Mott, *The Seven Mountains of Thomas Merton* (Boston: Houghton Mifflin, 1984), 77.

22. *HGL,* 516.

23. David Cooper, *Thomas Merton's Art of Denial: The Evolution of a Radical Humanist* (Athens, Ga.: University of Georgia Press, 1989).

24. *The Seven Mountains of Thomas Merton,* xxv.

25. Thomas P. McDonnell, "An Interview With Thomas Merton," *Motive* 27 (1967): 32–41.

26. Working Notebook 76, "1965, second half," Thomas Merton Studies Center collection, Bellarmine College.

27. See George Kilcourse, "The Monk as a 'Marginal' Person," *The Merton Annual* 2 (1989): 175–89.

28. Schoonenberg, *The Christ: A Study of the God-Man Relationship in the Whole of Creation and in Jesus Christ* (New York: Herder and Herder, 1971), 176–79.

29. See John J. Higgins, *Merton's Theology of Prayer* (Spencer, Mass.: Cisterican Publications, 1971), x–xi; and Elena Malits, *The Solitary Explorer: Thomas Merton's Transforming Journey* (New York: Harper & Row, 1980), 100.

30. *CWA,* 126–27.

31. Cf. Johann Baptist Metz's use of this term in *Faith in History and Society: Toward a Practical Fundamental Theology* (New York: Crossroad, 1980), especially chapter 5, "The Dangerous Memory of the Freedom of Jesus Christ," 88–99.

32. Laporte, *Patience and Power,* 136.

33. "The Historical Consciousness," *Contemplative Review* 1:2 (1968), 2.

34. "A Letter on the Contemplative Life (21 August 1967)," *MJ,* 171.

35. "First and Last Thoughts," *A Thomas Merton Reader,* ed. Thomas P. McDonnell (New York: Harcourt, Brace & World, 1974), 18.

1. ABUNDANCE OF THE HEART:
MERTON'S EXPERIENCE OF SALVATION

1. *MAWG,* i–ii. Although published posthumously in 1975, this novel was written in 1941 while Merton was a Columbia University graduate student.

2. *MAWG,* 142 where Merton mentions the work of Karl Barth admired by "Professor H.", along with that of William Blake, Jakob Boehme, and Gautama Buddha.

3. *MJ,* 169–70.

4. Anne E. Carr, A *Search for Wisdom and Spirit: Thomas Merton's Theology of the Self* (Notre Dame, Ind.: University of Notre Dame Press, 1988); Walter Conn, *Christian Conversion: A Developmental Interpretation of Autonomy and Surrender* (New York: Paulist, 1984).

5. See David Cooper, *Thomas Merton's Art of Denial,* 67–88; Michael Mott, *The Seven Mountains of Thomas Merton,* 23–26; Robert E. Daggy, "Birthday Theology: A Reflection on Thomas Merton and the Bermuda Menage," *The Kentucky Review* 7 (1987): 62–89.

6. Conn, 209, 211.

7. Ibid., 232.

8. "Wrestling with God," *Commonweal* 111 (October 19, 1984): 556.

9. *SJ,* 362.

10. Camille-Antonio Doucet, *The Trappists of Oka: Their History from the Foundation of Their Abbey in 1881 until the Present Day* (Oka, Que., Canada: Bibliotheque National du Quebec, 1981), 13.

11. *CP,* 155–56.

12. Michael Mott, *The Seven Mountains of Thomas Merton,* 78–79.

13. *CP,* 104–5. The line, "Until I come again to my beginning" appears so close to lines from T. S. Eliot's *Four Quartets* (the opening line of "East

Coker," and ll. 214–16) that a reader could easily conjecture about Eliot's significant influence on Merton's autobiographical recollections in this poem.

14. *CP,* 95–96.

15. *SSM,* 224–25.

16. Ibid., 107–10.

17. *SJ,* 74.

18. *SSM,* 206–10.

19. Ibid., 211.

20. Ibid., 198.

21. Ibid., 186.

22. Ibid., 53–54.

23. *CP,* 36.

24. Ibid., 38.

25. Ibid., 51.

26. Ibid., 52–53.

27. Cf. *SSM,* 204 where Merton remarks about his appropriation of Maritain's and Gilson's philosophical worldview: "I not only accepted all this, intellectually, but now I began to desire it."

28. Ibid., 111–13.

29. *SSM,* 22–24, emphasis mine.

30. Ibid., 113–15, emphasis mine.

31. Ibid., 57.

32. *CP,* 176.

33. *CP,* 182–84.

34. Ibid., 186–87.

35. Ibid., 193.

36. *SJ,* 5–6.

37. Ibid., 6.

38. Ibid., 330.

39. Ibid., 8–9.

40. 1961, though written five years earlier as noted in *The School of Charity,* ed. Patrick Hart (New York: Farrar, Straus & Giroux, 1990), 132.

41. *NM,* 3–4.

42. Ibid., 5.

43. Jean-Marc Laporte, *Patience and Power: Grace for the First World,* 105, 136.

44. *DQ,* 15.

45. *SSM,* 220–21.

46. Cf. Scotus, *Oxoniense,* 3 sent. d. 20 q. 1. For a thorough appreciation of Scotus's contribution, see Allen Wolter's *The Philosophical Theology of John Duns Scotus,* ed. Marilyn McCord Adams (Ithaca and London: Cornell University Press, 1990).

47. *SSM,* 3.

48. Ibid., 3.

49. Ibid., 191.

50. Ibid., 135.

51. James Finn Cotter, *Inscape: The Christology and Poetry of Gerard Manley Hopkins* (Pittsburgh: University of Pittsburgh Press, 1972), 122–23 summarizes the influence of Scotus on Hopkins: "The originality of Hopkins's development of a Christocentric myth through scriptural, patristic, and Scotist studies cannot be exaggerated. . . . [Scotus] hoped, by establishing the purpose of God's creative act as genesis in Christ, to show the unity and perfection of the divine concern for creatures. This unity is the Father's love for man made manifest in the likeness of his Son. The natural order is existentially oriented toward Christ who is its masterpiece and culmination. Christ's priority of nature, as Hopkins examined it in his 'Creation and Redemption,' places him first in the order of causality, which is counterpointed to the order of time: 'And as for the prophecies of his death, these are like histories written beforehand and are in nature after the event they tell us of'. . . . The Lamb is slain from the beginning. . . . Such in summary was the sublime myth Hopkins saw as the integrating force of his life and which he found confirmed and profoundly interpreted in Scotus."

52. *CP*, 187–89.

53. Ibid., 217.

54. *LF*, 63.

55. This needs to be balanced with Merton's appreciation of Bernard's devotion to the full humanity of Christ, including the Passion. It would lead to the new school of spirituality which was to be called *devotio moderna*, typified by *The Imitation of Christ*. He calls Bernard's devotion to Christ's humanity more than a pious aid to the monastic meditation. "It is simply a rediscovery of the Christ of the Fathers and of Saint Paul" (*LF*, 50). Merton amplifies this mystery to include the Passion and Cross: "At the very heart of Cistercian spirituality lies a poignant devotion to the sufferings of Christ and to His death on the Cross. St. Bernard and his disciples entered deeply into the mystery of the Passion—more deeply than any one before their time, except perhaps St. Paul. They saw in the Passion the greatest proof of God's love for men." [*The Waters of Siloe* (New York: Harcourt, Brace, & Co., 1949), 29.]

56. *LF*, 64.

57. *TMSB*, 148.

58. Ibid., 108.

59. Ibid., 107.

60. Ibid., 109.

61. Merton credits Bernard with the language of "false self" as the hermeneutical key for spirituality. See *The Waters of Siloe*, 349: "In St. Bernard's language, our true personality has been concealed under the 'disguise' of a

false self, the *ego* whom we tend to worship in place of God. The monastic *ascesis* is entirely directed against this *ego.*"

62. *CP,* 90.

63. *TMSB,* 114, n6.

64. Ibid., 114.

65. *TMSB,* 37; a similar observation is recorded on page 218.

66. See Michael Casey, *Athirst for God: Spiritual Desire in Bernard of Clairvaux's Sermons on the Song of Songs* (Kalamazoo, Mich.: Cistercian Publications, 1988).

67. "The Humanity of Christ in Monastic Prayer," *MJ,* 92. The original article appeared in *Monastic Studies.*

68. See Edward Cuthbert Butler, *Western Mysticism: The Teaching of Augustine, Gregory and Bernard on Contemplation and the Contemplative Life,* 3rd ed. (London: Constable, 1967).

69. *MJ,* 20.

70. Ibid., 26–27.

71. Ibid., 22.

72. Ibid., 24–25.

73. Ibid., 20–21.

74. Ibid., 23.

2. SHY WILD DEER: PERSONIFICATIONS OF THE INNER SELF IN MERTON'S POETRY

1. Boris Pasternak, *Doctor Zhivago* (New York: Pantheon, 1958), 3–5, 9–10.

2. *DQ,* 13.

3. Thomas Merton, "Standards for Poets," *New York Herald Tribune Book Review,* May 8, 1938, p. 10. Also available in *LE,* 462–63.

4. "Sincerity in Art and Life: from a letter of Owen Merton," *Good Work* 30 (1967): 58–59.

5. George Woodcock, *Thomas Merton: Monk and Poet; A Critical Study* (New York: Farrar, Straus & Giroux, 1978).

6. Ibid., 55–62, 75.

7. *Commonweal* 42 (1945): 240–42.

8. Michael Mott, *The Seven Mountains of Thomas Merton,* 242.

9. *SC,* 7.

10. *LE,* 462–63.

11. See, for example, *The Secular Journal* (New York: Farrar, Straus & Cudahy, 1959), 140; *SJ,* 77.

12. *SSM,* 139–40.

13. Ibid., 202.

14. See Merton's revisionist reading of Blake, "Blake and the New Theology," *LE*, 3–11.

15. "Nature and Art in William Blake," *LE*, 387–453. Anne E. Carr, *A Search for Wisdom and Spirit*, 27–32 attributes significant influence upon Merton's spirituality of the inner self to Maritain's *Scholasticism and Politics:* the individual vs. person/community. Merton's philosophy studies with Dan Walsh coincided with his attempt to analyze Blake. It was Walsh who introduced Merton to Maritain at a 1939 lecture (*SSM,* 219).

16. "Nature and Art," *LE*, 451.

17. *SSM,* 110.

18. Cf. David Cooper's *Thomas Merton's Art of Denial,* 24–29, 133–38; and David Cooper, "A Duck in a Chicken Coop: Thomas Merton and the Missing Years," *Cithara* 20 (1981): 5–14; and George Kilcourse, "The Crossroads of Myth and Irony: Thomas Merton's 'Change of Address,'" *Cithara* 20 (1981): 15–23.

19. *SJ,* 233.

20. John Howard Griffin, "Thomas Merton: Man as Believer," Thomas Merton Studies Center lectures, Bellarmine College, 1973.

21. *SJ,* 233.

22. Ibid., 11.

23. Ibid., 89.

24. This presumes that *Tears of the Blind Lions* was written over an extended period prior to publication in 1949, and that *The Strange Islands* selections were written late, in 1956 and 1957. See David Cooper, "A Duck in a Chicken Coop," 7.

25. *SJ,* 15.

26. *Commonweal* 59 (1958–59): 89. Cf. Merton's 1953 resolution of the ongoing argument over contemplation versus action, in "Action and Contemplation in St. Bernard," *TMSB,* 63 [italics Merton's]: "We must *harmonize the two* [action and contemplation], achieve a perfect balance between them, give each one its due. . . . [The soul] is able to *seek* and *prefer* contemplation before all else, while devoting itself (when necessary) to that which is less great in itself but which has a more intimate claim upon its time and energies: the care of souls and the other responsibilities of its office. . . . The solution to the problem goes far to explain why St. Bernard can say that contemplation is, in itself, superior and preferable to action, while on the other hand action is 'more necessary' and 'better' than contemplation." With such nuances, Merton roots action in a contemplative source, and avoids the pitfalls of activism.

27. *SSM,* 171–75.

28. Paul Tillich, *Dynamics of Faith* (New York: Harper & Row, 1957), 55–73.

29. *BW,* 53. Merton continues to pursue this New Criticism theory of

poetry: "Like all great works of art, true poems seem to live by a life entirely their own. What we must seek in a poem is therefore not an accidental reference to something outside itself: we must seek this inner principle of individuality and of life which is its soul, or 'form.' What the poem actually 'means' can only be summed up in the whole content of poetic experience which it is capable of producing in the reader. The total poetic experience is what the poet is trying to communicate to the rest of the world."

30. Ibid., 74–75.

31. "The Inner Experience: Some Dangers in Contemplation (VI)," *Cistercian Studies* 19 (1984): 147–48.

32. Ibid., 147–50.

33. *MZM*, 245–46.

34. *LE*, 29–36.

35. Ibid., 128–30.

36. *TMR*, 18.

37. *CP*, 6–7.

38. Ibid., 73–74.

39. Ibid., 143–46.

40. Ibid., 221–22.

41. Ibid., 3.

42. Ibid., 202–3.

43. Ibid., 96.

44. Ibid., 209–10.

45. Ibid., 99–100.

46. Thérèse Lentfoehr interprets many of these same poems as Zen poems, with the same appreciation of solitude and contemplation. See *Words and Silence: On the Poetry of Thomas Merton* (New York: New Directions, 1979), especially chapter 4.

47. *CP*, 317–18.

48. Ibid., 319–21.

49. Ibid., 215–17.

50. Ibid., 289–90.

51. Ibid., 239–45.

52. Ibid., 337–38.

53. The imagery of this poem recurs in a 1968 poem, "Rilke's Epitaph" (*CP*, 620): *"Rose, O pure / Contradiction / Longing to be nobody's / Sleep under so many / Lids."* Merton reverses this opening imagery: "Pierced by an innocent / Rose, (O pure / Contradiction) / Nobody's lids / And Everybody's sleep."

54. *CP*, 344–45.

55. Ibid., 353.

56. Ibid., 29–30.

57. *SSM,* 279–83.

58. A remarkable parallel to the imagery of "Song for Our Lady of Cobre" occurs in chapter 19 of *MAWG,* 183–84 ("Journal: Paris"). Just before recording the 1941 poem, Merton remarks: "I remember the wide hats and bagpipes and the black rocks crowned with huge statues of the Blessed Virgin. . . ." The poem is as follows:

> The moon smiles like a queen
> (says the voice in my vision)
> The star sings in the gate,
> (shines the speech in my ear)
> The waves all clap hands
> (says the voice in my vision)
> And the sleeping capes
> (shines the speech in my ear)
> Awake as shrill as children,
> The sleeping capes awake as innocent
> as children, lifting up their
> Hands to high heaven,
> (says the voice in my vision).
> The queen of light comes shining like a ship.
> The green hills sing hymns.
> The rocks cry out like glass.
> Leviathan plays in the gates of the ocean.
> The man on the mast cries land!
> (shines the speech in my ear)
> The man on the mast cries land!

59. *CP,* 35–36.

60. Ibid., 288–89.

61. The *Selected Poems of Thomas Merton,* with an introduction by Mark Van Doren (New York: New Directions, 1959), xi.

62. Ibid., p. xii. For an intriguing comparison, see Merton's poem, "In Silence," in the same collection, *The Strange Islands* (*CP,* 280–81). The themes parallel the more dramatic "Elegy for the Monastery Barn" but lack Merton's existential transformation. So "In Silence" remains abstract and dry. Cf. *SJ,* 325 where Merton records an April 22, 1951 entry: "This morning was like the morning of that first poem, the retreat in the guest house, ten years ago. The barn—that is, the garden house, which from my room seemed to me beautiful and mysterious—had become the very mystery in which I was hidden."

63. *CP,* 35.

64. Ibid., 84–85.

65. Merton recorded a conference to novices in which he offered an explica-

tion of Rilke's "Carrousel." It would not be unlikely that this particular poem, "Dirge for a Town in France," was influenced directly by that poem and its central metaphor.

66. Other early examples of Merton's sustained use of the innocent child imagery to symbolize the inner self of paradise consciousness are: "The Winter's Night" (*CP,* 38); "Evening" (ibid., 41–42); "Birdcage Walk" (ibid., 275–77); "Landscape" (ibid., 277–79); "The Fall" (ibid., 354–55). His "Aubade—Harlem" (ibid., 82–83) implies the child's paradisal innocence in the environs of Harlem's "cages of keyless aviaries." "The lines and wires, the gallows of the broken kites, / Crucify. . . ." Merton develops this crucifixion imagery with Pilate and Judas allusions, personifications of the false self; he contrasts them with the children who are present symbolically in "The ragged dresses of the little children." The paradise consciousness is directly evoked in "A Psalm" (ibid., 220–21).

67. Ibid., 330–31.

68. Ibid., 351–52.

69. Griffin, "Thomas Merton: Man as Believer," Thomas Merton Studies Center lectures, Bellarmine College, 1973.

70. *CP,* 631–32.

71. Perhaps the only equally eccentric monk at Gethsemani, Father Peter, had trained his turkeys to walk in single file like Trappists marching to work in the field. He paraded the turkeys for visitors at the monastery, and reports have it that he attired them with blessed medals. When some of the younger monks' embarrassment got beyond tolerance they hi-jacked the turkeys in a truck and advised Father Peter that they were stolen. He demanded that a deposition be given to the local sheriff. The monks had to find a confederate in the person of a neighboring farmer on whom they pinned a sheriff's star. At the formal meeting in the monastery, the "sheriff" interrogated Father Peter, beginning with the questions, "Where did the crime take place?" and "Can you describe the missing victims?"

72. "The Inner Experience: Notes on Contemplation (I)," *Cistercian Studies* 18 (1983): 3–5.

73. *VOC,* 90.

74. Ibid., 114–15.

75. Ibid., 130.

76. Ibid., 162.

77. Ibid., 165.

78. *CP,* 736–37.

79. I am reminded of John Updike's recent observation in his memoirs, *Self-Consciousness* (New York: Knopf, 1989): "A writer's self-consciousness, for which he is much scorned, is really a mode of interestedness, that inevitably turns outward."

80. *VOC,* 6.

81. Ibid., 88.

82. See Mott, *The Seven Mountains of Thomas Merton,* 228ff.; 286ff., where Mott records Merton's attraction to the forest solitude, eventually being named the abbey's forester. In an early (1947) poem, "Poem in the Rain and the Sun," *CP,* 741–42, he would write: "Owning the view in the air of a hermit's weather. . . . " Two early poems which were analyzed earlier in this chapter under the category "poetry of paradise consciousness," "Trappists Working" and "St. Alberic," are situated in the forest and foreshadow this symbolism of a deeper freedom.

83. *VOC,* 159.

84. Ibid., 112.

85. *Eighteen Poems* (New York: New Directions, 1985) [no pagination].

86. "Rain and the Rhinoceros," *Raids on the Unspeakable* (New York: New Directions, 1966), 10.

87. *VOC,* 156.

88. Ibid., 107.

89. Ibid., 207–8.

90. Ibid., 6.

91. "As kingfishers catch fire, dragonflies draw flame," *Gerard Manley Hopkins, Poems and Prose,* selected and edited by W. H. Gardner (Baltimore: Penguin Books, 1967), 51.

92. T. S. Eliot, "The Dry Salvages," line 215, *The Four Quartets* (New York: Harcourt, Brace & World, 1943).

93. "Elegy for a Trappist," *CP,* 631.

94. "Merlin and the Deer," ll. 10–13, *CP,* 736–37.

3. DANCE OF THE LORD IN EMPTINESS:
MERTON'S KENOTIC CHRIST

1. *CWA,* 159.

2. *CGB,* 141.

3. Cf. Sidney H. Griffin, "Thomas Merton, Louis Massignon, and the Challenge of Islam," *Merton Annual* 3 (1990): 151–72. See also Madeline Abdelnour, "Le Point Vierge in Thomas Merton," *Cistercian Studies* 6 (1971): 153–71.

4. *CGB,* 141.

5. "Hagia Sophia," *CP,* 363–71.

6. *SJ,* 347.

7. A late entry in *CGB* develops Merton's new appreciation of the integrity of his experience and reflections: "It is slowly . . . that I work my life

into another dimension . . . and there is a growing liberty from the succession of events and experiences. They are more and more woven into the great pattern of the whole experience of [hu]mankind and even something quite beyond all experience. I am less aware of myself simply as this individual who is a monk and writer, and who, as monk and writer, does this, or writes that. It is my task to see and speak for many, even when I am speaking for myself" (245).

8. See Rahner, *Theological Investigations* 13 (New York: Crossroad, 1975): 213–22. See also Leo O'Donovan, "The Word of the Cross," *Chicago Studies* 25 (1986): 69, where he remarks on Rahner's self-criticism in 1974 when he "puzzled over the possible discrepancy between his earlier speculative theology of the incarnation and his later reflections on the life of Jesus moving towards the cross."

9. Michael L. Cook, *The Jesus of Faith: A Study in Christology* (New York: Paulist, 1971), 203.

10. See David Cooper, *Thomas Merton's Art of Denial*, 50–60.

11. *HR,* 65.

12. *SJ,* 66.

13. Ibid., 84.

14. Ibid., 243.

15. Ibid., 191.

16. Ibid., 125, 178.

17. Ibid., 341.

18. Ibid., 234.

19. Ibid., 255.

20. Ibid. 68.

21. *NM,* 114.

22. Ibid., 96, 237. Merton intimated in an October 16, 1954, letter to his literary mentor at Columbia University, Mark Van Doren, that the book was then being aptly, if less catchingly, titled "Existential Communion" (*The Road to Joy,* ed. Robert E. Daggy [New York: Farrar, Straus & Giroux, 1989], 26).

23. See Merton's discussion of the limits of discursive reason in *AT,* 274–87.

24. *A Search for Wisdom and Spirit: Thomas Merton's Theology of the Self.*

25. "The Historical Consciousness," *Contemplative Review* 1:2 (1968), 2.

26. In a September 19, 1946, letter to Mark Van Doren, Merton wrote enthusiastically about Scotus, a vital influence from his 1938–39 study with Dan Walsh at Columbia University, even expressing the intention of writing a book. Given the contents of the chapter, "Things in their Identity," and the sacramental vision of the book, it is plausible that *Seeds of Contempla-*

tion has evolved as a semblance of the desired Scotus book. Merton's letter exclaimed:

> Duns Scotus and St. Bonaventure are tremendous. A book on that Scotus is brewing, I can see that: it will take time, though, and God will have to give me a lot of special graces if am going to do it well, because Scotus is something big. The thing is: while St. Thomas got off with Aristotle and tended to be intellectual and systematizing, Scotus knew how to take Aristotle and leave him alone and he keeps the full tradition of St. Augustine and St. Anselm — which keeps love in the first place all down the line — in its purity. Also he is the one who most glorifies Christ, that is, gives to the *Incarnate* Word, the Man-God [,] the full limit of everything that can be given Him. Living in the same house with Him we get to find out that this is the way to talk! I think that is everything.

This paragraph has disappointingly been edited out of the letter's published form, *The Road to Joy,* 20–21. My source for this highly significant missing paragraph is the Mark Van Doren Collection, The Butler Library, Columbia University.

27. *SC,* 24. Publisher J. Laughlin commented that the burlap cover of *Seeds of Contemplation* was made of the same fabric used to decorate trendy New York bars.

28. Ibid., 25.

29. Ibid.

30. Ibid., 111.

31. Cf. Merton's early poem, "The Blessed Virgin Mary Compared to a Window," *CP,* 46–48, employs the same metaphor. It imitates Hopkins's more effective metaphysical conceit in "The Blessed Virgin Mary Compared to the Air We Breathe."

32. Verbal commitments to a social reality appear in *SC,* but they lack the conviction of Merton's later work. For example, "I must look for my identity, somehow, not only in God but in other men" (41). He implies the same in his description of "the world" as "the unquiet city of those who live for themselves" (57). Therefore, one flees to the desert, "Not to escape people, but to learn how to find them" (58). Christ must be "found in others, or else He will not live in you" (115). See also his recommendation that monks experience poverty in solidarity with the poor (166–68).

33. *SC,* 91.

34. Ibid., 29.

35. Ibid., 46.

36. Ibid., 47, 59.

37. *AT,* 22.

38. Ibid., 26–27.

39. Ibid., 113–14.

40. Ibid., 131.

41. Ibid., 145–46.

42. Ibid., 243.

43. Ibid., 318.

44. Ibid., 261, 278.

45. *No Man Is an Island* (New York: Harcourt, Brace and Co., 1955), xxii. He later refines this mystery: "To find 'ourselves' then is to find not only our poor, limited, perplexed souls, but to find the power of God that raised Christ from the dead and 'built us together in Him unto a habitation of God in the Spirit' (Ephesians 2:22)," p. 15.

46. Ibid., xi, xvi.

47. Ibid., 92–93.

48. Ibid., 95–96.

49. Ibid., 53.

50. *Thoughts in Solitude* (New York: Farrar, Straus & Cudahy, 1958), 94.

51. Ibid., 87.

52. Ibid., 64. See also 37, 40–41 for reflections on "poverty" and "immolation" that characterize Jesus' kenosis. It is significant that he phrases the mystery in terms of compassion: "[W]e cannot have true compassion on others unless we are willing to accept pity and receive forgiveness for our own sins," (37).

53. Ibid., 83.

54. Ibid., 96.

55. Ibid., 122–24, emphasis mine.

56. *NM,* 114.

57. Ibid., 96, 237.

58. Ibid., 12.

59. Ibid., 18, emphasis mine.

60. Ibid., 135–36.

61. DeLubac's *Catholicism* is cited, *NM,* 5. See also Merton's reading notes on Hans Urs Von Balthasar's *La Liturgie Cosmique,* trans. L. Lhaumet and H.-A. Prentout (Paris: Aubier, 1947), a study of the seventh-century Greek Father, Maximus the Confessor. This volume and notes are especially helpful in appreciating Merton's development of the terms "in Christ" and "recapitulation." He records this influence in his unpublished lecture notes for a 1954 course he presented at the Abbey of Gethsemani, "Sanctity in the Epistles of Saint Paul" (Thomas Merton Studies Center collection, Bellarmine College).

Von Balthasar wrote an "Afterword" (*Nachwort*) to a German translation of a collection of Merton's poetry, *Grazias Haus: Gedichte* (Einsiedeln: Johannes Verlag, 1966). Merton enthusiastically reviewed Von Balthasar's *Word and Revelation* (*Commonweal* 81 [1964], 357–59) and corresponded with Von Balthasar (*The School of Charity,* ed. Patrick Hart [New York: Farrar, Straus, Giroux, 1990], 218–19, 226–27, 241, 287–88, 312). While there are obvious differences of interest in their spirituality and theology (as well as temperament) between the two, it is striking to note Von Balthasar's scholarly research on kenosis as a christological emphasis. He composed the entry on "Kénose" in the *Dictionnaire de Spiritualite, Aesthetique et Moral,* and his *Mysterium Paschale: The Mystery of Easter,* trans. with an introduction by Aidan Nichols (Edinburgh: T. and T. Clark, 1990) centers his christological reflections on kenosis.

62. *NM,* 134.
63. Ibid., 136–38.
64. Ibid., 106–7, 73–77.
65. Ibid., 41–44.
66. Cf. Donald Grayston, *Thomas Merton, The Development of a Spiritual Theologian* (New York and Toronto: Edwin Mellin Press, 1985); and Ruth Fox, "From Seeds to New Seeds," *Merton Annual* 1 (1988): 249–70.
67. *NSC,* 7, emphasis Merton's.
68. Ibid., 61–62.
69. Ibid., 72–75, emphasis Merton's.
70. Ibid., 141.
71. Ibid., 150.
72. Ibid., 152–53, emphasis Merton's.
73. Ibid., 209–10; cf. 154, where he identifies Christ as "present in the depths of our own being as our Friend, and as our other self."
74. Ibid., 227.
75. Ibid., 281–82.
76. Ibid., 290–93.
77. Ibid., 294.
78. Ibid., 295.
79. Ibid., 296–97.
80. *CGB,* v, vi.
81. Ibid., 3–4.
82. Ibid., vi.
83. Ibid., 144, 182.
84. Ibid., 289. There is evidence that Merton had read Henri Bouillard's *Karl Barth* (3 vols., Paris, 1957). While he read much of Hans Urs Von Balthasar, it would appear that he did not study this Swiss theologian's landmark study, *The Theology of Karl Barth* (New York: Holt, Rinehart and Winston, 1971) in its original German edition of 1962 because of his difficulty in reading German. However, it is important to note Von Balthasar's critique: Barth operated with a mistaken notion of "the analogy of being"; he eventually

developed an appropriate sense of grace building on nature that made his theology compatible with Catholic theology. Thus, Von Balthasar points to Barth's theological system as christocentric, with ecclesiology and sacramental theology flowing from the christology. Two affirmations Von Balthasar makes about Barth coincide with Merton's attraction to him: "The natural order, for all its inner laws and conditions, ultimately rests upon *a gratuitious happening (the Incarnation) and the history that flows from it*" (266, emphasis mine); "The real happening for Barth is now the Incarnation, *not the vertical descent of God's atemporal Word into the world*" (267, emphasis mine).

85. "St. Anselm and His Argument," *American Benedictine Review* 17 (1966), 238–62. Merton's essay reviews two recent Anselm studies, David Knowles's *The Evolution of Medieval Thought* and Richard W. Southern's *St. Anselm and His Argument.*

86. "Reflections on Some Recent Studies of St. Anselm," *Monastic Studies* 3 (1965): 222.

87. *CGB*, 312–13, emphasis Merton's. Cf. Merton's discussion of Anselm's theology in *CGB*, 298–302, 311–12, 315–16.

88. "St. Anselm and His Argument," *American Benedictine Review* 3 (1966), 258.

89. Ibid., 257.

90. *CGB*, 50.

91. Ibid., 59.

92. Ibid., 254–55.

93. Ibid., 244.

94. Ibid., 88.

95. Ibid., 174 where he criticizes the "Satanic theology" of "gnostic incarnation" which denies the God-Man in Christ. See later his statement: "The loveliness of the humanity which God has taken to Himself in love is, after all, to be seen in the humanity of our friends, our children, our brothers, the people we love and who love us. Now that God has become Incarnate, why do we go to such lengths all the time, to 'disincarnate' Him again, to unweave the garment of flesh and reduce Him once again to spirit? As if the Body of the Lord had not become 'Life-giving-Spirit'" (193).

96. Ibid., 231.

97. Ibid., 274.

98. Notebook #76, "1965—second half. Readings, etc. August to November" (emphasis Merton's), Thomas Merton Studies Center, Bellarmine College. Cf. notebook #88, "Working Notebook—1968" for six pages of Merton's reading notes on Bonhoeffer's *The Letters and Papers from Prison.*

99. "Orthodoxy and the World," *Monastic Studies* 4 (1966): 108.

100. Ibid., 110–11.

101. Cf. "Letter to a Greek Writer," *Seeds of Destruction* (New York: Far-

rar, Straus & Giroux, 1964), 312–14: "Here is where I think there are great possibilities in the Greek Orthodox tradition: the theology of St. Gregory Palamas, for example, with the belief in the 'divine energies' and their transfiguring effect in the world of matter. This has not yet been explored, and I think a great work will be done when the hidden possibilities of this theology are made known to the world." Merton's context is a discussion of the new demands being made on "religion" in our day. He characterizes the age as one where the "much more difficult task is not that of having a pure soul but also of spiritualizing matter."

102. *CGB,* 40, 294.

103. *RT,* 43.

104. "Letter to a Priest," *Seeds of Destruction,* 318–26.

105. *RT,* 52, 55, 59. In a later essay on "Blake and the New Theology," *LE,* 3–11, Merton returns to his aversion to Process Theology: "Afflicted as I am with an incurable case of metaphysics, I cannot see where the idea of Godhead *as process* is more dynamic than that of Godhead as *pure act.* To one who has been exposed to scholastic ontology and has not recovered, it remains evident that *the activity of becoming* is considerably less alive and dynamic than the *act of Being.* Far from regarding 'pure Being' as static quiescence, traditional metaphysics is in accord with Blake regarding it as the source and ground of all life. . . . Surely Blake's God is Creator who is present and immanent in his creation, not remote from it and solitary" (9).

106. Merton, "The Universe as Epiphany," *Love and Living* (New York: Farrar, Straus, & Giroux, 1979), 171–84.

107. *Commonweal* 87 (1967): 109–11.

108. *Albert Camus' The Plague: Introduction and Commentary,* Religious Dimensions in Literature 7 (New York: Seabury, 1968), 39–42.

109. *Seeds of Destruction,* xiii–xv, 195; cf. Merton's "Letter to a Priest," *Seeds of Destruction,* where he replies to charges that he and Rahner take a defeatist attitude of withdrawl with this concept of the diaspora. He passionately protests against a superficial church in the modern world that would reduce Christian optimism to the Rotary Club's cult of success and visible results, or to "the spurious radiance of clerical Babbits" (323).

110. Ibid., 89–90.

111. Ibid., 94.

112. Ibid., 96, 101.

113. Ibid., 176–83.

114. "The Humanity of Christ in Monastic Prayer," *MJ,* 87–88.

115. Ibid., 9, 13, 16, 19, 20, 21, 22, 24.

116. Ibid., 20, emphasis Merton's.

117. Ibid., 20, emphasis mine.

118. Ibid., 22, emphasis mine.

119. *VOC,* 42.
120. Ibid., 87.
121. Ibid., 106.
122. Ibid., 156–57.
123. Ibid., 182–83.
124. Merton's prefaces and introductions to foreign translations have been collected as *"Honorable Reader": Reflections on My Work,* edited by Robert E. Daggy (New York: Crossroad, 1989).
125. Ibid., 39–40.
126. Ibid., 41.
127. Ibid., 51.
128. Ibid., 65–66.
129. Ibid., 91.
130. Ibid., 135.

4. SON OF THE WIDOWED GOD: MERTON'S SAPIENTIAL INTERPRETATION OF FICTION

1. "The Inner Experience: Problems of the Contemplative Life (VII)," *Cistercian Studies* 19 (1984): 279.
2. *MZM,* 273, 280.
3. *SJ,* 241.
4. *Opening the Bible* (Collegeville, Minn.: Liturgical Press, 1970), 76, 42.
5. *CWA,* 357. Merton continues: "The imagination is something which enables us to discover unique present meaning in a given moment of our life. Without imagination the contemplative life can be extremely dull and fruitless."
6. "The Inner Experience," 269–71.
7. Ibid., 274–75.
8. *CGB,* 242; 99. See Merton's parallel discussions of the post-Christian consciousness in: *FV,* 142, 244, 263; *CGB,* 301, 305, 306; *LE,* 218, 229, 230. There are seeds here that would blossom in Merton's Bangkok address, given on the day of his death. On that occasion Merton described a Tibetan abbot's reply to a lama's question whether to escape Tibet to save his life. The "strange message" the abbot sent back was described as "very significant" by Merton—"'From now on, Brother, everybody stands on his own feet.'" He interpreted the statement to mean "that we can no longer rely on being supported by structures that may be destroyed at any moment by a political power or a political force. You cannot rely on structures" (*AJ,* 338).
9. *RT,* 7.
10. Ibid., 56.

11. See Nathan A. Scott, Jr., "Criticism and the Religious Horizon," *Humanities, Religion and the Arts in the Future* (New York: Holt, Rinehart and Winston, 1972), 39–60.

12. *MZM,* 258–62. Merton praised O'Connor for her existentialist voice:

> Yet as we read Flannery O'Connor we find an uncomfortable feeling creeping over us: we are on the side of the fanatic and the mad boy, and we are against this reasonable zombie [Rayber]. We are against everything he stands for. We find ourselves nauseated by the reasonable, objective, 'scientific' answer he has for everything. In him, science is so right that it is a disaster.
> Such is the dire effect of reading an existentialist.

> . . . .

> This, in brief, is the existentialist case against the scientism and sociologism of positivist society. It is a brief for the person and for personal, spiritual liberty against determinism and curtailment (260–61).

13. *RT,* 41. See also Merton's "Symbolism: Communication or Communion?" *Love and Living,* 54–79.

14. As quoted in William H. Shannon, *Thomas Merton's Dark Path* (New York: Farrar, Straus & Giroux, 1981), 97.

15. *CGB,* 204, italics Merton's.

16. "Symbolism: Communication or Communion?" 79.

17. *LE,* 26.

18. As quoted in Ross Labrie, *The Art of Thomas Merton* (Fort Worth: Texas Christian University Press, 1979), 13.

19. "Notes on Sacred and Profane Art," *Jubilee* 4 (November 1956): 26, 31.

20. *LE,* 16.

21. Ibid., 18, 22.

22. Ibid., 27–28.

23. Ibid., 148.

24. Ibid., 152.

25. Ibid., 371–74.

26. Ibid., 378. Cf. Merton's article, "Art and Morality," *New Catholic Encyclopedia* (New York: McGraw-Hill, 1967), I:864–67.

27. *LE,* 98.

28. Ibid., 99.

29. "The Inner Experience," 147–50.

30. *LE,* 382.

31. Ibid.

32. *HGL,* 542.

33. Mott, *The Seven Mountains of Thomas Merton,* 354–58.

34. See *Boris Pasternak/Thomas Merton: Six Letters* (Lexington, Ky.: "The King Library Press," University of Kentucky, 1973).

35. *DQ,* 46.

36. Ibid., 12.

37. Merton qualifies this with an important comment on kenosis: "Like Dostoevsky, Pasternak sees life as a mystic, but without the hieratic kenoticism of *The Brothers Karamazov.* The mysticism of Pasternak is more latent, more cosmic, more pagan, if you like. It is more primitive, less sophisticated, free and untouched by any hieratic forms. There is therefore a 'newness' and freshness of his spirituality that contrasts with the worn and mature sanctity of Staretz Zossima purified of self-consciousness by the weariness of much suffering. Pasternak's simple and moving poem on 'Holy Week' illustrates this point. It is the death and resurrection of Christ seen in and through nature" (*DQ,* 13).

38. Ibid., 15. Merton goes on to note that one of the greatest sins attributed to Zhivago, the doctor and poet, is his belief in intuition (20).

39. Ibid., 8.

40. Ibid., 48. See *NSC,* 232 for a striking parallel where Merton concludes his chapter "The Gift of Understanding" with the description of passing out of ourselves into the joy of emptiness and nothingness, into a light which tastes of Paradise. He identifies this light with Christ, "Who stands in the midst of us and we know Him not."

41. Ibid., 49.

42. Ibid., 61–62.

43. Ibid., 62.

44. Ibid., 65–66.

45. *LE,* 182, 211, 218, 232, 258. See Merton's retreat conferences to women religious, published as *The Springs of Contemplation* (New York: Farrar, Straus & Giroux, 1992), where Merton attributes to C. S. Lewis his use of the term "post-Christian."

46. Ibid., 232.

47. Ibid., 239.

48. Ibid., 240.

49. Ibid., 235.

50. Ibid., 239.

51. Ibid., 241.

52. Ibid., 244, emphasis mine.

53. Ibid., 247.

54. Ibid., 248.

55. Ibid., 275.

56. Ibid., 282.

57. Ibid., 288.

58. Ibid., 289.
59. Ibid., 286.
60. Ibid., 290.
61. Ibid., 258.
62. Ibid., 260.
63. Ibid., 259.
64. Ibid., 262.
65. Ibid., 272.
66. Ibid., 274.
67. Ibid., 220, 225.
68. Ibid., 231.
69. Ibid., 230.
70. Ibid., 221.
71. Ibid., 222.
72. Ibid., 231.
73. Ibid., 181. In a late poem, "With the World in my Blood Stream," from his 1968 collection entitled *Sensation Time at the Home,* Merton echoes this metaphor of "the death dance in our blood." The poem is surrealistic and marked by reveries during a hospital confinement. It suggests an autobiographical recapitulation with references to "my lost childhood," his admission that he has "no more sweet home," and "my lost Zen breathing." At two intervals in the poem Merton mentions Christ: saying that all his veins run with Christ, and that Christ's frail body sweats in the hospital bed where Merton himself is Christ's "lost cell." (See *CP,* 615–18.)
74. Ibid., 202.
75. Ibid.
76. Ibid., 196.
77. Ibid., 212–13.
78. Ibid., 204.
79. Ibid., 205.
80. Ibid., 191.
81. Ibid., 215–16.
82. Ibid., 299.
83. Ibid., 293.
84. Ibid., 298–99.
85. Ibid., 298.
86. Ibid., 291.
87. Ibid., 118.
88. Ibid., 119.
89. Ibid., 120.
90. Ibid.
91. Ibid., 106.

92. I use "appropriation" in the technical sense of Paul Ricoeur's *Interpretation Theory: Discourse and the Surplus of Meaning* (Fort Worth: Texas Christian University Press, 1976).

93. Ibid., 523.

94. Ibid., 530.

95. Ibid., 534–36.

96. Ibid., 498.

97. *Opening the Bible*, 45.

98. *LE*, 512.

99. Ibid., 514.

100. *Opening the Bible*, 48.

101. Ibid., 45.

102. *FV*, 258, 284.

103. *LE*, 115.

104. Ibid., 45.

105. *FV*, 156, 208.

106. Ibid., 273.

5. A SUMMA OF OFFBEAT ANTHROPOLOGY:
MERTON'S ANTIPOETRY AS CHRISTOLOGY

1. See Anthony Padovano, *The Human Journey: Thomas Merton, Symbol of a Century* (Garden City, N.Y.: Doubleday, 1982), 111 for an interpretation of these three garden motifs in this poem (number 80) from *Cables to the Ace* (*CP*, 449).

2. Notebook #84, p. 16, Thomas Merton Studies Center collection, Bellarmine College.

3. "Queen's Tunnel," n. 50, *CP*, 516.

4. *Letters From Tom*, ed. W. H. Ferry (Scarsdale, N.Y.: Fort Hill Press, 1983), 62.

5. This elusive term, antipoetry, has been defined variously. Babette Deutsch early defined the "antipoetic" in terms of Wallace Stevens's line, "that truth, that reality to which all of us are forever fleeing." [*Poetry Handbook: A Dictionary of Terms*, rev. and enlarged ed. (New York: Funk and Wagnalls, 1962), 109.] Deutsch attributed the proliferation of such antipoetry to William Carlos Williams. Merton's appreciation of antipoetry came largely through the works of Nicanor Parra, who was writing antipoems as early as 1938. He found a summary definition in Miller Williams's "Introduction" to Parra's *Poem and Antipoems* (New York: New Directions, 1967), vii: "We want to ask, of course, what antipoetry is, and for an answer we get what we always get when the thing we're talking about is not definable: we get description.

Antipoetry is flat, is understated and relaxed; antipoetry 'returns poetry,' as Parra likes to say, 'to its roots,' is honest; antipoetry is unadorned, is unlyrical, is nonsymbolist; in antipoetry what you see is what you see; antipoetry is chiseled, solid."

6. John Howard Griffin, "Thomas Merton: Man as Believer," Thomas Merton Studies Center lectures, Bellarmine College, 1973. See also *The Nonviolent Alternative* (New York: Farrar, Straus, Giroux, 1980), "[T]he effort of someone such as Lenny Bruce to restore to language some of its authentic impact was a service despairingly offered to a public that could not appreciate it. One might argue that the language of this disconcerting and perhaps prophetic comedian was often less obscene than the 'decent' but horrifying platitudes of those who persecuted him."

7. "News of the Joyce Industry," *LE*, 12–22.

8. John D. Crossan, *The Dark Interval: Towards a Theology of Story* (Niles, Ill.: Argus Communications, 1975).

9. Northrop Frye, *Anatomy of Criticism: Four Essays* (Princeton: Princeton University Press, 1957), 34.

10. *MJ*, 172.

11. William F. Lynch, *Images of Faith: An Exploration of the Ironic Imagination* (Notre Dame, Ind.: University of Notre Dame Press, 1973), 89.

12. Ibid., 85.

13. For a sense of myth as "broken" by demytholigization see Paul Ricoeur, *The Symbolism of Evil* (Boston: Beacon, 1967), 3–10.

14. *CGB*, 223, 235–43.

15. Merton offered a definition of myth which leads to his uneasy attitude toward contemporary cultural myths: "By 'myth' I do not mean a lie. A myth is an imaginative synthesis of facts and intuitions about them, forming an interpretative complex of ideas and images. This complex of 'values' then becomes central in a meaning-system or world-view, a norm of judgement and of practice. The myth of progress is a synthetic and imaginative evaluation of man and of society which assumes that man is always getting better (qualitatively) as a result of his quantitatively increasing control over matter and nature. This 'progress' tends to be regarded as an absolute value in itself. Actually the myth of progress, contemporaneity, etc., have become the centre of superstitions which are fully as tenacious and absurd as any religious superstitions of the past" (*RT*, 30). Cf. *FV*, 274n.

16. *CGB*, 24.

17. *HGL*, 164.

18. *The Behavior of Titans* (New York: New Directions, 1961), 14, 16, 18. He introduces two other mythic characters: Atlas, who "speaks to the night as to a woman," which is to say that he "speaks of his heart" (27); and the Fatman, who is a mechanical persona, one enamored of systems (27–47, 62).

19. Ibid., 76.

20. Ibid., 79.

21. Ibid., 87.

22. Ibid., 91–92.

23. Ibid., 56, 59.

24. "A Letter to Pablo Antonio Cuadra Concerning Giants," *Blackfriars* 42 (1962): 69–81; also available in *CP,* 372–91. See also Merton's article of this same period, "Is the World a Problem?" *CWA,* 143–56.

25. *CP,* 380, italics Merton's.

26. Ibid., 382–83.

27. Ibid., 384.

28. *FV,* 199–204. For an illustration of Merton's analysis of German nationalism displacing the church, see his three essays, "Auschwitz: A Family Camp," "A Devout Meditation in Memory of Adolf Eichmann," and "Danish Nonviolent Resistance to Hitler," in *The Nonviolent Alternative,* 150–67.

29. *FV,* 206–9. The reflections of Third World Liberation theologians have subsequently suggested this same privilege of nonbelievers. See, for example, Juan Luis Segundo's *The Community Called Church* (Maryknoll, N.Y.: Orbis, 1973), where he suggests that lukewarm church members who refuse to commit themselves wholeheartedly to the mission of the church thereby jeopardize their own salvation. Such persons, Segundo judges, would be better off outside the church, where salvation would depend upon the reality of love within their lives and not ecclesial responsibilities for mission. Segundo speaks of the sacramental life of the church as instrumental, not primary. The danger he sees is that the emancipation of human persons in history becomes aborted, or subordinated. Paul Lakeland offers a concise analysis of Segundo in *Theology and Critical Theory: The Discourse of the Church* (Nashville: Abingdon, 1990), 229–32: "Segundo of course is not arguing that salvation is to be identified with justice or with emancipation, but rather that salvation is encountered within the struggle for justice and emancipation carried out in history" (231).

30. *FV,* 211–13.

31. Ibid., 213–14.

32. *LE,* 162–67.

33. Ibid., 167.

34. *HGL,* 218. Cf. *Letters to Tom,* 21, 26, 38–39, 41, 46, 53–54, 58, 61, where Merton scolds the hierarchy and church officials in unequivocal language.

35. *HGL,* 585.

36. Ibid., 609.

37. Ibid., 651–52.

38. Ibid., 178. For Merton's enthusiastic review of Hans Küng's *The Church,*

Reunion, and Reform see his letter to an unidentified Benedictine studying in Germany, *Seeds of Destruction,* 289–92. He includes the comment: "There is really a breath of new life about this book and about his outlook. It is awake and frank, not wild, but objectively Catholic in the finest sense — not the sense of the poor good people who have been paralyzed for ages by rigidities and conventions" (290).

39. *HGL,* 651.

40. Thomas P. McDonnell as quoted in Padovano, 48.

41. *Letters to Tom,* 57, 59.

42. For a useful appraisal of Merton's appreciation of these new poetic voices, see Stefan Baciu, "Latin America and Spain in the Poetic World of Thomas Merton," *Revue de Littérature Comparée* 41 (1967): 288–300; reprinted in *The Merton Annual* 3 (1989): 13–26.

43. Nicanor Parra, *Poems and Antipoems,* ed. and trans. Miller Williams (New York: New Directions, 1967).

44. *AJ,* 117–18.

45. Ibid., 286. Italics Merton's.

46. *LE,* 271–72.

47. Ibid., 273.

48. Mott, *The Seven Mountains of Thomas Merton,* 380.

49. Ibid., 380–81.

50. *The Nonviolent Alternative,* 234–35.

51. Ibid., 238–39.

52. Padovano, 113.

53. Cf. *RT,* 82–92.

54. See Merton's review of William Melvin Kelley's *The Legend of Tucker Caliban,* in *LE,* 168–77, for an appreciation of Kelley's appropriation of the Caliban figure in his fiction.

55. Merton quotes Caliban's early speech, *The Tempest* (I.ii.444–46), to compose cable 6: "Your taught me language and my profit on't / Is, I know how to curse. The red plague rid you / For learning me your language!"

56. Mark Van Doren, *Shakespeare* (New York: Henry Holt, 1939), 323.

57. *A Catch of Anti-Letters* (Kansas City, Mo.: Sheed, Andrews & Mc-Meel, 1978).

58. "East Coker," IV, line 1.

59. Ibid., lines 11–12.

60. "The Love Song of J. Alfred Prufrock," lines 10, 43–44.

61. *The Waste Land,* II ("A Game of Chess"), lines 115–16.

62. "Nothing of him that doth fade / but doth suffer a sea-change / Into something rich and strange" (I,ii.485–87).

63. *NSC,* 296.

64. Anthony Padovano has cogently remarked that for Merton the Re-

demption myth has not functioned effectively because the Creation myth has been ignored. At the center of the Creation myth is an affirmation of equality among all persons. Its ironic inversion throughout *Lograire* heightens this dilemma. See Padovano, *The Human Journey,* 144.

65. See Merton's poem, "Advice to a Young Prophet," *CP,* 338–39 for a similar poem about Klansmen. In *Lograire* he emphasizes the insatiable racial anger lurking in the South: "TEN GUNS ARE OUT OF WORK UP ANGER HOLLOW" (line 37); "AND KEEP CAIN OUT OF THAT HOLLOW" (line 42).

66. For a prose analysis shedding important light on Merton's poetic mosaic of the Mayan turmoil in *Lograire,* see his two essays in *Ishi Means Man* (Greensboro, N.C.: Unicorn Press, 1976). "Ishi: A Meditation" and "The Cross Fighters" examine the genocide (25) of Mayan Indians in the mid-nineteenth century. "Ishi" translates as "man," to symbolize the fact that the native California Indians never revealed their names, or those of others (32). He ponders over the word "genocide," which technology has made "easier, not new." His intent is to reflect on the "structure of these happenings," the genocide in Yucatan, because they leave a haunting and disturbing imprint upon the mind.

67. Merton integrates a brief interlude of the 1855 Kane Arctic relief expedition to conclude the "North" canto; and the fourteenth-century Muslim, Ibn Battuta's travels to Asia and Africa, to begin the "East" canto. The latter builds on Merton's theme of Cain and Abel enmity between Shi'ites and Sunnites in Islamic religious culture.

68. "Cargo Theology," 4, 37, emphasis Merton's. This is the author's revised manuscript taken from a May 11–12, 1967, tape recording which Merton made (Merton Studies Center, Bellarmine College). A subsequent edition appears in *Love and Living,* 80–94, and is entitled "Cargo Cults of the South Pacific."

69. "Cargo Cults" (manuscript), 49, 52–53, 44, 42.

70. Ibid., 56. Cf. "A Letter to Cuadra," 385, where Merton diagnoses the same divisive conflict and estrangement: "The desecration, desacralization of the modern world is manifest above all by the fact that the stranger is of no account. As soon as he is 'displaced' he is completely unacceptable. He fits into no familiar category. Everything not easy to account for must be wiped out, and mystery must be wiped out with it. An alien presence interferes with the superficial and faked clarity of our own rationalizations."

71. *Ishi Means Man* (Greensboro, N.C.: Unicorn Press, 1976), 9, 11–12, 14–15.

72. *Raids on the Unspeakable* (New York: New Directions, 1966), 72, 75.

73. Ibid., 2, 4–5.

74. Ibid., 18. He uses explicit kenotic language from Philippians 2:5–11 to define the eschatology inaugurated by Christ. "He has indeed emptied

Himself, taken the form of God's servant, man. But he did not empty Himself to the point of becoming mass man, faceless man. It was therefore right that there should be no room for him in a crowd that had been called together as an eschatological sign. His being born outside that crowd is even more of a sign. That there is no room for Him is a sign of the end" (68).

75. *FV,* 162–64.

76. *FV,* 252–55, 246, 248–49, 253, 254, 256.

77. *FV,* 258.

78. *Raids,* 32.

6. A COMMON SPIRITUAL CLIMATE: MERTON'S CHRISTOLOGY IN INTERRELIGIOUS DIALOGUE

1. As quoted in John Moffitt, "Memories of Thomas Merton," *Cistercian Studies* 14 (1979), 73.

2. *HGL,* 535–36. For further references to Merton's interreligious dialogue with Judaism see his correspondence with Abraham J. Heschel, *HGL,* 430–36; Erich Fromm, ibid., 308–24; and his unpublished "The Cold War Letters," Thomas Merton Studies Center collection, Bellarmine College.

3. *ZBA,* 5. For further references to Merton's interreligious dialogue with Islam and Sufism, see *HGL,* 43–67, for his correspondence with Abdul Aziz, especially pp. 56–57; see also M. Abdelnour, "Le Point Vierge in Thomas Merton," *Cistercian Studies* 6 (1971), 153–71.

4. *HGL,* 561–62. For a brief description of his 1964 meeting with Suzuki at Columbia University in New York, see *ZBA,* 59–66.

5. *HGL,* 566, 562–64.

6. Ibid., 564–65.

7. *ZBA,* 100.

8. Ibid., 102; cf. 123, 129.

9. Ibid., 116–18.

10. Ibid., 125, 128.

11. Ibid., 136–37, 118.

12. *Gandhi on Non-Violence* (New York: New Directions, 1965), 3, 5–6.

13. Ibid., 7–10.

14. Ibid., 11–13.

15. Ibid., 18–20.

16. *The Way of Chuang Tzu* (New York: New Directions, 1965), 9–10.

17. Ibid., 11.

18. Ibid., 15, 16, 23, 24.

19. Ibid., 25, 27, 29, 30.

20. *MZM,* viii–x.

21. Ibid., 7, 9–10. It is important to remark Merton's description of the tea ceremony as a contemplative exercise and not a religious ritual. This is reinforced later in the book when he notes the tendency of all institutional religion toward formalism and degeneration (251).

22. Ibid., 12–14.

23. Ibid., 17–20, 25.

24. Ibid., 50, 65, 70.

25. Ibid., 83–85, 90.

26. Ibid., 203–4.

27. Ibid., 214, 208.

28. Ibid., 212–14.

29. Ibid., 251, 237, 239–40, 236.

30. Ibid., 242, 247, 236.

31. Ibid., 282–83, 286.

32. *ZBA,* 75–76, emphasis Merton's.

33. Ibid., 18–20, 15–17, emphasis Merton's.

34. Ibid., 22, 24.

35. Ibid., 28–29, 31.

36. Ibid., 2, 3, 8, 21, 31, 33, 46, 62.

37. Ibid., 8–9, 12–13.

38. Ibid., 55–56.

39. *AJ,* 314–15.

40. Ibid., 296, 325, 310.

41. Ibid., 312–13.

42. Ibid., 308, 316.

43. Ibid., 332, 334.

44. Ibid., 342.

45. *MZM,* ix.

46. *ZBA,* 210.

47. Ibid., 118–19.

48. Ibid., 135.

49. Ibid.

50. Ibid., 8.

51. Ibid., 42.

52. *HGL,* 56–57.

53. *ZBA,* 57–58.

54. It is important to note Merton's dramatic shift in describing Zen, first as static and later as dynamic, in *ZBA,* 139, 222. For a helpful analysis of several such lacunae in Merton's Zen studies, see Joseph Chu-Cong, "Thomas Merton and the Far East," *Cistercian Studies* 14 (1979), 45–58, reprinted in *The Legacy of Thomas Merton,* ed. Patrick Hart (Kalamazoo, Mich.: Cistercian Publications, 1986), 49–65. Chu-Cong also comments on Suzuki's dis-

satisfaction with Merton's identification of Zen "emptiness" with Cassian's "purity of heart." Merton wrote to Suzuki in 1959, in a rather untypically patronizing manner, "What you are saying really belongs to the authentic Christian tradition" (*HGL,*, 566).

CONCLUSION

1. *HGL,* 500–501.
2. Ibid., 637.
3. Ibid., 642–43. Emphasis mine.
4. Ibid., 643–44.
5. Ibid., 644.
6. *TMSB,* 12. It could be argued, perhaps, that Leclercq overstates the immediate theological context as an "infatuation with the Christologies 'from below.'" Nonetheless, he clearly states that christology "begins in an act of faith in Christ's divinity and everything else we can perceive is illuminated by that light." This in no way truncates Merton's kenotic christology but makes more evident his development of a kenotic motif that integrates the christology "from below."
7. *ZBA,* 76–77. Cf. *AJ,* 72, where Merton advises that it is "false to make mysticism consist essentially in visions."
8. Ibid., 19.
9. Ibid., 17–18. Cf. *CGB,* 153, where Merton identifies the "crucial problem" as "the *conversion of the good* [persons] *to Christ.*" "But 'the good' are solely tempted to believe in their own goodness and their own capacity to love, while one who realizes his own poverty and nothingness is much more ready to surrender himself to the gift of love *he knows* cannot come from anything in himself" (emphasis Merton's).
10. *CGB,* 127.
11. *LE,* 159–61.
12. "The Inner Experience: Notes on Contemplation (I)," *Cistercian Studies* 18 (1983): 14–15.
13. Merton reiterated his preference for the existential voice in two late letters. Writing to June Yungblut, January 16, 1968, he deprecates his work: "I do think that my overall work is such a mess and contains so much that is trivial and inconsequential, and hopelessly useless, that it would make a rather deadly project if you had to go through even most of it, not to mention all of it." On March 6, 1968, when he again writes to Yungblut, he qualifies his earlier, blanket self-condemnation. He describes his "editorializing" about Christianity, monasticism, social justice, and peace as "thin and often a bit alien." "The work I feel more happy about is at once more personal, more

literary, more contemplative," he says. "Books like *Conjectures, New Seeds, Sign of Jonas, Raids,* or literary essays, or poetry, or things like introductions to Chuang Tzu, Gandhi, Desert Fathers, etc." He speaks of writing "in a creative manner" as what "really suited me. Working on the long Cargo etc. poem I feel much more in my right element. Though *Cables to the Ace* is in ways deficient, I feel it is also another right approach, though dour and perhaps sallow" (*HGL,* 639, 641–42).

14. "For My Brother: Reported Missing in Action, 1943," *CP,* 36.

Index of Names

Index of Subjects

Index of Merton Works